SHOULD WE CHANGE HOW WE VOTE?

Should We Change How We Vote?

Evaluating Canada's Electoral System

Edited by

ANDREW POTTER, DANIEL WEINSTOCK,

AND PETER LOEWEN

*Published for the McGill Institute
for the Study of Canada*
by
McGill-Queen's University Press
Montreal & Kingston · London · Chicago

ISBN 978-0-7735-5062-9 (cloth)
ISBN 978-0-7735-4882-4 (paperback)
ISBN 978-0-7735-5082-7 (ePDF)
ISBN 978-0-7735-5083-4 (ePUB)

Legal deposit third quarter 2017
Bibliothèque nationale du Québec

Printed in Canada on acid-free paper that is 100% ancient forest
free (100% post-consumer recycled), processed chlorine free

McGill-Queen's University Press acknowledges the support of the
Canada Council for the Arts for our publishing program. We also
acknowledge the financial support of the Government of Canada
through the Canada Book Fund for our publishing activities.

Library and Archives Canada Cataloguing in Publication

Should we change how we vote? : evaluating Canada's electoral system /
edited by Andrew Potter, Daniel Weinstock, and Peter Loewen.

Published for the McGill Institute for the Study of Canada.
Includes bibliographical references.
Issued in print and electronic formats.
ISBN 978-0-7735-5062-9 (hardcover). – ISBN 978-0-7735-4882-4 (softcover). –
ISBN 978-0-7735-5082-7 (ePDF). – ISBN 978-0-7735-5083-4 (ePUB)

1. Voting – Canada. 2. Elections – Canada. 3. Canada. Parliament – Elections.
4. Proportional representation – Canada. 5. Representative government and
representation – Canada. 6. Election law – Canada. I. Potter, Andrew, editor
II. Weinstock, Daniel, 1963–, editor III. Loewen, Peter John, 1979–, editor
IV. McGill Institute for the Study of Canada, issuing body

JL193.S5 2017   324.6'30971   C2017-900223-6
                                    C2017-900224-4

This book was typeset in Minion.

Contents

Acknowledgments ix

Preface: A Note from Charles Bronfman xi

Introduction: The History and Politics of Electoral Reform xiii

PART ONE: GUIDING PRINCIPLES

1. Evaluating How We Vote – Again 3
Ken Carty

2. The Complex Normative Landscape of Electoral Systems 14
Daniel Weinstock

3. Democratic Stability, Representation, and Accountability:
A Case for Single-Member Plurality Elections in Canada 23
Peter Loewen

4. Electoral Reform Is Not a Rights Issue 33
Emmett Macfarlane

5. The Imaginary Worlds of Electoral System Reform 42
Christopher Cochrane

PART TWO: EVIDENCE AND EXPERIENCE

6. Voter Choice and Accountability:
A Case for Caution about Electoral Reform 49
Elizabeth Goodyear-Grant

7. Electoral System Reform:
Implications for Internal Party Democracy 63
William Cross

8. Democratic Deliberation and Electoral Reform 74
Colin M. Macleod

9. Can Proportional Representation Lead to Better
Political System Performance? 86
Mark E. Warren

10. What Is the Problem that Electoral Reform Will Solve? 94
Lydia Miljan

PART THREE: ISSUES AND ALTERNATIVES

11. The Electoral System and Parliament's Diversity Problem:
In Defense of the Wrongfully Accused 111
Erin Tolley

12. Indigenous Representation, Self-Determination,
and Electoral Reform 126
Melissa S. Williams

13. Addressing Representational Deficits in Canadian Legislatures 139
Angelia Wagner and Elisabeth Gidengil

PART FOUR: HOW SHOULD WE DECIDE?

14. Public Consultation on Electoral Reform Through Referenda
or Plebiscite: Recent Experience in British Columbia 155
Keith Archer

15. Should We Have a Referendum? 166
Dominique Leydet

16. A Modest Case for Constitutional Limits on
Electoral Reform in Canada 177
Hoi L. Kong

17. Which Procedure for Deciding Election Procedures? 188
Arash Abizadeh

Notes 197
Contributors 229

Acknowledgments

This book is the result of a collaboration between the McGill Institute for the Study of Canada, the School of Public Policy and Governance at the University of Toronto, and the James McGill Professor Chair in Law at McGill University. It was conceived in response to Prime Minister Justin Trudeau's promise that the 2015 federal election campaign would be the last one held under Canada's "first-past-the-post" electoral system.

The papers in this collection are largely the proceedings of two conferences we organized in fall 2016. The first was held in Ottawa on October 28; the second, in Montreal on November 1. One exception is the paper by Ken Carty, who was unable to attend either conference. Instead, he submitted his paper in advance as a "target" paper, giving some historical context to guide conference participants in formulating their arguments.

We are grateful to David Lametti, the Liberal member of Parliament for Lasalle–Émard–Verdun, who was the parliamentary sponsor for the Ottawa conference. We would also like to thank the journalists who served as panel moderators, including Paul Wells, Heather Scoffield, Kate Heartfield, Martin Patriquin, and Celine Cooper. We would also like to thank the staff at MISC, Adriana Goreta and Mercedes Taboada, Mr. Lametti's assistant, Gillian Nycum, as well as Jesse Hartery and Dorinne Ah-Kam for their work organizing the events.

We are very grateful to Natalie Blachere of McGill-Queen's University Press for her enthusiasm and patience. Julie Pattee gave the contributions a helpful first read, while Kelly Hope did an outstanding job on the manuscript.

Finally, our deepest appreciation to our sponsors: the Donner Foundation, the Faculty of Law at McGill University, the Dean of Arts Development Fund at McGill University, the Macnaughton Lecture Fund, the Faculty of Law, McGill University, and the Research Group on Constitutional Studies, McGill University.

Preface

The subject of this collection of papers is an intriguing one, and it is one that is extremely important to all Canadians. While it is useful to compare electoral systems, we should avoid copying other systems or making a change for the sake of change. In my view, the citizens of each nation should adopt a voting system that is unique, and which serves the particular values and makeup of their society.

The way Canadians vote in the future will have a major impact on the character of our country. We should have a voting system that reflects our values and our priorities, as well as who we are as a people. If we decide that this requires changing how we vote, then we should proceed, but with caution. On the other hand, if we conclude that the current system serves our purposes, we should keep it.

Charles Bronfman

Introduction:
The History and Politics
of Electoral Reform

The Electoral Reform Process Thus Far

In June 2016, with his party languishing in third place in the polls and a general election looming, Justin Trudeau released a thirty-two-point plan aimed at "restoring democracy" in Canada. At the heart of that plan was a bold – some would have said foolhardy – commitment to changing Canada's electoral system. He pledged that, if his party was elected, the 2015 election would be the last in Canada's history to be run under the "first-past-the-post" system. Specifically, the party dedicated itself to striking an all-party committee that would report to Parliament, so as to allow legislation on electoral reform to be tabled within eighteen months of its accession to power.[1]

As we all know, the Trudeau Liberals climbed from (almost) worst to first in a matter of weeks, and were elected to a majority government on October 19, 2015. This placed the new government up against a tight electoral reform agenda. When Trudeau first presented the Liberals' electoral reform platform plank, Chief Electoral Officer Marc Mayrand warned that legislation would have to be in place in time to provide Elections Canada with two years in which to reorganize the institutional infrastructure on the basis of which elections occur in Canada. May 2017 was put forward as a deadline beyond which it would be difficult for Elections Canada to deal with the reforms that the legislation would set in motion.

From the beginning, the government's approach differed from recent attempts at electoral reform at the provincial level. In British

Columbia and Ontario, the government had convened citizen's assemblies and tasked them with proposing new electoral systems. These quasi-randomly selected assemblies then had their recommendations put to referendums held parallel to elections. British Columbia held two referendums in successive elections (2005 and 2009). The first achieved majority support for reform but not the super-majority required by the government. The second referendum failed. In Ontario, a sole referendum on reform held in 2007 also failed. Likewise, a proposal for electoral reform in PEI – the result of a special committee and then a legislative committee – failed in 2005. More recently, however, a plebiscite on electoral reform resulted in a public preference for reform. Whether reform is to be implemented remains an open question. In New Brunswick and Quebec, extensive consultations and draft legislation never successfully passed either legislature.

Against this backdrop of failed reforms, Trudeau took a different course. He named a political unknown, first-time MP Maryam Monsef of Peterborough, to a cabinet position as Minister of Democratic Institutions, and thus, as leader of the electoral reform process. The subsequent process of consultation and debate, initiated by Monsef and backed by the whole government, was beset by inept communications and chaotic implementation. Monsef had to backtrack on her nomination of the all-party committee, which had initially been composed majorly of Liberal MPs. Elected officials and pundits pointed out that there was more than an air of hypocrisy in a committee aimed at introducing more proportionality to the electoral system while reflecting the lack of proportionality in the system it was being asked to replace. Later, Trudeau got himself into an embarrassing public relations pickle when in a wide-ranging interview he declared that there was no longer any great urgency in reforming the electoral system, given how happy the population of Canada now was with his government. By this time, the committee had almost completed its consultations. Trudeau's comments raised the suspicion that what had really motivated the Liberal commitment to electoral reform was political calculation rather than a concern with electoral fairness. (There is nothing new in this. Paul Martin's famous promise to fix the "democratic deficit" was itself a reaction to Jean Chrétien's increasingly centralized control of the party and of Parliament. Promising to reform Canada's political institutions as a response to political impotence is a long-standing part of our heritage.)

When the all-party committee finally reported on the prospects for electoral reform in Canada, Monsef took the opportunity to dump all over the committee and its report in the House of Commons. She claimed that its main recommendation, which was that whatever system ended up being chosen by Canadians and their representatives fall within a certain range of proportionality as measured by a standard tool known as the Gallagher index, was too complicated for Canadians. (Oddly, the Liberal members of the committee dissented from this, recommending, in effect, that the government break its promise of making the 2015 election the last fought under first-past-the-post, giving rise to the paradoxical position in which opposition members seemed more inclined to fulfill the government's platform on electoral reform than the government itself did.)

Finally, a consultation document that the Liberal government put online in early December 2016 in order to gauge the values and preferences of Canadians with respect to electoral reform was almost universally panned. Critics charged that the survey itself offered false choices, contained nonsensical questions, and revealed unacceptable bias insofar as it did not ask of Canadians that they express their views with respect to the main alternatives to first-past-the-post. The suggestion that the survey was well designed and succeeded in its goal of getting Canadians to think about the outcomes of various electoral systems went largely unheeded.[2]

As things evolved, Monsef herself was moved as part of a more general cabinet shuffle in early 2017. She was replaced by an even younger and equally inexperienced MP, Karina Gould of Burlington, Ontario, which simply raised anew the question of how serious Trudeau was about getting any movement on the file. That question was answered at the beginning of February 2017, when Gould called a press conference to announce that in the absence of a "consensus" on how to proceed, changing the electoral system was no longer in Canada's interest or her mandate. The prime minister later repeated these talking points in the House of Commons, asserting that he would not do something that was "wrong" for Canada "just to tick off a box on an electoral platform." And with that, electoral reform was off the table, with no expectation that it will return under this government.

Refocusing the Debate

As this quick summary of the steps and stumbles that have been taken by the Liberal government in trying to enact (or, as it turned out, to step away from) its commitment to electoral reform makes clear, public debate has been dominated by questions of process rather than of substance. This is unfortunate. The decision to reform an electoral system (or indeed not to reform it) is among the most important that any democratic society has to make. This is because the electoral system does not merely reflect the political landscape. Rather, it profoundly shapes that political landscape, creating incentives for political actors to coalesce into parties in radically different ways, and for ordinary citizens to deliberate about electoral options by attending to quite different ranges of considerations. The kind of democracy we have is a function of the kind of electoral system we choose.

As a modest contribution to raising the level of debate surrounding electoral reform, and to refocusing it on issues of substance, the editors of this volume convened two meetings in the fall of 2016 in order to ask some leading academic and non-academic observers of the Canadian electoral scene to highlight what they saw as the main issues confronting Canadians. These meetings were held in Ottawa on October 28, 2016, and at McGill University in Montreal on November 1. The papers presented in this volume are drawn from these events. Rather than asking authors to rewrite their papers and to present them in full academic regalia, we have sought to capture them largely as they were delivered on the day, in order to give readers a sense of the lively debates that our invitation gave rise to, and to produce a volume that could contribute in a timely manner to the fundamental issues that ought to be framing the Canadian debate over electoral reform.

What are those issues? They are legion, and too numerous to capture in the pages of a single volume. But very quickly we felt that debate and discussion needed to coalesce around three ranges of issues. First, many of the contributors felt that before making any steps in the direction of reform, we needed to proceed on the basis of a clear reckoning of the values at stake in the choice of electoral systems. Democracy is not one value. Rather, it is a way of organizing a plurality of values, and the choice of electoral systems is of crucial importance precisely because different systems organize and prioritize those values in different ways. Electoral reform should occur with all relevant values in full view.

Second, many of our participants expressed the view that before a decision is taken to do away with our present system, we should have a full appreciation of its strengths and weaknesses, as assessed on the basis of relevant democratic values. Government in this system is typically formed by the political party whose candidates win the greatest number of seats. A seat is won by a candidate who receives the highest number of votes in a territorially defined constituency. Opponents of first-past-the-post tend to focus on its lack of proportionality. When such a system is in operation, a political party can achieve majority status without a majority of voters having chosen it. Conversely, parties with significant support can fail to achieve any representation whatsoever. Thus, the first-past-the-post system is viewed by many as failing before the value of proportionality. But how does it fare in relation to other relevant values? We must gain a better appreciation of this question before we decide on a new electoral path.

Finally, the question of *how* we ought to change our electoral system was raised by a number of participants. There are a number of options that are relevant here. At one extreme, our electoral system might be changed by a simple act of Parliament, since the electoral law of Canada is not enshrined in the constitution. (The question of whether a change to the electoral law might be challenged on constitutional grounds is a separate one.) At the other extreme, we might imagine the choice of a new electoral system being put to a referendum. What, exactly, does it mean to change a democratic electoral system *democratically*? This was a question that attracted the attention of some of the participants at these events.

Canadian society is sufficiently mature and politically sophisticated to consider these issues seriously and responsibly, just as they have been considered at the provincial level in British Columbia, in Prince

Edward Island, and in Ontario. But in order to do so Canadians need to have the relevant issues put before them in a manner that invites rather than inhibits substantive deliberation. Throughout this ill-fated exercise in reform, neither Trudeau nor his ministers made any real effort to provide Canadians with the resources with which to engage in such deliberation. Instead, they allowed the debate to become mired in procedural quandaries and political machinations.

Electoral reform is off the table for now, but it will return eventually. And when it does, we hope that these essays will contribute to righting the focus of this important societal discussion.

PART ONE

Guiding Principles

Evaluating How We Vote – Again

Ken Carty

Electoral reform is back on the agenda, a consequence of the winning Liberals' campaign promise that 2015 would be the last national election conducted under first-past-the-post. The Liberals first embraced electoral reform at their 1919 leadership convention (the one that chose Mackenzie King) and much has changed since then – the franchise has been broadened, multi-member districts have been abolished, constituency boundaries are now drawn by non-partisan commissions, elections are managed by an independent officer of Parliament, election dates have been fixed, and electoral finance is publicly regulated – but first-past-the-post remains. Over the century, several provinces have experimented with alternate vote and single transferable vote electoral systems, singly or in combination, but all have returned to first-past-the-post. So why, and with what realistic prospect, is it back on the agenda now?

As the Liberals' old 1919 commitment suggests, a concern for reforming the way elections are conducted is hardly new. About a decade ago, from 2003 to 2007, much of the country was caught up in the debate as five of the provinces launched major reform exercises. Considerable time, resources, and energy were spent on each initiative and in every case the outcome was a recommendation to replace first-past-the-post with something "better." Yet a decade later, despite the clear commitment of those governments to taking up the issue in a serious fashion, none of those proposed reforms have led to a change. That surprising outcome ought to make us pause and consider what the experience can teach us about the processes and prospects for a productive electoral reform debate in Canada.

Five (Recently Failed) Provincial Electoral Reform Initiatives

The electoral system is one of the central institutional lynchpins of any democracy, so a proposal to abandon a long-tried-and-true system is inevitably a radical one. More often than not, enthusiasm for such a change comes from an opposition that believes the existing system discriminates against them. So the fact that five strong sitting provincial governments should have simultaneously launched such an exercise in the early years of the new century was surely quite unexpected. Yet in Prince Edward Island, New Brunswick, Quebec, Ontario, and British Columbia, the governing premiers deliberately put the issue on the public agenda and created a process designed to lead to change.

Several aspects of this sudden development deserve to be noted. The first is that there was no obvious common partisan flavour to it. Both Liberal and Progressive Conservative party governments instigated reform exercises and New Democrat and Parti Québécois opponents generally supported them. A second striking feature of the initiatives was the absence of any specific reform proposal from any of the sponsoring government leaders or their parties. In both Prince Edward Island and New Brunswick, the reform agencies established by the governments were directed to consider more proportional electoral systems, but in none of the five cases had the government identified or committed to a particular change. Although constitutional reality dictated that the respective legislatures would have the final say, there was some ambivalence about who ought to decide the issue. In the end, three of the provincial governments resorted to referenda and a fourth was defeated before it could hold one.

These separate reform exercises overlapped one another, starting in Prince Edward Island in early 2003 and effectively ending with the Ontario referendum in the fall of 2007. Not surprisingly, there was a good deal of interaction among the principal actors involved. Staff members of each group were welcome visitors at each other's offices and meetings, and they often served together on discussion

4

panels at national and provincial conferences. This ensured a considerable exchange of ideas about both process and substance among those involved. Perhaps the most obvious example of the influence of this interaction was the impact that the British Columbia Citizens' Assembly process had on Ontario, which borrowed heavily from that experience in designing and managing its own process.

In this short period of furious activity, all five provincial governments managed to mount reform exercises that conducted independent research, held extensive public consultations, and then came to the common conclusion that first-past-the-post ought to be abandoned for a proportional electoral system. Yet behind these apparent similarities lay important differences in the definition of respective problems (or objectives sought), the process used to contemplate change, and the alternative electoral system.

Table 1: The Five Provincial Electoral Reform Initiatives

Precipitating Issue	Process	Proposal
PEI Lopsided legislature	One-man commission Eight-person Electoral Future Commission Plebiscite	MMP Provincial closed lists
NB Lopsided legislature	Eight-member Bipartisan Elite Commission Possible referendum	MMP – four big regions Candidates run on one side only

Precipitating Issue	Process	Proposal
QC Wrong winner rooted in "linguistic gerrymanding"	In-house policy making to minister Legislative committee (supplemented by citizens)	MMP One vote only Many small regions
ON Perceived democratic deficit	Independent Citizens' Assembly Referendum	MMP Provincial closed lists Larger legislature
BC Wrong winner Lopsided legislature	Independent Citizens' Assembly Referendum	Single Transferable Vote DM 2-7

During the period when the provinces were preoccupied with reform, there was considerable national debate about a perceived "democratic deficit" (an issue Paul Martin made his own in seeking the leadership of the national Liberal Party), and a recognition that voter turnout was in sharp decline. There is no doubt that immediate cases of the well-known anomalies possible under first-past-the-post drove the agenda. In two provinces – British Columbia and Quebec – the system had recently produced "wrong winners" (a government elected with fewer votes than its opponent), challenging the legitimacy of those outcomes.[1]

In Quebec, an additional phenomenon known as "linguistic gerrymandering," which flowed from the geography of partisan distributions across a single-member constituency map, made this a recurring problem. In the two Atlantic provinces, the small size of their legislatures made them vulnerable to extraordinarily lopsided parliamentary outcomes. Without enough members to mount an effective opposition, the very principle of responsible government had recently been rendered moot for whole electoral cycles in both. Only in Ontario was one of these obvious precipitating outcomes absent, though there the new premier had won an election in which democratic reform was one of his campaign themes.

The province of Quebec, where the confounding issue of the linguistic gerrymander was seen as essentially a technical problem, pursued a traditional approach to policy-making by relying on experts to devise an improved electoral system. The two smaller Atlantic provinces, focused on the need to strengthen their legislative oppositions, relied on the tried-and-true processes of independent commissions populated by the interested and the expert. British Columbia, where the vitriol of adversarial politics was strongest, opted for the radical strategy of handing decision-making about the electoral system completely over to ordinary citizens meeting together in a year-long assembly with the authority to propose a specific alternative.[2] The Ontario premier, anxious to promote his credentials as a reformer, decided that his province would follow the "more democratic" path charted by British Columbia.

One of the striking features of the reform exercises was the decision of four of the respective provincial governments and legislatures to abdicate ultimate responsibility for the issue by leaving its resolution to a popular referendum.[3] In part this reflected a principled position that politicians were inevitably in a position of clear conflict of interest on questions of electoral change. But it also reflected a deep ambivalence on the part of politicians who had made electoral promises to consider electoral reform but now saw their interests to have changed.[4] In British Columbia, Premier Campbell attempted to resolve this tension, and balance the interests of rural and urban caucus members, by establishing a double threshold for the referendum: it required an overall vote of 60 per cent as well as a majority vote in 60 per cent of the districts. In Prince Edward Island, the elected politicians were happy to seize on this precedent, and a month before its "plebiscite" the premier announced that the British Columbia standard would apply. And, despite reformers' vigorous objections that the standard was undemocratic, the Ontario government indicated it would also follow this lead and use the same criteria. Only in New Brunswick was a premier apparently willing to accept 50 per cent plus 1 as the measure of success, but he was turned out of office before he was able to hold the promised referendum.[5] For many stakeholders this recent history would appear to have established a new constitutional precedent, one that demands that any change to the electoral system now requires a public referendum.

With almost all of this activity happening simultaneously, there was little opportunity for strong demonstration effects that might have seen provinces copying successful institutional innovations from one another. Still, it is striking that none of the debates led to a recommendation to maintain the familiar first-past-the-post electoral system, even in some reformed or improved version. Nor did any advocate majoritarian systems such as the Australian Alternative Vote (once used in several provinces) or the French two-round system. All were clear that some element of proportional representation was desirable in a system that maintained traditional notions of local representation. With four of the five recommending a mixed-member proportional system, it seemed that there was some general perception that it was indeed what some have called the "best of both worlds."[6]

However, these separate processes produced four very different mixed-member systems. The specific features of the Quebec proposal seemed perfectly designed to solidify the province's bipolar politics by increasing the number of safe seats and making it difficult for minor parties to get elected. Prince Edward Island's proposed system would have strengthened the position of party leaders and made it difficult for voters to turn out the parties' preferred personalities. By contrast, New Brunswick's regionalized system seemed likely to increase both the level and location of intra-party competition in that province. Thus, any consensus on the virtues of a mixed-member proportional system was quite superficial; the sharp differences among the proposals reflected both the distinct definitions of the electoral system problem that the reform processes were working from and their approach to the idiosyncratic political traditions and practices of their respective provinces. Had these proposals been adopted, they would have had very different impacts on the various party systems and the way political parties went about structuring and organizing electoral competition in them.

This is a quite remarkable story. A span of three busy years saw serious, detailed proposals that would have reshaped electoral organization and completion in half the provinces suddenly on the public agenda. Given that the work that led to them had been initiated and supported by the respective governments, one might have expected that at least one or two might have been adopted. But none were. It is unlikely that the process was at fault, for there was no common element of the respective policy paths that might account for this. What then might this story tell us about electoral reform as an issue in Canada?

Electoral Reform on the Agenda

In all five cases, the governments that put electoral reform on the agenda had come to office (two re-elected, three newly elected) having made campaign promises to do so. In British Columbia and Quebec, the promises were made largely to satisfy activist partisans upset by how the system had treated them; in New Brunswick and Ontario, they were a consequence of the party leaders' personal belief that the issue was important; in Prince Edward Island, it was done to sustain a process launched under a previous mandate. It appears that electoral reform emerged simply because the respective party leaders, in government or in opposition, had made it one of many public promises during a campaign and then felt obligated to make good on it by launching a formal review process. In no case were the promises made because the issue was central to the competitive electoral process or because more than a few reform enthusiasts were generally concerned (or even knowledgeable) about it. There is simply no evidence that there was any widespread public interest or concern for the subject, even after the reform exercises got underway.

In none of the cases did the premier opening the debate have any reason to expect that a different electoral system would be politically advantageous for them, although the Quebec Liberals surely had an incentive to try to find a way to mitigate the impact of the province's linguistic gerrymander. Indeed, few premiers appear to have any sophisticated appreciation of the working and potential impact of different systems, let alone any particular one. One premier was prepared to acknowledge and accept the potential upsets of a first-past-the-post "wrong winner" outcome, saying, "We knew the rules – and having been willing to win by them we were prepared to lose by them."[7] But knowing little about the complex rules of other systems, the politicians who initiated the debate never offered, or campaigned for, a preferred alternative.

Without an engaged public, or clear proposals from the politicians most affected by the electoral system, no common debate on what the real problem of first-past-the-post might be, or how it might be addressed, ever emerged. In part this reflected the reality that the rather different processes adopted by the provinces led them to focus on the specifics of their provincial political dynamics rather than broader systemic issues. But it also reflected the reality that the absence of a directed debate on the merits of a particular alternative inevitably led each to a temptation to design a made-at-home variant. Given that no two countries use an identical electoral system, it was easy to conclude that one had to be fashioned to meet unique local circumstances.

If five of the provincial reform exercises could conclude that first-past-the-post had to be replaced, and by a system that incorporated some element of proportional representation, they could not identify or generate any agreement on what that system should look like. Four of the provinces recommended some form of mixed-member proportional system but the differences among them were very large: the matter of ballot form, the number of votes an elector would have, the basis (regional or system wide) and the control of party lists, the relative weight of the two sides of the system, where candidates might run, and more technical questions of counting rules, overhangs, and by-elections.[8] These significant variations made it clear that the mixed-member proportional label covered a wide variety of very different systems, each bound to produce very different operating practices and outcomes. The obvious absence of any agreement across the country – among politicians, activists, or citizens – on what an appropriate mixed-member proportional system would consist of undoubtedly made it harder to create a consensus in favour of any reform.

The decision of a majority of the premiers to stand aside from the reform processes they had initially championed, by leaving a decision to a referendum, drained the movement of the dynamic political leadership necessary for such a significant change. And in a number of cases it allowed individual members of the parties' legislative caucuses to assert their personal interests, defending first-past-the-post and the politics of local representation that had seen them elected. In Quebec, members of the Liberal caucus appear to have strongly opposed the reform proposal despite the fact that it would appear to have been in the long-term interest of the party as a whole. In British Columbia, caucus members concerned with defending the perceived interests of rural districts led to its extravagant set of referendum hurdles that politicians in both Prince Edward Island and Ontario then readily embraced. These were clear cases of individual district politicians allowing their personal electoral interests to trump their publicly declared values or even the collective interests of their parties.

Most working politicians may not have wanted any electoral reform. The same might be said for the citizens of the provinces. In the three cases where the recommendations for change went directly to referendum, the voters turned it down. Advocates for the reforms naturally claimed that referendum thresholds were too high, and analysts pointed at an unsympathetic media in Ontario, and an unprofessional organization of the referendum mechanics in Prince Edward Island.[9] But the simple truth is that, across three provinces, in three referendums, the voters turned down the proportional alternative. Only in British Columbia, and then only the first time, did the yes vote ever exceed 50 per cent. With none of the established parties' leaders championing reform, voters apparently were not convinced of the need to abandon first-past-the-post for something new.

The lessons of the provincial electoral reform initiatives of a decade ago seem straightforward. Setting a reform agenda, agreeing on a basic value such as proportional representation to guide it, launching well-resourced processes, and activating advocacy groups in civil society was not sufficient to accomplish electoral reform in even one of the five cases. What was lacking in each was focused political party leadership determined to carry it to the public and see it through.

National electoral reform may be more difficult. It must take into account the constitutional provision for the representation of the provinces in the House of Commons. At a minimum, the continuing overrepresentation of some of the smaller provinces and territories ensures that the votes of the population in those parts of the country count more in electing representatives – thus a vote in Prince Edward Island is worth three times that of one in British Columbia as far as its contribution to electing an MP is concerned. Until that anomaly is corrected, any ambition to create a reform that will have "all votes count equally" is likely to be stymied. Nothing in the current electoral reform exercise seems aimed at dealing with this entrenched constitutional reality.

Most enthusiasts for reform have long identified a mixed-member proportional system, with its provision for continuing local representation, as the desired outcome.[10] However, the recent inability of the detailed provincial initiatives to agree on the central features of an appropriate system must give pause. It reflects the realization that the very many elements of a mixed system need to be tailored to the imperatives of local circumstance. As long as the constitution specifies that representation in the House of Commons is structured provincially, this is likely to make the creation of a common national mixed-member proportional system difficult. The balance of elements that would be acceptable in the larger provinces with dozens of seats would not work in the smaller provinces or territories with only a handful of representatives. It might be that different arrangements of a mixed system could be created for different provinces, but generating nation-wide agreement that different rules would govern parties and elections in different parts of the country would be hard to sell, given that the political leadership has yet to identify the problem it is designed to solve.

In British Columbia, the Citizens' Assembly, which spent a year considering its options, recommended a single transferable vote system. It did so because its members concluded that it provided for the best balance among the three competing values that speak to the three central aspects of any electoral system: proportionality, local representation, and voter choice.[11] The latter criteria focused on the electoral system's ballot form, the element that many believed maximized their opportunity to have an effective say in the choice of their representative. A single transferable vote system could easily be adopted for use in all the provinces by simple amalgamations of existing constituencies. However, the reality is that a transferable vote ballot increases the influence of the voter at the expense of the political parties and so is rarely favoured by professional politicians.

Major national electoral reforms in the past have been carried through Parliament. However, the use of referendums to deal with the Charlottetown Constitutional Accord and the more recent proposed electoral system changes in British Columbia, Ontario, and Prince Edward Island have, for many, created an expectation that any significant alteration in the way in which parliaments are chosen would require a referendum. Whether those precedents are sufficient to create a constitutional convention is an open question – but it is certainly a live political one. Given this history, in the absence of a popular referendum, it would surely take a substantial parliamentary majority, determined and committed to a proposal that commanded wide support, to legitimate the replacement of first-past-the-post with some new system.

All five provincial reform proposals failed for want of committed leadership. In its absence the same fate would seem most likely for any significant national reform.

2

The Complex Normative Landscape of Electoral Systems

Daniel Weinstock

There are no perfect electoral systems. As we here in Canada embark upon a path that may lead us to changing the way we vote, we should be careful not to be misled into thinking that there is some correct way of organizing the translation of votes into political representation to which we should aspire. Choosing an electoral system is a question of emphasizing certain considerations that are relevant to that choice, and of sidelining others. Inevitably, as we live under an electoral system, our attention turns to the considerations that we have set aside, and the system we have is judged wanting when assessed on their basis. We need to take a step back in thinking about whether or not to change the electoral system under which we presently operate, and consider the range of values that are relevant to the choice. My intention in this paper is to contribute to this task by laying out what I take two main families of considerations to be, and to point to some of the trade-offs that choosing an electoral system unavoidably involves. As will emerge, trade-offs occur within, as well as between, these families of values.

Some Initial Remarks

Before embarking on this task, however, I want to make a number of prefatory remarks that should also be kept in mind as we think about the matter of electoral reform.

The first is that voting systems narrowly understood, which include the way we elicit information from voters and the way we transform the aggregated preferences into distributions of seats in representative assemblies, are embodied in a larger set of democratic institutions. A thorough discussion not just of the way we vote, but of the way we organize our democratic systems, should include not just electoral systems, but the full range of institutions through which societies that call themselves "democratic" attempt to realize democratic values.[1] This broader range of questions includes the following: Should we be represented in one or in two legislative assemblies? If the latter, what should be the principle that distinguishes representation in what have traditionally been called the "lower" and "upper" houses?[2] How should campaign financing be regulated? What should the minimum voting age be? Should political parties be required to include specified quotas of candidates drawn from diverse groups? These and countless other questions need to be addressed in order to come up with an institutionally grounded theory of democratic practice. An electoral system is an important part of the total set of institutions through which societies attempt to realize democratic values, but it is not the only part.

This is particularly important in the present context for the following reason. As we shall see, electoral systems are answerable to a wide range of relevant political values. If we frame the question of how best to realize those values as being equivalent to the question of how best to reconcile them within a voting system, we risk hitting up against a lot of tragic dilemmas. But if we view our democratic system as made up of a plurality of institutional spaces, it might be possible to reconcile these values by embodying them in different places within this complex set of institutions.

My second observation is that the question we should be asking ourselves is not what the best electoral system is, given the plurality of values that we need to try to embody in our democratic system, but rather, what the best electoral system is *for us*, given the specific set of circumstances – historical, demographic, and geographical – to which an electoral system is to be applied. One manifestation of this broader concern has to do with the fact that electoral *change* is not the same thing as electoral *choice*. Electoral systems do not just reflect sociological facts on the ground. They are also productive of some of those facts. This is so in (at least) two ways. First, electoral systems, such as Canada's, that define constituencies territorially create territorial identities where none may have existed before. Indeed, if people are bundled together by what might at first blush seem like arbitrary electoral lines, they will have strong incentives to discover shared interests and concerns, to use the political leverage that finding themselves within a political unit represents to promote causes that people within those lines share. From that, identities follow over time. Now, this may not be the best way to define electoral constituencies. Andrew Rehfeld has, for example, defended the idea that electoral constituencies ought from election to election to be defined by a randomization process bringing people together across various lines, including territorial ones.[3] However, once the decision has been made to define constituencies in ways that are creative of territorial identities, these identities have *pro tanto* moral importance. In other words, there may be reason, all things considered, to make changes to our electoral systems that disrupt these identities. But they need to be part of the moral ledger as we go about deciding whether or not to change an electoral system, and they obviously would not be were we choosing a system from scratch.

Not only do political systems create territorial identities; they also create political identities, and in particular, partisan identities. After elections, analysts will often misleadingly calculate how the parties contesting the election would have done under another electoral system. Such analyses are misleading because different electoral systems generate different party systems, rather than simply aggregating their electoral yields differently. A single-member plurality system like Canada's gives rise to what are colloquially referred to as "big tent" parties. Such parties bring together people of quite different political profiles under the banner of a large political party bound together by very general, abstract political principles. Proportional representation systems give rise to a plethora of smaller parties that can all hope to achieve representation even where their support is modest and territorially spread out.

Though they may at present be in a state of crisis for a variety of reasons that I cannot get into here[4], parties ground valuable forms of political identity. Some of these are committed to partisanship, but many also lead to the creation of identities based on political proposals presented to the broader public in the context of democratic debate and deliberation. Now, I have argued elsewhere that there is value in "big tent" parties that cannot easily be replicated in the smaller parties that tend to be generated by proportional representation.[5] But the point for present purposes is that there is *pro tanto* moral value to the identities created by diverse political systems, value that must be placed in the moral ledger before the decision is taken to disrupt them through the choice of a new electoral system.

There are of course other parameters about polities that should be taken into account when determining which electoral system best suits them. They reinforce the notion that what we are talking about is choice of an electoral system *for this or that polity*, with its specific history, geography, demography, and so on, rather than reflecting on the abstract normative merits of different systems.

Three Values

So what *are* the values that we ought to be taking into account as we make the contextual judgment as to whether or not a given polity ought to change its electoral system? The scope of this article prevents me from offering a sketch of more than a couple of them. But I believe that they are the most important ones to be kept in view.

Pundits and politicians who live in a single-member plurality system such as Canada's tend to emphasize the system's lack of representativeness in urging for a move toward a more proportional system. They note, correctly, that such systems tend to distort the vote, in the sense that as little as 37 per cent of the vote has been enough for parties to receive more than 50 per cent of the vote in Parliament, whereas parties with as much as 15 per cent of the vote can be shut out of Parliament entirely if their support is spread evenly across the country. All things equal, it seems that the share of seats that a party receives in Parliament should be in proportion to the share of the popular vote that it manages to attract during an election.

But the claim is not as obvious as it may seem at first glance. Indeed, should the share of the vote that a party gets in an election determine the share of seats that it should get in Parliament, or the extent of influence?

As is well known, proportional representation systems give rise to situations in which parties must engage in coalition-making. A result of this is that parties that have only managed to attract a relatively small number of voters are able to exert great influence on the platforms of coalitions because of the need to secure the votes of the representatives they have managed to elect in order to form a working majority.

But putting that concern aside – and assuming for the sake of argument that the disproportion between votes and seats that single-member plurality systems generate is, all things equal, a problem – all things are not, in fact, equal. Vote/seat proportionality is not the only value that those choosing whether to change electoral systems ought to keep in view. In fact, it is not even the only consideration to place under the general rubric of "representativeness."

There is an argument that can be made that in a large country like Canada, regions should also be fairly represented in Parliament. In particular, care should be given lest a sole concern on vote/seat representation set in motion something that some might see as a vicious cycle disempowering rural regions in Canada. Canada is a highly urbanized society, and rural areas have had trouble dealing with the rapid exodus toward cities. To make representation in Parliament strictly mirror vote shares risks taking away tools, in the form of elected representatives capable of shaping policy at least to some minimal degree, that already vulnerable regions need in order to act in a politically effective manner for the interests of their constituents.

Now, some might argue that the disproportion between number of votes and seats that characterizes the Canadian Parliament is not morally justifiable, and that it creates its own morally problematic disproportions. Thus, for example, Michael Pal and Sujit Choudhry have pointed out that, as immigrants tend to be largely concentrated in urban centers, the overrepresentation of rural areas gives rise to a problematic undervaluing of immigrant votes.[6] Now, it could be that the overrepresentation of rural votes is, all things considered, difficult to justify. But this is not to say that regional representation has no *pro tanto* weight needing to be taken into account when making overall judgments as to the way in which representativeness should be calibrated as between individual and region.

The value of representativeness has also been invoked by commentators who have worried about the *group* representation of historically marginalized populations.[7] These include racialized minorities such as African-Americans in the United States, and indigenous populations all over the colonized world. The concern has also been voiced with respect to women, who have been underrepresented in legislatures around the world. Neither regional nor vote/seat representativeness will increase the representation of such groups, which tend to be territorially dispersed.

Thus, representativeness, the value on the basis of which many have found the Canadian system of single-member plurality to be wanting, is itself an internally complex value. Arguments have been made to the effect that concerns with proportionality should track power and influence rather than seats, and they have also suggested that the value of representation should as well be applied to regions, and to groups. Different electoral systems stack up differently depending upon whether one focuses on one or the other of these dimensions of representation.

A second set of normative considerations which are relevant to the evaluation of electoral systems are *epistemic*. This rubric, as I am defining it, encompasses a range of considerations that have to do with the epistemic quality of the electoral process, the degree to which electoral systems elicit considered judgments from voters rather than just uneducated preferences and give rise to well-reasoned policy outcomes.[8]

Here again, trade-offs abound. Let's assume that the epistemic quality of the vote depends in at least some significant measure on the incentive that voters have to seek out information about the platforms that political parties put forward during electoral campaigns, and to reflect and deliberate upon the desirability of those platforms. One of the reasons that people may have to do so is the thought that parties that form government will actually act on the basis of the platforms that they present to the electorate. If citizens have reasons to think that platforms only provide a very imperfect sense of what governments will do, then they have less reason to base their vote on epistemically relevant considerations such as platforms. A virtue of the single-member plurality system from this point of view is that, by tending to produce majority governments because of the very high rate at which the party with the most votes can translate their votes into seats in Parliament, it removes one of the reasons that parties have not to act on their electoral platforms when they come to power, namely that they need to compromise and to drop some of their platform planks in order to obtain the cooperation of coalition partners.[9] All things equal, if voters know that parties will have to compromise on their platform promises in order to form workable coalitions, they may be less inclined to pay attention to platforms, which in systems that tend to produce the need for coalitions can be seen more as opening gambits in coalition talks than as promises made to an electorate.

Electoral systems that are designed to increase reflection and deliberation among citizens will, however, tend to reduce the need, and perhaps even the desirability, of deliberation in parliamentary institutions. Democratic systems designed to incentivize reflection and deliberation among voters will, for example, view positively an institution such as party discipline, in the absence of which voters have as much reason to fear that platforms will not be acted on as they do in systems that generate coalitions. Of course, if what is wanted is greater deliberation in parliamentary institutions themselves, then such institutional mechanisms will come to be seen as suspect. Different electoral systems, and more broadly different democratic systems, create incentives for deliberation, and thus presumably for epistemic work in different institutional locations. Systems that incentivize such work in one region of the democratic system will tend to disincentivize reflection and deliberation in others.

There are other epistemic considerations that need to be taken into account. It has, for example, often been observed about single-member plurality systems that they tend to elicit strategic voting from the electorate. This is because such a system gives little incentive for citizens to vote for parties that match their political preferences perfectly (and little incentive for the party system to generate such parties in the first place), and more reason for them to vote in a way that will make it more likely that the party they least like achieves power. Votes in this kind of system potentially are epistemically vacuous, since they do not express the political preferences of voters. They provide us with very little information about what voters really think, and largely prevent voters from expressing fine-grained preferences.

At the other end of the spectrum, systems such as the single transferable vote (which allows voters to rank candidates rather than just providing one preference), or systems inspired by the Borda count (which invites voters to engage in pair-wise comparisons) elicit far more information, as they allow voters not just to express a preference, but to have the way in which they see candidates as comparing to one another impact on the final result of the election.[10]

The kind of epistemically fine-tuned vote that systems of ranked ballots allow must of course be calibrated to the epistemic carrying capacity of the electorate. Ranked voting systems presenting a large number of candidates to the electorate, and requiring of voters that they rank all of them, risk giving rise to a fair degree of noise. The degree to which voters are capable of making meaningful choices in ranked ballots is a function of the degree to which the electoral system in which they find themselves incentivizes reflection and deliberation among the choices presented to them. And so, epistemic considerations relating to the amount of information elicited by the ballot interact in complex ways with considerations relating to the system's tendency to promote reflection. Electoral systems must calibrate the fine-grained nature of the information they elicit from voters on the basis of the quality of the reflection and deliberation voters can be expected to have engaged in, given the nature of the voting system in place. Different versions of ranked ballot systems identify the epistemic optimum in different places. However, how these different proposals fare at balancing relevant epistemic considerations falls well beyond the scope of this paper.

Conclusion

I've only been able to quickly describe two of the families of considerations that are relevant to the evaluation of electoral systems. Hopefully, this is enough to show that there are a number of relevant values, and that they are sometimes in tension with one another. A more thorough inventory would include other families of values as well. Accountability, the capacity of a system to generate the sense among elected officials that they are morally bound to their electorate to attempt in good faith to meet voters' legitimate expectations, and to give rise to sensible judgments among the electorate as to whether or not they have met reasonable standards of accountability, is such a relevant value. Stability, the tendency of a government to be adequately resilient before both endogenous and exogenous shocks to the system, is another.

There is no single right way to rank all of these values. Choosing to change an electoral system is a deeply contextual matter, in which choices have to be made among various values in the context of particular polities' history, geography, demography, and the like.

If there is no single right way of ranking the relevant values, is there a right way of *deciding* on what the ranking of these values should be? In Canada, electoral law can in principle be changed by parliamentary votes, since the voting scheme is not enshrined in the constitution. But it has been held by some that it does have "quasi-constitutional" status, and that a more demanding procedural hurdle should be cleared by any proposal for electoral change. This could mean a super-majoritarian requirement in Parliament, a referendum, perhaps preceded by a constituent assembly of the kind that was organized in British Columbia's experiment with electoral reform.[11]

There may be as many theoretical quandaries involved in deciding how to decide as there are in the evaluation of the various electoral systems on offer. In particular, there are dangers of exceeding the epistemic capacity of whatever body is tasked with making the decision, and of a kind of elite capture, a situation in which groups that have devoted a lot of time and energy defending a particular direction for change end up dominating debate and deliberation. Here as well, care must be taken lest superficially attractive options hiding serious normative shortfalls be chosen as the "best" way in which to decide whether or not to change how we vote.

3

Democratic Stability, Representation, and Accountability: A Case for Single-Member Plurality Elections in Canada

Peter Loewen

Should we change our electoral system? I argue that we should not. To begin, I argue that what we should want – what we should prioritize – in our electoral system are three related characteristics: stability and long-term viability, responsiveness, and accountability. Because democracy is precious and because free and fair elections are central to democracy, we should want an electoral system that is robust against breakdown. Because citizens' preferences and interests matter, then we should want an electoral system that leads to responsive governments. Finally, because politicians are not perfect, we should want a political system that allows for citizens to punish and remove underperforming politicians.

In this chapter, I argue first that Canada's electoral system has proven robust against breakdown, despite a difficult starting position. I then argue that on grounds of democratic responsiveness, a plurality system such as Canada's performs as well as a proportional representation system. Finally, I argue that given the deep flaws of voters, we should want an electoral system that does not reward appeals to the worst nature of people while still allowing them to hold governments accountable. On this score, Canada's current system once again performs well.

The Robustness of Our Electoral System

The first criterion on which we might evaluate our federal electoral system is its robustness against breakdown, or what Nassim Taleb calls "anti-fragility."[1] I argue that the best evidence we have for the anti-fragility of a system is its tenure and its ability to incrementally rather than radically reform itself in response to existential threats.

Tenure can be assessed through a simple counting exercise, and Canada performs well if we take this approach. Canadian representatives have been chosen by democratic means without interruption since Confederation in 1867. Our first peaceful transfer of power occurred just four years later. Only two countries have a longer record of democratic selection and peaceful transition[2]: the United Kingdom (since 1660 with the crowning of Charles II and the assertion of parliamentary supremacy) and the United States (arguably in 1801, with the first transfer of power from Adams to Jefferson). Of course, countries have not faced equally difficult circumstances, so one might reasonably object, for example, that the suspension of the democratic selection of leaders in various European countries in the Second World War says nothing at all about the robustness of their democratic institutions; rather, it is merely a case of breakdown after invasion and occupation by a foreign force. This is fair enough, though it perhaps unnecessarily downplays the pressures toward the suspension of democratic norms that Canada, the United States, and the United Kingdom have faced over the past century and a half.

One might also argue that such a counting exercise is meaningless, as Canada began from an advantageous position. From the beginning, it had a strong economic base, a set of basic democratic norms in its political culture, and no great shadow of the past hanging over its politics. Compared to more complex places, it had a much better starting position. Surely, it is no great achievement for Canada to have maintained democratic selection of leaders and to have staved off breakdown. Such an argument, however, ignores two broad sets of facts. First, Canada's starting position was a difficult one – political survival was never assured. Second, Canada's political system has been in a state of constant if modest reform to address the fundamental, genetic[3] challenges that it faces.

On the first point, consider the following stylized facts about Canada. First, Canada's starting position was one of deep divisions between people. Those divisions were over matters fundamental to self- and group-understanding. From the arrival of the first Europeans, Canada was populated by a mix of Catholics and Protestants, with the latter group occasionally divided internally over important debates. Overlaid on this were ethnic and linguistic divisions, sometimes neatly organized and other times not. To begin, divisions were between the French, Irish, and British, the last group having its own internal divisions to boot; then, further divisions sometimes emerged with the addition of German-speaking and Eastern European immigrants through the late nineteenth century. In the shadow of all of this were objectively awful actions toward Aboriginal Canadians. Divisions of identity were not the only ones. Economic interests were often directly opposed in some parts of the country over others. The interests of the commercial class in the Maritime provinces diverged from those in central Canada. With the eventual opening of the west and the explosion of Prairie agriculture, the interests of exporting farmers came up directly against the protectionist preferences of manufacturing interests in central Canada.

Such social divisions can often find expression in political parties.[4] However, the political system places sharp limits on the number of parties that can be expected to reasonably compete. The canonical findings here are those of Duverger[5] and, most centrally, Cox.[6] Duverger noted that majoritarian systems (like Canada's) tend toward a smaller number of parties (he said two), while proportional systems generate multiple parties. Cox articulated the conditions under which the multiplication of parties increases, characterizing it as a joint function of two factors: an electoral system that does not punish smaller parties, and multiple salient social divisions. Clearly, this later condition has obtained in Canada from the start. Much is often made of the fact that Canada is not "Israel or Italy."[7] I take this to mean that if Canada had adopted a system of proportional representation, it would not display the fragmentation and occasional sclerosis of those two political systems. The comparative data and serious analytical work suggests something different. In a more permissive electoral system, we have good reason to believe that Canada would have fragmented into a large number of political parties making not only regional appeals, but also direct appeals to ethnicity or language. Such is the tinder to the fire of identity politics.

The consequence of political parties fragmented along ethnic and confessional lines was obvious to early observers of Canadian politics, not least the French social scientist André Seigfreid, who undertook a comprehensive early account of the Canadian party system[8]:

> Aware of the sharpness of certain rivalries, they [the major political parties] know that if these are let loose without any counter-balance, the unity of the Dominion may be endangered. That is why they persistently apply themselves to prevent the formation of homogeneous parties, divided according to race, religion or class – a French party, for instance, or a Catholic party, or a Labour party. The clarity of political life suffers from this, but perhaps the existence of the federation can be preserved only at this price.[9]

Johnston provides clear examples of the efforts of parties to contain rather than exploit such deep divisions, even when they directly pitted some groups against others.[10] On matters as diverse as "the disposition of Jesuits' Estates in Quebec; the Manitoba schools controversy; and Northwest schools," national party leaders "strove to contain the passions, as each electoral coalition embodied conflicting forces."[11] As he notes, "Provincial politicians and provincially minded federal ones rubbed at sectarian sores, as did extra-parliamentary groups...," but "neither Macdonald nor Laurier sought to exploit them even covertly."[12] This was not just a matter of norms. It was a matter of responding to the electoral and governance incentives of our electoral system.

Critics of our electoral system often note the occasionally regional nature of some parties. Let us take them at their word that the concentrated expression of regional grievances within regional parties is a normatively bad thing. Two facts should not be ignored. First, regional parties that wish to experience governing invariably need to stop being regional. Those that do not are often punished by voters, though perhaps too slowly. Those who do wish to govern most often find themselves putting water in their wine as they broaden out their coalitions or collapse into other parties altogether. Second, the historical record is clear: in the thirty-three elections since 1904, the party that has won the most seats in most of Canada's five regions has formed government on twenty-seven occasions.[13] In short, parties that resist the well-known temptations to fragment and instead pursue the building of a diverse, permanent, national voter base are those who are most likely to form government. Our electoral system just might have something to do with the ability of our politics to avoid falling into fragmentation, regional grievance, and zero-sum national politics.

Critics of our current electoral system have misunderstood how effective it is in limiting party fragmentation. By ignoring the counterfactual of how fragmented the system would be under a different system, they mistakenly identify our limited regional parties as a failure, rather than as evidence of success. Critics have also given insufficient due to how other institutions have evolved to address concerns of a regional matter. Our electoral system is just one element of our system of federal political representation. Focusing only on it and ignoring other institutions misses the second important element of our national political institutions. Namely, while our electoral system has remained essentially unchanged,[14] other practices have emerged to better address national needs of representation. For example, when assembling cabinets, prime ministers used to give careful consideration both to regional balance and to religious and ethnic balance within regions. This has evolved appropriately over time, with various ethnic groups moving up or down the pecking order, while religion has largely disappeared as a basis for cabinet membership. At a higher level, the practice of federalism has evolved, for example in the creation of provincial secretariats and in meetings between first ministers.[15] Finally, at moments of acute crisis, we have considered massive overhauls to our constitutional structure, though for better or for worse these have been rejected. All of this is just to say that our system of political representation has evolved over time to address the unique needs of our country. This recommends against radical reform of the central institution for at least two reasons. First, comparative evidence on how the whole system will react to a change of a central component is uninformative, as no other country has the same set of unique and slowly constructed institutions that we do. Second, in the choice between slow evolution and exogenous shock, we should choose the latter only if we believe we are cleverer than evolution. We are not.[16]

Single-Party Government and Effective Representation

A second basic consideration when evaluating an electoral system is its ability to translate the preferences and interests of voters into policy. Absent this function, the advantage of democracy is less clear. I argue that our electoral system and the governments it produces allow for the effective representation of public preferences while also allowing for the manoeuvring room necessary to pursue fundamental policy reforms.

There is a common trade-off expressed in the literature on electoral systems, perhaps best articulated by Powell.[17] In this account, choosing an electoral system is about optimizing across two dimensions, which largely exist in trade-off with one another. The first is representation, broadly understood as the translation of voters' political preferences into legislative representation and eventually policy. The second is effectiveness and accountability, which can be understood as the ability of governments to set out and pursue clear policy agendas (effectiveness) and for voters to know which party was responsible for policy decisions (and failures) in the next election (accountability). I address the accountability element more in the next section.

Why would there be better political representation in a proportional representation system? First, because proportional systems are less punishing of small parties, they are more likely to be present in a legislature. This is an empirical reality.[18] With a greater diversity of parties comes a greater diversity of views. However, this is only one stage in many.[19] A government has to be formed from among those parties. Again, the empirical regularity is uncontroversial: proportional systems are more likely to lead to coalition governments (whether a minority or a majority)[20] and those coalitions likely represent a majority of voters. We can compare this with plurality systems, where a party often wins a majority of seats and thus all government power with sometimes far less than a majority of the vote. Coalition governments in a proportional system will form on the basis of a majority of votes; they will then negotiate over a policy agenda which will balance the priorities of the coalition partners. In theory, this is thought to produce policy outputs that are closer to the median voter and/or average ideal point. Advocates of proportional systems will contrast this with a plurality system, where a party elected to a majority with four in ten votes may then pursue policy some distance from the average voter's ideal point.

It is on this basis that many advocates of proportionality make their case. However, this account ignores three other empirical regularities. First, policy does not result directly from the expression of voters' preferences in an election.[21] The parties that form a coalition government need to come to an agreement over which policies will be pursued. In this negotiation process, there is no guarantee that power is divided with perfect proportionality between these parties. To the extent that it is not, distortions in policy outputs can occur, moving policy away from the ideal point of the average voter. Second, public preferences change. In light of events, what citizens want can often change, and dramatically so. Because coalitions are often built on tight policy agreements and mutual monitoring of coalition partners, it may well be the case that coalition governments are not able to respond to changing preferences with sufficient speed. So, while they may be closer to the average voter at the start of a mandate, it is not apparent that they can track changes in voters' preferences with any ease. Third, it is an empirical fact that governments do not last as long in proportional representation (PR) systems.[22] This is not a result of more frequent elections, but of mid-election changes in first ministers or, more relevant to this argument, in the complement of parties forming the coalition. What do such changes say about policy congruence? It seems unlikely that governments would change merely to enact the same suite of policies as the previous government. So, perhaps new governments are formed to move closer to the average voter's ideal point, but for this to be true the previous government would need to be off that ideal point.

Consider now policy representation under the single-party governments that are the norm in plurality systems. Such governments are unquestionably powerful, often to the point of abuse.[23] However, with power comes greater room to manoeuvre. A single party majority elected on one platform might be supported by only a minority of the population. However, they can, without fear of immediate sanction, move closer to the average voter's ideal point, especially given the lack of a constraining coalition agreement. Moreover, such governments are also able to swiftly pursue major policy reforms without fear of losing government before the next election. In the Canadian case, we need only think of the goods and services tax, the aggressive deficit reduction in Jean Chrétien's first mandate, or the phasing out of income trusts in Stephen Harper's first term. Such decisions were objectively good on efficiency and equity grounds, but were politically unpopular and largely contrary to party policy. Perhaps such policies would have been passed under coalition governments. Certainly, PR countries are not free of examples of political courage. But it certainly does seem easier to make such moves in the kind of single-party governments that result in plurality systems.

Until now, my argument has been largely one of hypothetical propositions. What do the data say on this point? A long line of work in political science examines the connection between the preferences of voters and the composition of governments and, sometimes, the policies they enact.[24] Earlier work often found a representation advantage for proportional representation.[25] However, some more current work suggests that there is simply not much overall difference between proportional and plurality countries.[26] Importantly, this is true both at the beginning of a mandate and at the end. Why proportional systems do not outperform majoritarian ones is not entirely clear, though it is reasonable to assume that it has something to do with the flexibility of coalition governments.

Accountability and the Limits of Voters

Until this point, I have argued at two levels of analysis. First, by considering the long-run performance of Canadian democracy, I have argued that Canada's majoritarian system performs well on something of a whole-system level. Second, by considering the representation of voters' preferences, I've examined the system at the level of the behaviour of parties and governments. Finally, I wish to examine our electoral system at the level of voters. There are three main arguments here. First, voters have severely limited capacities and we should approach these with sufficient realism. Second, voters are nonetheless central to accountability, and so we should ask under what conditions they can best exercise this function. Third, voters are humans and as such they are as prone to conflict as they are to compromise and conciliation. We should consider, at a normative level, how electoral systems appeal to the best and worst of voters.

To begin, we must acknowledge that voters are far from the perfectly rational agents assumed in many models of politics.[27] Instead, they are most often uninformed about the details of politics and public policy.[28] They make up their public opinions off the top of their heads.[29] When they do engage in active reasoning about politics, it is often poorly motivated and deeply biased. More often than not, their policy preferences follow from their partisanship, not vice versa.[30] Less formally, they are seemingly no more capable of always making good choices than they are of resisting the worst of hucksters and conmen.

Perhaps our only hope then is that voters might serve as agents of accountability. Whatever we think about the capacity of voters to reason over policy and to vote in an enlightened fashion, we have to at least believe that they have the capacity to throw out leaders whose policies and performance they do not approve of. Absent this belief, what exactly is the justification for democratic selection of leaders and parties?

In general, the evidence here is not inspiring. As Achen and Bartels painstakingly demonstrate, voters are not good at assigning blame and credit.[31] Nonetheless, we do not have an apparently better method than elections for enacting the peaceful removal of leaders. Is this better or worse in a proportional system? The most relevant evidence here likely comes from recent work by Raymond Duch and colleagues, using both observational work[32] and work in laboratory experiments.[33] They take seriously the cognitive limits of voters. Their work suggests that accountability – which we can understand to be correctly identifying and punishing those responsible for policy failure – is best in systems where there is a clarity of responsibility. These conditions best obtain when voters have to consider the actions of a single party, rather than a coalition made up of several, each of whom may try to escape blame.

Finally, we must acknowledge some hard truths about humans. As Niebuhr put it: "Man's capacity for justice makes democracy possible, but man's inclination to injustice makes it necessary."[34] Voters are not all bad, of course, but neither are they all good. In particular, as individuals whose identities are largely group-based, they are as inclined to seek differences with other groups as they are to look for similarities.[35] This is as true in politics as in other domains.[36] Moreover, at least some individuals take pleasure in the ruination of others, whether that destruction is material, spiritual, or political. Given this, what exactly should we hope for from political parties? Two broad possibilities exist. First, a small number of parties who take as their raison d'être the incorporation and downplaying of differences. Second, a large number of parties seeking to articulate sharply the differences between groups of citizens, even when those differences were previously unknown or unimportant to those voters. In the extreme, such articulations are not an appeal to a capacity for justice. If proportional systems do not have an advantage on matters of representation and if they do not have an advantage in accountability, what exactly is their appeal? One hopes that proponents do not see virtue in the politicization of small differences.

Conclusion

That Canada's electoral system is not perfect is self-evident. It often exaggerates the power of the largest party. It occasionally elects governments that quickly prove to be unpopular. It is occasionally an object of great discontent. But this is no basis for reform, because no other system is perfect. If we wish to assess our electoral system against some alternative, I argue that there are three reasonable and simple conditions. First, is the existing system as likely to ensure the continued democratic selection of rulers as any proposed alternative? On this measure, our existing system performs well. Moreover, we should accept that there is substantial uncertainty involved in the effect of shifting to a whole new system, particularly on all the other institutions and practices that have slowly evolved alongside our electoral system. Second, does the existing system represent voters' preferences as well as an alternative system? Once we consider the various stages involved in converting preferences to policy, the answer seems to be yes. Third, which system is better suited to a realistic understanding of voters, not least in their ability to hold governments to account? Again, our existing system scores respectably. We ought not change.

4

Electoral Reform Is Not a Rights Issue

Emmett Macfarlane

Some proponents of electoral reform claim that basic civil rights are infringed by the existing first-past-the-post (FPP) electoral system. The implication is that vote equality and the right to vote under the Charter of Rights and Freedoms necessitate changing to a system of proportional representation (PR). The claim is also used in response to arguments in favour of a referendum on electoral reform: because rights are implicated, it would be "immoral" to permit the public to vote on the issue.[1]

After examining these arguments in light of the electoral reform debate as well as existing Charter jurisprudence on democratic rights, I argue that the central claim is without merit. Established interpretation of the Charter explicitly recognizes that the choice of electoral system involves weighing different, sometimes competing, values and objectives, and that Parliament ought to enjoy significant latitude in determining the voting method and related electoral rules. While advocates of electoral reform have legitimate (and debatable) concerns about the purported fairness of the existing system, and there is considerable room for reasonable disagreement about the values FPP privileges relative to PR systems, these concerns do not rise to the level of rights infringements.

The paper also explores why this unsupportable and misguided argument is so popular with advocates of reform. I argue that their claims are an example of inflationary "rights talk," something Mary Ann Glendon describes as the "increasing tendency to speak of what is most important to us in terms of rights and to frame nearly every social controversy as a clash of rights."[2] The dangers of rights talk are that policy issues and values debates are immediately elevated to the level of absolutist entitlements. In the context of the Canadian debate on electoral reform, rights talk is explicitly employed to delegitimize arguments in favour of the status quo or of putting the issue to a referendum. As a consequence, political consensus over the issue is more difficult to achieve, in turn making the legitimacy of any changes more likely to be cast in doubt.

Transforming a Values Debate into a Rights Claim

The notion that rights are implicated by electoral reform is advanced by politicians, academics, and lobby groups. Green Party leader Elizabeth May describes the central electoral reform issue as follows: "We are essentially talking about a rights issue: the right that every voter knows that their vote will count. Essentially, in getting to a proportional representation system of some kind we're looking after minority rights."[3] Political science professor Dennis Pilon explains it from the perspective of vote equality:

> [O]ur current voting system privileges geography, though geography is not the basis informing that vote. Thus proximate voters – voters who live close to each other – are privileged by our system, while dispersed voters are discriminated against. This violates the voters' rights to have their votes count equally. This issue actually affects all parties. Voters of all parties find themselves marooned in different parts of the country, unable to make common cause with voters who agree with the kinds of things they would like to see represented. This leads to wasted votes, distorted representation of parties, and typically a legislative majority government that a majority of Canadians do not actually support.[4]

And Fair Vote Canada, a lobby group that argues in favour of implementing proportional representation, argues that "Canada's Charter of Rights and Freedoms asserts that Canada is a free and democratic society and that all citizens deserve equal treatment under the law. Canada needs to make every vote count equally."[5]

These arguments share something in common, in that they each assume their starting premise – proportionality is the primary value that should be privileged in a voting system – in order to conclude that the existing system violates rights by not resulting in proportional outcomes. While criticisms of disproportionate outcomes produced by FPP are fair and legitimate, the arguments advanced by proponents end up framing the entire electoral reform debate through the lens of how popular national vote share is translated. This is done to the exclusion of other attributes and values, when the debate is actually about the competing values or principles reflected in each system.

As a result, these electoral reform advocates employ dubious rhetoric about "making every vote count" or "wasted votes" that simply do not treat majoritarian systems fairly on their own terms. Federal elections in Canada under FPP are effectively 338 distinct electoral contests. It is facile to suggest that votes that do not result in one's favoured candidate winning are wasted or do not count. Similarly, the talking point that FPP produces "false majorities" is true from the perspective of the proportionality of national vote shares, but it is false from the perspective of a system where the relevant unit of measurement is the number of riding-level contests a party can win.

The electoral reform debate is a question of values, and FPP privileges parties that have broad enough appeal to win geographic-based ridings. It also allows voters to hold single-party governments to account in a more straightforward manner than might be the case under a proportional system that encourages coalition governments. In a large, diverse federation like Canada, an appeal to such values is not inherently unfair or unreasonable. It is perfectly legitimate to argue that proportionality ought to take precedence over geographic-based modes of representation, but advocates of PR engage in shallow and trite analytical reasoning when they rhetorically reframe the way FPP operates – indeed, is intended to operate based on the underlying principles it advances – into claims about vote equality and rights.

If certain advocates of PR find the notion of competing values underlying the electoral reform debate unpersuasive, then they need to consider how their arguments would translate into an actual rights claim under the Charter. The next section explores this in light of the existing Charter jurisprudence on voting rights.

Voting Rights under the Charter

In its brief to the parliamentary committee on electoral reform, Fair Voting BC argues that the "need for voting reform should be seen primarily as a civil rights issue aimed at ensuring equal treatment of all voters and delivering effective representation to the greatest extent possible."[6] The lobby group supports this claim by stating that the FPP system "leaves upwards of half the voters without an MP they have voted for, which has the practical effect of denying these voters a voice in parliament."[7] Under PR, the argument goes, every vote is counted equally. Thus by "making every vote count," the system would "nearly double the number of voters represented in Parliament."[8] The logic that voters who do not directly elect the winning candidate somehow go unrepresented is dubious at best, but Fair Voting BC asserts that the nature of party discipline in Canada renders any broader conception of representation a misunderstanding of the system.[9]

But would an argument that under FPP voters are "effectively disenfranchised"[10] succeed under the Charter? Section 3 of the Charter states that "Every citizen of Canada has the right to vote in an election of members of the House of Commons or of a legislative assembly and to be qualified for membership therein." The major jurisprudence under section 3 has seen courts deal with a variety of issues implicating rules surrounding the electoral system. Courts have invalidated restrictions that prohibit certain categories of people from voting, including judges[11] and prisoners,[12] but have upheld residency requirements.[13] The Supreme Court has upheld laws that advance equality of participation in the electoral process in challenges to federal third-party advertising legislation[14] and a ban on the dissemination of election results before polls in other parts of the country have closed.[15]

As it relates to the constitutionality of the existing system, three cases stand out for their elaboration on the meaning of the right to vote. These cases involve electoral boundaries,[16] restrictions on benefits for political parties,[17] and a direct challenge to the FPP system in Quebec.[18] The most consequential elements of the first two cases are the elaboration of the twin pillars of the right to vote, which the Supreme Court has said include the right to effective representation and the right to meaningful participation. In the third case, these were applied to determine that the FPP system does not violate voting rights or a principle of vote equality.

In *Reference re Prov. Electoral Boundaries (Sask.)*, changes to electoral boundaries in Saskatchewan were subject to constitutional scrutiny. The changes introduced quotas for urban and rural seats, resulting in ridings that were permitted to vary by up to 25 per cent of a "provincial quotient", with the two northern ridings varying by up to 50 per cent. A majority of the Court eschewed a "one person, one vote" rule, determining that the right to vote "is not equality of voting power *per se*, but the right to 'effective representation.'" The majority also concluded effective representation includes a consideration of many factors, including geography, parity of voting power, community history and interests, and minority representation. Absolute voting parity is impossible in practice, and so it is reasonable, the Court concluded, to take into account other values "to ensure that our legislative assemblies effectively represent the diversity of our social mosaic." In the context of electoral boundaries, the variance in riding sizes did not amount to a violation of section 3. The Court's logic that legislative consideration of factors other than vote parity is both necessary and legitimate no doubt applies to electoral reform as well.

Federal restrictions on benefits to political parties that do not nominate at least fifty candidates were struck down as unconstitutional in *Figueroa v. Canada*.[19] The Court determined that in addition to effective representation, section 3 encapsulates a right to meaningful participation in the electoral process.[20] Iacobucci rejected the government's argument that parties that run fewer than fifty candidates do not advance the objective of effective representation. He characterized section 3 as "participatory in nature,"[21] stating further that "the electoral process has an intrinsic value independent of its impact upon the actual outcome of elections."[22] The members and supporters of political parties can play a meaningful role in the election process even if they put forward fewer than fifty candidates. Here, a meaningful role in the electoral process is not limited to a party's ability to provide a genuine "government option."[23]

Justice LeBel agreed with the overall argument advanced by his colleague but wrote a concurring opinion about how meaningful participation should be defined. Specifically, he disagreed with Iacobucci's emphasis on the individual aspects of meaningful participation, arguing that communitarian features, such as national representation and inter-group alliances, were relevant.[24] LeBel argued that other values relevant to the electoral process, including cohesiveness and aggregation, ought to be recognized in the section 3 analysis.[25] Citing the existing FPP electoral system as "perhaps the most significant example" of the constitutional relevance of these values,[26] LeBel noted that while FPP creates biases in favour of larger, mainstream parties and "distorts" the translation of votes into seats, it represents broad communities of diverse interests and creates stable majorities connected to the Canadian tradition of responsible government, thereby fostering a strong political centre and reducing factionalism.[27] Importantly, especially in light of the question of the current electoral system's consistency with section 3, LeBel wrote:

> It should be emphasized that I do not intend to express any opinion about the consistency of our FPP electoral system with s. 3 of the Charter. Any challenge to that system will have to be evaluated on its own merits. Nor would I wish to give the impression that I consider stability, majority governments or aggregation to be more important than fair participation. Nevertheless, within the boundaries set by the Constitution, it is the legislature's prerogative to choose whether to enhance these values over other democratic values, or not. Still less should I be taken as suggesting that FPP or any feature of the electoral system that favours larger parties is constitutionally *mandated*. On the contrary, I would argue that *the government has a fairly wide latitude in choosing how to design the electoral system and how to combine the various competing values at play.*[28]

For his part, Iacobucci noted that "the Charter is entirely neutral as to the type of electoral system in which the right to vote or to run for office is to be exercised. This suggests that the purpose of s. 3 is not to protect the values or objectives that might be embedded in our current electoral system, but, rather, to protect the right of each citizen to play a meaningful role in the electoral process, whatever that process might be."[29]

Despite an apparent disagreement about the level of analysis as it concerns particular values and how meaningful participation is applied, it is noteworthy that the fundamental agreement between Iacobucci and LeBel regards the degree of latitude the electoral system itself ought to be afforded under any section 3 analysis.

This was precisely the result in a 2011 constitutional challenge to the FPP system in *Daoust v. Quebec*. Drawing on the Supreme Court's analysis in *Figueroa*, the Quebec Court of Appeal rejected claimants' arguments that the FPP system prevented effective representation and meaningful participation. Notably, this decision upheld the decision of the lower court. Noting that no electoral system is perfect, Justice Dufresne concluded that "effective representation is not dependent on the electoral system, and the evidence does not justify asserting that the first-past-the-post system that prevails in Quebec makes the representation of citizens ineffective. On the contrary, the expert evidence tends to demonstrate that every system has shortcomings. Therefore, it cannot be concluded that the principle of effective representation is violated solely as a function of the electoral system."[30] For an electoral system to be valid, it "must confer on the electorate or assure it of a minimal, albeit significant, degree of representation."[31]

Judicial reasoning as it relates to voting rights simply does not accord with the proposition advanced by electoral reform advocates that FPP infringes rights. PR proponents' arguments do not reflect existing or reasonable interpretations of the Charter.

The Rights Claim as Rhetorical Tactic: Rights Talk in Action

Rights talk, as noted above, elevates a debate about principles and values to a question of rights and is a tactic employed to end discussion and disagreement. As Glendon argues, rights talk represents a claim to an entitlement, constraining opportunities for consensus or compromise, and markedly increasing the chances for conflict.[32] In this context, rights are used as trump cards to delegitimize the arguments of those who disagree.

Some PR advocates adopt this tactic explicitly, such as in the context of arguing against a referendum on electoral reform: "Putting our current system to a vote in a national referendum won't give it democratic legitimacy, it will just violate the rights of voters to have their votes count equally. The higher order principle here is voter equality and you don't put such principles to a vote."[33] The overt assumption here is that vote equity is not just a more important feature of the electoral system than other considerations, like geography, accountability, aggregation or efficiency, but also that there exists a right to it in spite of other values. While advocates articulate the importance of vote equality or proportionality, they are unsuccessful at explaining why these values ought to be regarded as rights while the principles privileged by other electoral systems are not.

Rights talk could easily be employed by defenders of the status quo, who might simply assert that they have a right to the geographically based, one-to-one relationship with their member of Parliament. Electoral systems that employ multimember ridings could be said to obfuscate the relationship between representative and voter, thereby infringing the principle of effective representation. Similarly, PR systems that use party lists to ensure proportionality could be said to infringe the right to meaningful participation, as a voter would have no idea whether their vote would result in the election of the third candidate on a party list or the twentieth. Surely the right to vote encompasses knowing who your vote might elect! Such arguments enjoy an internal logical coherence premised on the idea that geographic representation holds special weight, but they lose their coherence entirely if other values – like proportionality – are given due recognition as legitimate contenders in the debate. And like the rights claims made by PR advocates, these hypothetical arguments have no realistic basis in existing constitutional law.

Indeed, not only are these rights claims unpersuasive in the context of the public debate about electoral reform, but they have also failed at court, as the *Daoust* case demonstrates. One of the additional risks of rights talk is that it encourages the transfer of responsibility for making policy choices to courts, a phenomenon recognized as the "judicialization of politics."[34] Unable to succeed in the political arena by convincing a majority of their fellow citizens that the existing electoral system is flawed, proponents of reform attempt to get the judiciary to compel reform by fiat. It is unfortunate for them that no reasonable reading of the Charter entertains such a claim.

The debate over electoral reform is in one sense a question of public policy. How should an electoral system translate votes into seats? How should the electoral system reflect the nature of representation in a large, diverse federation? In another important sense, these are questions about competing principles and values. While it is certainly possible to imagine scenarios where certain proposals run up against the democratic rights in the Charter – the right to be eligible for membership for office, for example, could be implicated by a system that gives complete control to parties and rules out independent candidates – neither the current system nor the major proposed alternatives are likely to do so.[35] An attempt to transform the current debate into one about rights is an attempt to end the debate before it starts. It is unprincipled and disingenuous. To cry rights infringement when one does not like the status quo or the outcome of an inherently political process is to devalue the very concept of rights. Worse still, it is undemocratic to presume that the most fundamental link between the state and society should be determined in any other manner than political deliberation and clear consensus.

5

The Imaginary Worlds of Electoral System Reform

Christopher Cochrane

Should we reform Canada's electoral system and, if yes, what alternative should we adopt? Many people answer this question like lawyers making a case for their client. They state a position, then follow with reams of evidence that support it, one hundred percent. The evidence heralds nothing good about the status quo and nothing bad about some proposed alternative. Or it reveals nothing good about some alternative and nothing bad about the status quo. There are entire chapters, articles, and books that proceed in this way. And many of the most vocal arguments are of precisely this form. This style is acceptable, of course, especially for arguments about values and morals, where insights usually emerge from a clash of perspectives. But it is not a convincing style when our decisions require nuanced and balanced assessments of messy evidence from the social world. And therein lies the problem: the debate about electoral reform is framed, first and foremost, as a question of values; in fact, it's mostly an empirical question.

Don't get me wrong. Given that no electoral system aspires to maximize all of the things that we want, while at the same time minimizing all of the things that we do not want, reforming the electoral system *is* to some extent about priorities. But we fixate on this aspect. Thus, for example, we start by outlining key values, and then move on to weighting the pros and cons of what each electoral system aspires to induce in the political environment. Do we want the greater government accountability fostered by single-member plurality (SMP) systems, or should we sacrifice some of this accountability in order to get more representativeness from a system of proportional representation (PR)? Should we aspire to the ideological diversity induced by PR, or should we give up some of this diversity in favour of the political civility promoted by alternative vote (AV)? Thinking about these types of questions is undoubtedly important, not least because it clarifies how more of some values implies less of others. We will not get very far if we trod off naïvely without regard to these interdependencies. Logic matters. But so does evidence.

Two assumptions underlie the view that electoral reform is primarily about values. The first is that we understand reasonably well the effect of the single-member plurality system on the way politics in Canada plays out. The second and even more questionable assumption is that we understand the consequences of changing the electoral system. When it comes to understanding the political world, our track record does not justify such a high degree of confidence, especially about the pristine theoretical worlds that we imagine some reform to produce. Let's face it: at the precipice of electoral reform, claims for and against taking the plunge are ultimately claims about the relative desirability of a real world state of affairs that we barely understand, and a bunch of imaginary alternatives that we understand less well still. We know little of how SMP affects politics in this country. We know less about what politics would look like under PR, AV, or any other system.

As always, the fog of uncertainty surrounds us. We should tread carefully. The remainder of this paper outlines five things that a comprehensive argument for electoral reform has to address, if it is to provide a convincing map for the way forward.[1]

I. A Description of the Best Political World Attainable

First, what political world do we hope to attain? Here, we outline the criteria that we use to judge political worlds, and then imagine their optimal instantiation. But this is not the best world imaginable; it is the best world attainable. And so we need to be explicit about our understanding of the relevant elements of that world, including things like the motives of citizens and politicians, the effects of institutions, the laws of economics, and so on. We also need to take into consideration that elements of the world are not independent of each other; they interact. At a minimum, we need to be explicit about the compatibility of our criteria with one another. Increasing the score on one criterion may entail decreasing our score on one or more other criteria.

Crucially, this ideal world will rarely have a direct link to the electoral system. Indeed, if our best possible political world is something like "a political system where seats are awarded in proportion to the share of the votes that each party receives in an election," or "a world where people get to vote with ranked ballots" – if that's our idea of the best possible world, then we need to get out of the house more often. In thinking about electoral reform, we need to stop focusing so closely on the nickels and dimes of electoral systems, and instead ask those for and against reform to be more explicit about the political world to which they aspire. Among other things, this will clear up misunderstandings before they are buried in the minutia of labyrinthine arguments.

II. A Description of the Current Political World

Second, what does the status quo look like and how does the current electoral system affect it? If we cannot answer this question, we have no basis for proposing reform or guesstimating the consequences. We don't want a "just so" story, either: we want evidence. It is possible that an SMP system might disadvantage women by allowing parties to set up female candidates in unwinnable ridings, but is that actually happening? If so, which parties are doing it? It is possible that an SMP system might turn people off the electoral system by making them feel like their vote is wasted, but is that actually happening? How many non-voters are disengaged from politics because they have calculated the futility of their vote under current electoral rules? More generally, do people's perceptions and feelings track actual, real-world conditions and institutional configurations? And if so, how closely?

III. Description of the Political World, if the Proposed Change Is Made

Third, what will the political world look like once our change is made? In other words, if we change the electoral system, what do we expect to happen? Note here that we can never change one and only one thing in a system. If we change one thing, we change many things. Thus, our description of what the world will look like implies an understanding of the interconnections between relevant features of the current world. These relevant features include the motives of politicians, the thought process of voters, the effects of institutions, and so on. The complexity is overwhelming. Thus, we need to model the system. Our model of this imaginary world may be more or less developed, but it is invariably less certain and reliable than our model of the current world. This is true for two reasons. First, we can actually observe the current world; we can only imagine the alternative. Second, the model of the imaginary world is just a model of the current world with additional assumptions about the effects of the proposed reform. These additional assumptions are never sure things, and so the model can only be less certain.

IV. Assessment of the Desirability of the Current and Alternative Worlds

Fourth, what are the benefits, costs, and risks of reform? What is the relative desirability of the current and alternative worlds in terms of the criteria outlined in Part I? In what ways is the imagined world better and in what respects worse than the current world? How much better (or worse) overall? According to our models, what are the risks and uncertainty?

It is impossible to make an informed decision without answers to these questions. We need to know about the rewards, the costs, and the risks.

V. A Map of the Proximity Between the Current World, the Alternative World, and the Best-Case Scenario

Finally, what is the proximity of the current and alternative worlds to the best attainable world outlined in Part I? It is important to note that proximity and desirability are not the same thing. Proximity is defined here as the inverse of the difficulty of moving from one state of affairs to another. Where there are multiple dimensions to consider and interdependencies between dimensions, the landscape is a "moderately rugged" terrain riddled with local optima. Thus, we may move in the direction of something better and away from our objective, or toward a local optimum and away from the global optimum. Given a reasonable understanding of the complexity of social and political phenomena, this possibility holds, no matter the criteria outlined in Part I. There's no ladder straight to the top. There's a rough landscape of peaks and troughs.

This is why we have to be careful about narrowly defining our ambitions – the nickel and diming that I mentioned above. Moving in the right direction, in a small window of reality, may be to move in the wrong direction, in the bigger frame. And once we move, there is no guarantee that we can move back. As hard it is to change institutions, it may be a lot harder, if not impossible, to change them in the new system. Institutional reform is sometimes a one-way street. Students of political history know this full well.

VI. Summary

In sum, arguments for (or against) electoral reform should include five things: I) A description of the best political world attainable; II) A description of the current political world (which must include the impact of the present electoral system); III) A description of the political world if the proposed change is made; IV) An assessment of the desirability of the current and alternative world; and V) a map of the proximity between the current world, the alternative world, and the best case scenario.

Notice the importance of careful science and evidence. Even at the very first step, where we lay out our vision of the best possible world we can imagine, much of the work is in the domain of logic and evidence. We need to think about the interdependencies of the things we want to maximize and minimize. We need to consider the limits of human nature, the legacies of institutions, and so on. The burden of evidence is clearer still in the second step, where we turn to rich descriptions, analytical models, and evidence. The third step is the modelling exercise that underpins the fourth step. And the fifth step is our understanding of how all the pieces fit together.

The debate about electoral reform is no straightforward question of values. We should talk more about the political world we want. And much more about what we do, and do not know, about the worlds off in the distance, is shrouded by the fog of uncertainty.

PART TWO

Evidence and Experience

Voter Choice and Accountability: A Case for Caution about Electoral Reform

Elizabeth Goodyear-Grant

There are multiple criteria against which to evaluate electoral systems. The classic literature points to two types: democratic criteria and state management criteria.[1] Current debates about electoral systems, including whether Canada should alter its system, typically emphasize the former, and do so narrowly given our preoccupation with disproportionality in the conversion of votes to seats, as well as the seeming contribution of single-member plurality (SMP) electoral rules to the underrepresentation of women, Indigenous peoples, and racial minorities (the latter two groups are not currently numerically underrepresented at the federal level in Canada).

This paper will provide a more comprehensive analysis, looking at a fuller range of democratic criteria, and focusing on the relationship between voter choice, government composition, and accountability under major electoral system types. The paper raises considerable doubt about whether connections between voters and governments are enhanced under alternate electoral rules. For PR systems and possibly for mixed systems, the coalition governments that would surely consistently result, given Canada's regional and ethnocultural divisions, would blur accountability between voters and government. Moreover, while PR systems excel at translating votes directly to seats, what matters most in systems of responsible government are governments. Current debates focus unduly, therefore, on legislative composition. Insufficient

attention has been paid to government composition and its relationship to voter preferences under alternate electoral rules. Post-election
coalition bargaining has the potential to create a policy chasm between
the mandate given to parties by voters during elections and the legislative agenda that multiparty coalitions actually pursue.

Ultimately, I make a case for greater caution about electoral reform
than has been seen thus far. Maybe Canada ought to change its electoral formula, although this paper suggests that great skepticism is
warranted on that front. Considering a fuller spectrum of democratic
evaluative criteria, not to mention government performance criteria –
which I leave aside in this paper – suggests that alternative systems have
critical shortcomings. This is no surprise to scholars of institutions,
because the literature is clear that there is no "best" electoral formula.
If Canada were to pursue electoral change, at the very least my paper
presents a compelling case for a more comprehensive analysis of the
full spectrum of implications using all the evaluative criteria on which
electoral systems are typically assessed. This would require us to move
away from lopsided debates that focus quite narrowly on a single criterion: proportionality in the votes to seats ratio.

Evaluating Electoral Systems

Revisiting the classic literature on electoral systems reminds us that there
is a suite of criteria against which to appraise electoral systems. Dunleavy and Margetts outline two major sets of criteria: democratic criteria
and state management criteria. Drawn from democratic theory, the first
theme contains several sets of criteria for judging the democratic quality
of electoral formulae (the way votes are translated into seats): political
equality, representation of viewpoints, accountability, and the importance of elections for determining government composition as the key
components. Within the state management theme, Dunleavy and Margetts identify three sets of criteria: governability, party system stability,
and handling of social conflicts. All these criteria are broadly reflective of
theoretical work on electoral systems,[2] so I will stick with Dunleavy and
Margetts's criteria in this paper for the sake of simplicity.

As is emphasized repeatedly in the theoretical literature on electoral systems, from Duverger onward, the different types of electoral

formulae reflect different visions of democracy.[3] Each major family of systems emphasizes different norms about the ultimate functions of elected representatives and governments. As such, systems vary in their performance on each of the individual items in the democratic and state management evaluative criteria. Majoritarian systems – which typically produce genuine or manufactured seat majorities at the legislative level – tend to perform better on most state management criteria than proportional systems. Proportional systems tend to perform better on most of the democratic criteria (though not all, as this paper will argue, particularly accountability). Less is known about mixed systems' performance because they are relatively rare, and because their use is relatively new,[4] and their effects vary depending on their configuration.

Public Opinion about Governance

In Canada, it seems premature to examine options for electoral reform and the mechanisms through which reform should occur (i.e., national binding referendum or not). Dissatisfaction with governance broadly among Canadians has been a concern for some time, but what we make of this is unclear. Trust and confidence in government have increased over the past year, perhaps as a result of a change in government. Environics reports that the proportion of Canadians who believe the federal government is working is 13 percentage points higher than it was two years ago, and the main changes Canadians would like to see in government are "better leadership, more accountability and more efficient spending."[5] Environics' Institute on Governance wrote a report in June 2016, entitled "Canadian Public Opinion on Governance 2016," drawing on the organization's ample data on the subject, which reveals that "Canadians express interest in changing the country's electoral system, but this does not reflect widespread or deep-seated desire for reform."[6] The report goes on to explain that:

> in terms of changing the country's longstanding "first past the post" method of electing MPs to Parliament, a majority favours changes, but only one in four Canadians believes that these should be major in scope. None of the alternative voting systems currently under consideration are clearly favoured, although the mixed member

proportional method is comparatively more popular than the others tested. The results suggest the public as a whole is not yet engaged in the issue of reforming the federal electoral voting system ...[7]

Arguably, support for electoral reform does not dwell deeply in the population, and is not the only or perhaps even the principal driver of dissatisfaction with governance. Even if public opinion data were sufficiently consistent to suggest that there is something "broken" about the way government operates, it is far from clear that the defective component is the electoral formula, or that its replacement is the solution.

In addition to the ambiguity around public opinion on electoral reform specifically and governance broadly, we can also see that that the electoral reform debate has advanced prematurely in this country. This is seen in our neglect of broad-based discussion about the sort of political system we want; which institutions are responsible for the current malaise; and, if it is the electoral system that is responsible, whether our electoral formula should be designed to promote democratic or state management ideals. We have heard little about the trade-offs involved in reform; for example, what we might be sacrificing if we move away from SMP electoral rules. We have not heard about the risks involved in institutional change more generally, especially important given the far-reaching consequences for the party system, government function, and political choice that may come from altering the electoral formula. The theoretical literature unequivocally states that we cannot have it all. A choice of electoral formula is a choice about our vision for democracy, and a change in electoral formula will not rid us of the system's shortcomings. Rather, fundamental change would simply require us to live with different shortcomings. There is no "best" or "ideal" electoral system; each emphasizes a different approach to democratic governance.

So, my first caution about our current trajectory is this: we must examine what sort of political system we want and what sort of values we want to prioritize before we can possibly know whether to keep or ditch our current electoral formula, and if the latter is the case, we must look at which electoral formula would best suit our political community. Under the heading "Criteria for Design," the International

IDEA Handbook of Electoral System Design strongly recommends that "when designing an electoral system, it is best to start with a list of criteria which sum up what you want to achieve, what you want to avoid and, in a broad sense, what you want your parliament and government to look like."[8] Canada has not had this debate, despite the fact that we think it is essential for new democracies to do so before adopting electoral rules. In contrast, the front page of the government of Canada's website on its current electoral reform consultations states that "the Government has committed to have a new voting system put in place before the next federal election. These reforms will be aimed at better representing the views of Canadians and improving public trust in our political system." Not only does the government appear committed to ditching SMP rules (though there are hints this may have changed recently), it also seems to be communicating that the core values at the heart of electoral rules should be mirroring the electorate's cleavages in the legislature (i.e., proportionality in votes to seats conversion) and generating public confidence. These might be good criteria, but without a fuller examination, it is impossible to know if these should be the values driving our choice of electoral formula.

Selective Focus on Disproportionality

My second caution relates to the selective terms of public debate regarding the comparative strengths and weaknesses of our current system and its alternatives. Public discussion of electoral reform in Canada focuses overwhelmingly on disproportionality. For example, the federal political parties that promote electoral change pay little attention to evaluative standards beyond disproportionality. The "Good Government" portion of the Green Party's platform says this about improving governance: "the critical first step in this process is to ensure we have a government that represents the will of the people – that means an end to first-past-the-post voting, an end to false majorities, and the creation of a voting system that ensures all Canadians have a voice in our government."[9] The NDP, which also campaigned in the last federal election on a platform that included electoral reform, likewise focuses on disproportionality – both parties do, in part, because they are disadvantaged in the conversion of votes to seats under SMP rules. Even the

Bloc Québécois, which used to benefit under SMP rules but has not in the last couple of electoral cycles, has started to publicly discuss electoral reform. In its platform, the NDP says that change is needed so that "Canada's electoral system truly·represents the expressions of voters, ensuring Parliament reflects real party support across Canada."[10]

Statements from these opposition parties reflect the first two of Dunleavy and Margetts' four democratic criteria: concern with political equality and the representation of viewpoints, interpreted here to mean the equal or proportional representation of diverse viewpoints. Proportional some mixed systems excel on these criteria, designed as they are to reproduce a microcosm of society in the legislature. By extension, the focus on equal representation of diverse viewpoints provides a strong basis for critiquing the disproportionality of SMP electoral systems. Disproportionality has become a common feature of Canadian election results, at all levels, and does not require further elaboration here.

Accountability

Popular discourse about electoral reform in Canada pays much less attention to Dunleavy and Margetts' other two democratic criteria: accountability and the idea that elections should determine government composition. And this is not to mention state management criteria, which I leave aside for this paper on account of space constraints. The current debate has focused narrowly on two of the four democratic criteria. It is the accountability criterion that needs examination in the Canadian context. Not only is this criterion critical to democratic governance, but Canadians are clear in their desire for greater government accountability, as discussed above. I focus primarily on relationships of accountability between voters and parties/government, rather than between the executive and the legislature (a distinction that is an important dimension of Westminster government, and germane to debates about electoral reform in Canada).

Increasingly, scholars of voting behaviour are asking how the vote calculus is conditioned by context,[11] which is central to the query of how different electoral rules would affect performance voting and relationships of accountability more generally. Why is accountability so important in our assessment of whether Canada should change its electoral system? First, some classic theory and much of popular discourse takes it for granted that proportionality in the conversion of votes to seats is what determines representativeness. As Manin, Przeworski, and Stokes note, the assumption is that "if the assembly is descriptively representative, then it will act to represent interests of the represented. As a consequence, discussions of representative institutions focus almost exclusively on electoral systems."[12] They go on to note that "the pathbreaking, and still unduly ignored, contribution of Pitkin (1967) was to problematize this connection: is it true that proportionality is the best way to secure representation?"[13] At the very least, we cannot assume that proportionality in the votes to seats ratio ensures representation. Indeed, the accountability view on representation suggests that without clear accountability – specifically, well-functioning mechanisms through which voters can punish and reward representatives and governments for their actions – representation may be incomplete or of poor quality. As such, we must not neglect how accountability functions under electoral formulae.

Manin, Przeworski, and Stokes summarize nicely what accountability is: "Governments are 'accountable' if voters can discern whether governments are acting in their interest and sanction them appropriately."[14] Two components, then, are required for accountability: clarity of responsibility for government action, and mechanisms of sanction. It is the first component that may prove problematic under alternate electoral formulae.

SMP electoral rules promote accountability fairly neatly. Accountability at the district level is simple in that there is one member of Parliament (MP) elected per district, who is answerable to voters in the district for his/her actions in the preceding term. Accountability is simple at the government level as well in that SMP tends to produce single-party seat majorities in the legislature, and thus single-party majority governments at the executive level, establishing clear responsibility for government actions. Performance voting is easy because policy responsibility is concentrated in a single party.[15] When governments perform well, the party is rewarded with continued support of the electorate, and when they perform poorly, the party is turned out of office.

What effect might alternate electoral rules have on voters' ability to assign policy responsibility? Certain types of electoral formulae – proportional and mixed systems, but also possibly preferential systems – tend to result in minority or coalition governments. Without the seat bonuses that plurality winners typically receive under SMP rules, single-party governing majorities would be rarer, and probably eliminated altogether given that no party has won a majority of the popular vote in a Canadian federal election in three decades, since 1984. The fragmentation of the party system post-1993 coincided with a similar division of the national vote. If multipartism is a feature of our electoral landscape now, despite our use of SMP rules, defying Duverger's prediction,[16] adoption of proportional or mixed rules would likely increase party system fragmentation, particularly given the entrenched regional and ethnocultural cleavages in Canadian society, as well as the variation in economic interests in a mixed economy with regionalized primary industries.

Minority governments are workable in Westminister systems – prime ministers Diefenbaker, Harper, and others have proven that. And while their durability varies, minority governments' policy records are respectable. Taking a closer look, however, the actions taken by minority governments in Canada to retain control of government have sometimes drawn criticism, such as Harper's 2008 prorogation of Parliament following a threat of non-confidence of the House as a result of the cooperation of three of the opposition parties (NDP, Liberal, Bloc Québécois). Harper's prorogation was constitutional, but drew widespread criticism nonetheless as a heavy-handed strategy to avoid facing the will of the House.

On durability, minority governments are tempted to resort to mechanisms such as prorogation because minority governments are in constant peril of losing the confidence of the House. There have been thirteen minority governments in Canada over our federal electoral history, and their average duration is 479 days, which is less than a year and a half. No minority government in Canada has lasted the standard four-year term.

It is likely that the persistent lack of a majority seat winner under proportional or mixed electoral rules, and possibly preferential voting rules, would lead over time to coalition governments. There would be every incentive for parties to cooperate in order to avoid the relatively short lives of minority governments, as noted above. It is difficult to speculate about the number and identities of parties that would come together to form governing coalitions in Canada, in part because we cannot assume that the current party system would hold under a new electoral formula. New parties might form and existing parties might wither. One thing is certain: we cannot simply predict parties' hypothetical seat counts under alternate rules based on votes cast under SMP rules. Some people most certainly would vote differently under alternative electoral formulae, changing the distribution of the vote across parties. As noted above, scholars have been adamant that both individual and contextual features influence the vote calculus, and electoral rules are central forces on the contextual side.

What does coalition government mean for accountability? Like some of the earliest scholars of voting behaviour,[17] I argue it diminishes accountability. This view is corroborated by the empirical literature, which finds that accountability is lower under coalition than single-party governments, and is actually inversely related to the number of partners in a coalition, independent of other factors.[18] Put simply, multiparty coalitions blur lines of responsibility for policy action, making it difficult for voters to assign blame and credit for a government's record, the central task involved in performance voting. When clarity of responsibility for government action is diminished, accountability will be diminished because voters struggle to divvy blame and credit for government action among coalition partners. Moreover, even when voters understand that blame and credit should not be assigned equally across coalition partners – for there is usually a "head of government" or lead partner – they struggle with how to weight the blame and credit by party.[19]

Post-Election Coalition Bargaining

Yet, it is not only accountability that suffers under coalition government. Accountability is a mostly backward looking or retrospective feature of democratic representation. We must also carefully consider the related issues of voters' prospective judgments about parties' campaign promises. Post-election coalition bargaining inevitably requires horse trading between coalition partners, in which policies are swapped, eliminated, watered down, or newly adopted, and all of this occurs after the electorate has cast its ballots. Before a new government even starts its term in office, its constituent partners may have abandoned or significantly altered key components of their election platforms.

This is conceptually related to the accountability section above, for the other key way to think about representation is through the conferring of mandates, rather than a retrospective reward-and-punish accountability model. The mandate view on representation suggests that ballots cast for parties provide affirmation of their electoral platforms as legislative blueprints for governing. Following on this, "elections emulate a direct assembly and the winning platform becomes the 'mandate' that the government pursues."[20] Certainly, there always has to be flexibility in allowing a party to revise its legislative agenda as circumstance require – economic and security crises occur, for example – but extensive alterations to a party's platform as a result of coalition bargaining after the electorate has cast its ballots can challenge the mandate model of representation, depending on how far the negotiated coalition agreement deviates from parties' election promises. Put simply, voters cast ballots for a set of campaign proposals, and coalition governments may pursue something that looks quite different.

Some may object to my characterization of coalition government, noting that coalition formation encourages compromise, flexibility, and a greater inclusion of interests. These points are likely true, but the response inevitably is that majoritarian systems require coalition formation too and are not bereft of compromise, flexibility, and inclusiveness. The difference is timing. Coalition formation happens within parties, prior to elections in majoritarian systems, versus between parties, after elections in proportional and most mixed systems. In Canada we have two large, fairly centrist parties, one of which will typically win a seat majority. Centrist parties are by their nature coalitions of societal elements. For much of its history, the Liberal Party was a well functioning coalition of Quebecers, Catholics, centre-left progressives, and racial and ethnic minorities. The US Democratic Party post-WWII was a New Deal coalition of blue-collar (especially unionized) workers, racial and ethnic minorities, farmers, intellectuals, and white southerners. In Canada, the fact that we described the two major parties using a brokerage analogy for much of our political history is consistent with this narrative of big tent politics, in which large centrist parties, built on complex coalitions of voters, alternated in and out of power. Carty's most recent book provides an apt analysis of the Liberal Party's use of brokerage politics and a franchise structure to forge and stabilize its coalition, for example.[21] The critical point for my purposes here is that coalition building occurs prior to election day in SMP systems, and the parties' platforms can be taken fairly literally as their blueprints for governance, facilitating accountability, in turn, to bring the discussion back to the previous section. Certainly, governing parties can deviate from their platforms if circumstances require, or they can disregard campaign promises, although the voters can hold them to account for this.

In contrast, coalition building in proportional and some mixed systems – indeed in any system that fails to regularly produce single-party seat majorities – occurs after elections. As Hobolt and Karp explain, "the instrumental goal of voting a specific government in office can thus become a highly challenging task because a vote for a particular party and its policy will never directly result in a government, but at best secure a party's membership in a coalition along with other parties with different policy agendas."[22] Voters do not know which elements of parties platforms will be compromised or negotiated away, or which of a rival party's proposals will be adopted. This introduces a higher degree of uncertainty and risk into vote choice, and combined with the blurring of accountability as a result of the diffusion of policy responsibility in coalition government, makes it difficult to hold parties to account for post-election coalition horse trading.

None of this is to say that coalition government does not work or is inherently undesirable. Indeed, in some systems, parties make formal pre-election alliances, reducing post-election uncertainty. However, the point here is that we have not mulled over these issues in our national electoral reform conversation. Moreover, to the extent that parties would continue to campaign independently following a change in electoral rules – and this is the case in many systems that regularly produce coalition government – the uncertainty and risk of post-election coalition bargaining is an important factor to consider before a major shakeup of electoral rules. If we value pre-election coalition building, simpler accountability between voters and government, and more, then examination of these issues needs to be included in the debate about electoral reform, and caution is warranted before we lightly dismiss our current electoral formula. Currently, we do not know if Canadians are aware of these possible outcomes, or whether they view them as reasonable trade-offs for the elimination of disproportionality in the translation of votes to seats.

Disproportionality in Coalitions

Keeping with the theme of coalition governments, while proportional and mixed electoral rules are designed to reproduce (to varying degrees) society's distribution of values, characteristics, and opinions inside the legislature, post-election coalition bargaining is not designed this way. In most instances, debates about the effects of electoral systems focus on their impact on legislative composition. This is certainly the case in Canada's current dialogue, which emphasizes representational considerations and SMP's disproportionality, as discussed above. Post-election coalition bargaining to form a government does not follow norms of proportionality, and several important distortions (we might think of them as elements of "disproportionality") can result.

Parties may have greater influence in coalition governments than their legislative numbers warrant, and sometimes even relatively small parties can play the role of kingmaker, giving them undue weight in government policy-making. The best known example is the Free Democratic Party (FDP) in Germany, which played kingmaker for Christian Democrats on the right and Social Democrats on the left for much of the post-WWII period in Germany, a role facilitated by the low rate of "grand coalitions" between major parties of the left and right in multiparty government.

Parties are also shut out of coalitions, and sometimes regularly, depending on the dynamics at play. Indeed, all parties cannot be part of forming a government. What would be worrisome in a country like Canada is if an important segment of the electorate – defined by regional or ethnocultural identity, for example – was regularly excluded

from coalition arrangements. It could be the case that the Bloc Québécois or some other Quebec-based, nominally separatist party is regularly excluded, for example. The backlash against the Liberals and NDP
for cooperating with the Bloc in the run-up to the 2008 prorogation
suggests that there are perils to cooperating with "a party dedicated to
the destruction of the country," as Andrew Coyne put it at the time.[23]
The Conservatives immediately began calling the partnership the "separatist coalition," claiming that the Liberals and NDP were "in bed with
the Quebec separatists."[24] Acrimony toward Quebec runs high in some
parts of the country, unfortunately. The point here is that while the
legislature is a mirror of the electorate under proportional and perhaps mixed rules, governments are not. In parliamentary systems in
particular, governments are the key drivers of legislative agendas. The
focus on proportionality in our electoral reform debate, on the inclusion of all voices, and on the elimination of "wasted votes" may give the
impression that alternative electoral formula are inherently fairer, and
will produce better representation on account of policy-making that
is more attuned to the "true" wishes of the majority. In the broadest
sense, from coalition formation onwards, this notion is on weak foot-
ing. Indeed, to cast the argument even wider:

> while the assembly may reflect interests proportionately, many
> decisions entailed in governing do not permit proportional allo-
> cations. Indeed, many are dichotomous, and in those the majority
> prevails while the minority loses. Hence, while proportionality allows
> all voices to be heard, it does not guarantee that all interests will be
> proportionately accommodated.[25]

Conclusion

Should we change how we vote? This paper does not propose an
unequivocal answer, but it does demonstrate that a fuller consideration
of the criteria for judging electoral formulae raises considerable doubt
about the wisdom of change. Pro-reform advocates have focused on
two of the seven democratic and state management criteria, and these
happen to be the ones on which SMP performs poorly compared to
alternatives, at least if we're looking at the composition of legislatures

(but not necessarily governments). That SMP distorts the conversion of votes to seats is uncontested. However, when we consider other democratic criteria, it is much less clear that alternate systems are superior. Indeed, single-party government is optimal for accountability. SMP may be the best model under a mandate view of representation as well, given that coalition formation occurs prior to elections and can be assessed by voters prior to casting their ballots.

Large-scale institutional change produces considerable risk and uncertainty, and the takeaway of my paper is this: a compelling case for reform may be possible, but it has not yet been identified. Until Canada engages in a full and comprehensive debate about how systems fare on all the criteria on which electoral formula are judged, a decision to pursue reform may be misguided and have negative consequences for the function of Canadian democracy.

7

Electoral System Reform: Implications for Internal Party Democracy

William Cross

The choice of an electoral system has far-reaching implications for democratic practice. The electoral institutions and practices in a state are all part of a democratic ecosystem, and change to something as fundamental as the electoral system has implications for many other parts of democratic life. Much of the popular and scholarly discourse concerning electoral reform focuses on questions relating to representational issues, such as who gets represented in Parliament, and on the details of how various systems operate, such as degrees of proportionality, district magnitude, and the ballot structure. Much less considered is how electoral systems influence the internal operations and organization of political parties.

Many of the key functions of parties, and of the nature of internal party democracy, are affected by the choice of electoral system. These include candidate nomination, election campaigning, government formation, and party leadership selection. In this paper, I briefly canvass how political parties operating under different electoral systems respond to the imperatives of these arrangements by organizing themselves in distinct ways. In doing so, I draw upon the experiences of parties in Australia, Ireland, and New Zealand. Together these countries utilize the principal electoral systems often proposed as alternatives to Canada's single-member plurality (SMP) system. Australians elect members to the House of Representatives under the alternative vote (AV), Ireland has long used the single transferable vote (STV), and since the 1990s, New Zealand has used the mixed-member proportional (MMP) system. For comparative purposes in considering how the adoption of different systems might influence party decision-making in Canada, it is instructive to look to countries with broadly similar political institutions, political culture, and democratic infrastructure so that we can observe the effect of the electoral system as a variable on the party practices studied.[1]

Candidate Nomination

The selection of candidates for the general election is the defining activity of political parties and is what differentiates them from other political organizations such as advocacy groups.[2] In parties in all of these countries, the two major and ongoing issues relating to candidate selection are the balance of authority between the local party branch and the party centre, and the challenge of nominating a representative pool of individuals, particularly in terms of gender. There are, however, important differences in candidate selection, particularly between Canadian parties and the practices of parties in New Zealand and Ireland.

In New Zealand's MMP system, parties need to develop processes for the selection of candidates both for the fifty members chosen from the party list and for the seventy selected in the single-member electorates. These are closed lists, meaning the parties develop internal processes to determine their composition. It is in the construction of these lists that parties in MMP systems face decisions different from those that parties are confronted with under SMP.

Discussion relating to closed-list proportional representation systems often includes concerns that parties, and not voters, will choose MPs since parties determine the list from which representatives are elected. Responding to this concern when it adopted MMP, New Zealand added a provision to its electoral law requiring that the lists be made using "democratic procedures" permitting party members to participate.[3] No further legal restrictions exist, allowing parties great leeway.

The two largest parties, Labour and National, assign a number of spots on their lists to each region of the country. Regional party conferences composed of delegates from the local branches then vote to select these candidates. A central party committee has the task of taking all the candidates selected at the regional conferences and rank-ordering them on the party's official list.[4] This is the key step, as being ranked in the top portion of the list is essential to one's chances of actually being elected. Considerable power then lies with the body given authority to construct the list.

By way of example, we can examine the process in Labour. A moderating committee (informally known as the knitting committee) meets after the conclusion of the regional conferences and has sole authority to compose the list. The issue of who is represented on this committee can be contentious. In 2013, as part of a party organizational reform movement, an attempt was made to reduce the size of this committee in order to allow for more strategic decision-making. After considerable consideration, this proposal was narrowly defeated as various groups fought to maintain their representation. The committee includes representatives of the parliamentary party, the national party executive, women, Māori, Pacific Islanders, youth, seniors, trade unions, local governments, rural communities, and the LGBT community. While the committee has absolute discretion in composing the list, party rules require it to pause after every five selections for an equity review. This review includes the aforementioned groups as well as persons with disabilities, geographic spread, and persons with "a range of skills." By way of contrast, the National party's process does not include such extensive concern with diverse representation and is dominated by regional representatives, the national executive, and the parliamentary party leadership.

The process works differently in other parties. The Greens, for example, also select the members of their list at a delegated conference. However, this is followed by a ballot of the entire party membership to determine the rank-order of the chosen candidates with the national party having the ability to adjust the results by applying "balance" criteria relating to Māori status, gender, age, and regional representation.

If MMP, or a pure closed-list system, were adopted in Canada, several decisions would have to be made. First, Parliament would have to decide if it is going to be prescriptive in placing restrictions on how the parties select their candidates. It is worth noting that Canadian parties now have absolute discretion as to how they nominate their candidates, allowing party leaders to appoint candidates when they so choose.[5] Second, the parties themselves would have to establish processes for list construction, determining whether these would be uniform across the country, what the balance of authority would be between member participation and central party officials, and any provisions regarding enforced diversity both in the group making the list and in its outcomes.

The STV system also raises unique issues for candidate selection. What's important here is that there are multi-candidate districts – in the Irish case, between three and five members. The locals choose their candidates in nominating conventions similar to those currently held in Canada, but do so under directives issued from the centre.[6] For example, the centre determines how many candidates the party will run in each electorate. This is a highly strategic decision and is often contentious between the two levels of the party. The locals often want to run more candidates than the centre will determine is the appropriate number to maximize their chances of electing TDs (*Teachta Dála,* the Irish equivalent to a member of Parliament). In recent elections, none of the parties have run a full complement of candidates, which reflects the logic of the system as parties do not want to disperse their first preferences too broadly, resulting in inefficient transfers and potentially lowering their overall success rate.

It is also not uncommon for the centre to dictate that the locals nominate one candidate fewer than the number it plans to run in the electorate. In this way, one position is held in reserve in case a favoured candidate of the centre is not chosen by the locals. The result is that in an electorate with five TDs, a party may decide to run three candidates and to allow the locals to nominate two.

The centre also often issues dictates regarding the geographic location of the candidates. For example, if there are two principal population centres in the electorate, and if the decision is made to nominate two candidates, the centre may demand that one candidate be chosen from both of these areas. This reflects the logic of the STV system, which is to maximize first preferences for the party and ultimately transfers. In addition, the centre may place gender requirements on the local electorate – requiring that at least one person of both genders be nominated.

From an organizational perspective, if STV were adopted, some mechanism would have to be put in place determining who in the party had the authority to decide how many candidates a party would run in each constituency; who, if anyone, would be able to put conditions on this nominating authority; and who would be represented in this decision-making body.

Campaigning

In the AV system, voters cast preferential ballots with winners required to reach a majority threshold. This often requires consideration of individual voters' second and third choices before any candidate achieves majority support. This leads to parties and candidates entering into deals concerning their allocation of second and lower preferences, which can be crucial to determining who is elected. In Australian elections for the House of Representatives, this results in parties distributing "how to vote" cards to their supporters. The deals can be different by constituency depending on the cast of parties and local dynamics. Sometimes it's easy and obvious; for example, support between Labor and the Greens and between the two parties on the right – National and the Liberals – is common place.

However, it is not always so straightforward. For instance, in the 2016 federal election, in the electorate of Melbourne, Adam Bandt was seeking re-election as the only Green incumbent. In a somewhat surprising move, the Liberals decided to formally give their preferences to the Labour candidate in order to defeat Bandt – but this strategy did not work out as many Liberal voters ignored the instruction and Bandt won. Nonetheless, a decision has to be made as to who will make the preference allocation decision. The 2016 contest in the electoral division of Melbourne Ports provides an excellent example of this. Incumbent Labor MP Michael Danby was in a tight three-way fight with the Green and Liberal candidates. A staunch supporter of Israel, Danby called on his supporters to oppose the Green candidate and instead give their second preferences to his Liberal opponent.[7] This was contrary to the position taken by the central campaign. The result was that some voters received party-issued "how to vote" cards encouraging them to rank the Greens second, and competing cards issued by Danby encouraging support of the Liberals as second preference.

In the Canadian context, in which we often have highly regionalized federal competition, with parties facing different primary opponents in different regions,[8] it is difficult to imagine that a single agreement would be reached nation-wide. The question then is who would make these decisions: Would provincial or regional party organizations make them, would individual electoral district associations (EDAs) be given this authority, or would the parties leave this to voters to determine for themselves?

The logic of the AV system also allows for the continued existence of splinter parties without there necessarily being any electoral cost. Thus, in Australia there is a permanent divide on the right between the Liberals and National Party in parts of the country. The two parties always govern together in coalition. They are free to run against each other because they almost always share preferences, so there is little risk of dividing up the vote and allowing Labor to win with something less than majority support. This is obviously very different than the logic of SMP, which penalizes vote dispersion. This is evident from the recently witnessed division on the Canadian right between the Progressive Conservatives and Reform parties, allowing the Liberals to win seats with less than 40 per cent of the vote, while the two right-of-centre parties sometimes had majority support between them. The SMP electoral system provided an irresistible incentive for the parties to merge.

In terms of election campaigning, what distinguishes STV from AV or SMP is that it involves intra-party competition during the general election. For example, in our hypothetical district with five TDs, Fianna Fáil might decide to run three candidates in hopes of electing two. The three Fianna Fáil candidates are then competing with one another as much as they are with those from Fine Gael or Labour or Sinn Féin for first and second preferences. This obviously adds an extra dimension to the campaign dynamic that parties need to carefully manage.

In MMP, voters cast two ballots – one for their preferred local MP and one for their preferred party. These two votes are often inconsistent. For example, in 2014 in the electorate of Auckland Central, Labour won 44 per cent of the electorate vote – in a losing effort – but only 22 per cent of the party vote, and it is the party vote that determines the overall number of seats a party gets in the legislature and thus is the key vote. Parties have struggled to execute their electoral strategies in a way that reflects this. In part, this is because incumbent electorate MPs want to preserve their electorate positions and in part because voters and party workers come out of an SMP tradition, as would be the case in Canada, and don't innately understand the logic of the system. Labour in particular has struggled with organizing a campaign that directs efforts and resources to the party vote campaign. In recent organizational reforms the party has created regional hubs for campaign purposes in an attempt to move some of the focus and resources away from the electorates in order to concentrate more broadly on increasing the all-important party vote. As the allocation of campaign resources is zero sum, this can be contentious: electorate party associations, and in some cases incumbent MPs, see resources and authority being shifted away from them to regionally based campaign teams.

If Canada should adopt MMP, parties would have to restructure their campaign organizations. List seats likely would be distributed at the provincial level, meaning that provincial campaign organizations would need to be strengthened and resourced likely at the expense of electorate campaigns, and there would almost certainly be significant tension between the two levels – particularly where incumbent MPs want resources at the local level – even though these might be largely irrelevant to the number of seats a party ultimately ends up with in Parliament.

Government Formation

Since Confederation, Canada has always had single-party governments, whether of the minority or majority type. The only exception was the "unity government" during the Great War. Single-party governments are now the exception in Ireland and New Zealand. Every election held in New Zealand under MMP has resulted in multiparty governance and this has been the norm in Ireland for several decades.[9] This results from the fact that these more proportional systems make it highly unlikely that any election will award a single party with a majority of the legislative seats. This is unlike the Canadian situation where majority outcomes are not uncommon and thus parties finding themselves in a minority position are willing to govern alone, believing they are an election away from achieving majority status.

The presence of multi-party governments in STV and MMP systems raises the issue of who in the party has the authority to enter into a coalition agreement and who has authority over the content of the agreement. There is significant diversity among the parties in terms of the approaches adopted.

In New Zealand, the process is highly centralized in the Labour and National parties, with the parliamentary leadership having significant authority. National's rules require that any agreement reached by the party leader is subject to approval of the party's national board, but in recent years this appears to be rather pro forma. The Greens take a very different approach and require approval from a specially called party congress before any coalition arrangement is formally approved. Similar division exists in Ireland. Both Fianna Fáil and the Greens require approval from a specially convened party congress while Labour grants this authority to its central council.[10]

Given the discussions around the possibility of a coalition arrangement in Canada surrounding the 2015 election, we can imagine this might be a contentious issue and might well be determined differently by different parties. The movement toward empowering party members, and in the Liberals' case, supporters, might well result in demands for some role for riding presidents or party members in approving a coalition agreement. This, of course, can make what is already often a difficult, and sometimes lengthy, task even more challenging. This also raises the issue of whether parties enter into an agreement before the election and campaign, accordingly, or wait until after the results are known. Again, some individual or group in the party has to be granted decision-making authority in this regard.

Leadership Selection

The relationship between the electoral system and questions of party leadership relates to the issue of government formation and specifically the presence of coalition governments. In cases where coalition formation is necessary for participation in government, party voters will give consideration to whether the prospective leaders are likely to be able to forge agreements with the other parties. If the system adopted makes it highly unlikely that a party can win a majority on its own, then parties need to think about whether they will be likely to win the necessary support of other parties to form government. The leadership campaign typically will flesh this out as well as the views of potential leaders toward deal making with what likely would be an increased number of parties, as more proportional systems typically lead to a fragmenting of the party system.

The presence of multiparty governments also raises the real possibility of one party exercising influence over the leadership of another party. While largely unheard of in the Canadian case, this has occurred in parties in Australia, Ireland, and New Zealand. Considering a few examples is illustrative of how this plays out.[11]

In Australia, after Liberal prime minister Harold Holt was presumed drowned and the party was in the process of selecting a successor, significant influence was exercised by the Country Party. William McMahon, then serving as treasurer in the Holt government, had widespread support among his fellow Liberals and was the presumed successor. However, there was significant opposition to McMahon within the Country Party, which was the junior partner in a coalition government with the Liberals. Country's leadership threatened that if McMahon was chosen as Liberal leader it would withdraw its support from the government. Ultimately, McMahon was forced to withdraw from the contest so that the Liberal government could survive.

In Ireland, two relatively recent leaders of Fianna Fáil, both of whom were serving as taoiseach at the time, were effectively removed from the party leadership by junior coalition partners. Charlie Haughey faced internal divisions within his parliamentary caucus throughout much of his leadership; nonetheless, he consistently managed to win these battles and fought off several internal attempts to remove him. Largely as a result of opposition to Haughey, one of his ministers, Desmond O'Malley, led others in forming a new splinter party, the Progressive Democrats (PDs). Fianna Fáil was dependent on the support of the PDs to remain in government. Ultimately, the PDs insisted that Haughey vacate the leadership in return for their continued support. In this way, O'Malley and the PDs accomplished what they could not from within Fianna Fáil – the ouster of Haughey as Fianna Fáil leader. Haughey's successor, Albert Reynolds, suffered a similar fate. Serving as taoiseach in a coalition government supported by the Labour Party, Reynolds found himself mired in a government scandal. While initially maintaining support within his own party, Labour announced that it would withdraw its support over Reynolds' continuing leadership. Within a day of this announcement, support for Reynolds melted away in his caucus and he was forced to resign the leadership.

New Zealand provides an example of the influence running in the opposite direction – from the principal governing party to a smaller support party. Prime Minister John Key's 2008 National Party government was supported by the small ACT party. ACT held two posts in the Key government. An internal party movement was afoot to remove ACT leader Rodney Hide. Key, a supporter of Hide, made it clear that he would not name Hide's replacement to his ministry and that he would remove the other ACT minister should Hide be dumped. Not wanting to lose its place at the government table, the would-be rebels in ACT ended their efforts to remove Hide.

With no tradition of coalition governments, the Canadian parties have no history of directly influencing leadership selection in rival parties. If an electoral system were adopted that resulted in multiparty governments, this might well change. This might prove particularly problematic in the Canadian case, in which parties have vested authority for both leadership selection and removal with their extra-parliamentary supporters. In all of the examples referenced above, the parliamentary parties controlled the process and could ensure swift action.[12] In the Canadian case, this could result in parties adopting the provisions of Michael Chong's Reform Act, giving the parliamentary parties the authority to remove a leader and quickly install an interim replacement.

Conclusion

This paper provides a brief overview of some of the issues relating to party organization and internal party democracy that parties face under different electoral systems. There are many unintended consequences that can accompany the choice of electoral system beyond how voters exercise their franchise and who gets represented in the legislature. As we think through a timetable for electoral system reform, and if the government is indeed committed to having a new system in place before the 2019 election, time needs to be set aside for parties to grapple with these issues. A change in system need not necessarily result in the party in the centre becoming more powerful vis-à-vis its local electorate associations, but this is the likely outcome if a new system is put in place, close to the commencement of an election campaign, without there being time for a party to discuss and debate these issues internally.

8

Democratic Deliberation and Electoral Reform

Colin M. Macleod

The Dismal State of Democratic Discourse

It's easy to be cynical about the discursive character of contemporary Canadian politics. Election campaigns are dominated by shallow slogans, spin, sound bites, and theatrics. Wildly exaggerated claims about the wisdom of party platforms by partisan pundits are matched only by the wholesale dismissal of proposals made by political rivals. Media commentary focuses obsessively on strategic facets of campaigns and gives short shrift to substantive analysis of issues, ideas, and arguments. The conduct of politicians in office that is most visible to the public only compounds the perception of political discourse as vapid rhetoric dominated by partisan rancour. Pertinent questions posed to politicians are evaded, and carefully crafted "talking points" are repeated ad nauseam. As one journalist recently quipped to me: "There's a reason it's not called Answer Period." Now this is not to say that our democratic processes are entirely dysfunctional from a deliberative point of view. A good deal of serious, reflective, and even collegial work goes on in parliamentary committees and in other settings. Policies, even if deeply flawed in some important respects, typically are not completely irrational and are usually developed via processes of consultation with experts and affected constituencies. Nonetheless, it's hard to escape the conclusion that the overall calibre of public political discourse is poor in a way that contributes to the alienation of many people from democratic politics.

Against this rather pessimistic depiction of our current situation, I will offer some reflections on electoral reform in relation to deliberative facets of democracy. More specifically, I consider whether the adoption of a system of proportional representation (PR) might help to improve the deliberative character of Canadian politics. There are different ways of securing proportional representation but I will not explore the details of different proposals here. Instead, I will adopt the working assumption that PR in whatever specific form it takes ensures that the seats held by parties in Parliament reasonably accurately reflect the share of votes parties receive in an election. I identify some deliberative defects of a first-past-the-post (FPP) electoral system and consider some deliberative advantages of PR. We have reason, I suggest, to favour electoral reform on deliberative grounds. Yet there is an important caveat: proportional representation cannot alone secure an ideally deliberative and respectful form of democratic politics. Many other factors influence the deliberative character of Canadian democracy. Nonetheless, PR does have deliberative virtues that the current Canadian electoral system lacks. To set the stage for the analysis, I shall begin by briefly reviewing contrasting accounts of the significance of reflective deliberation by citizens for democratic legitimacy.

Aggregation, Deliberation, and Democratic Legitimacy

The degree to which the phenomenon of vacuous public political discourse poses a serious threat to healthy democratic politics depends, to some important degree, on one's conception of democratic legitimacy. If we accept a broadly aggregative conception of democracy in which democratic legitimacy is secured principally through fair procedures for the aggregation of the preferences of citizens then the vacuity of political discourse will not be especially troubling. On the aggregative conception of democracy, political parties vie for the support of the electorate and citizens support parties that best reflect their antecedent political preferences. Legitimacy is achieved mainly by ensuring that the electoral system aggregates preferences in a way that both respects the equal standing of citizens and accurately represents the degree of support that different parties have from voting citizens. In the simple case where one party commands a majority of votes cast, that party forms the government. In turn, the government and its legislative agenda have legitimacy in virtue of the procedural fairness of the electoral system in translating votes into seats in Parliament.

Of course, in contemporary Canadian politics, where more than two parties field candidates for office, it is now rare for any party to secure a majority of votes cast. A procedurally fair electoral system that aims at respecting democratic equality and representativeness needs to determine how government is formed when no party commands a majority of votes. As many advocates of systems of PR point out, a significant procedural defect with our FPP system is that it does not and cannot reliably generate results that represent voters' preferences accurately, and it flouts the basic ideal of democratic equality. So even from an aggregative point of view FPP is deeply flawed. Procedural unfairness of this sort frequently threatens the democratic legitimacy of governments formed under FPP.

I note this important objection to FPP not by way of suggesting that it provides a decisive democratic argument in favour of PR. Rather, I want to emphasize that the argument rooted in procedural fairness does not focus on the democratic significance of the conditions under which citizens form their political preferences, or the degree to which political legitimacy depends on the articulation of reasons for favouring or opposing policies or parties.

Deliberative democratic theorists argue that fair processes for the aggregation of the preferences of citizens are not sufficient to secure political legitimacy.[1] A legitimate political outcome is one that citizens have good reason to accept even if they disagree with it. Recognizing that one has reason to accept an outcome is partly a matter of being able to acknowledge that reasonable efforts have been made to justify the outcome substantively, and that the grounds offered as justificatory speak to the common good, not merely to narrow private or sectarian interests. Also in order for citizens to view a political outcome as justified, there must be meaningful opportunities to critically scrutinize rival positions and to reflectively assess them. So for deliberative democrats, legitimacy depends crucially on the respectful exchange of reasons between citizens and their political representatives.

Deliberative democrats also emphasize the significance of diversity and disagreement in contemporary political communities. The consideration and development of public policy should be sensitive to the plurality of reasonable political perspectives in the community. Debate and discourse between political rivals should be thoughtful and aimed at (rational) justification on terms that all can acknowledge as reasonable. Deliberative democrats disagree about exactly what kinds of reasons are pertinent to public justification.[2] Suitable political reasons aimed at justifying policies and laws must be ones that diverse citizens can all acknowledge as germane to respectful political argument. Processes of reason-giving and reason-taking do not magically resolve political disagreement and they do not supplant the need for fair systems of voting to arrive at final decisions. However, the exchange of suitably public reasons contributes to legitimacy by orienting political discussion to substantive, rather than merely procedural, justification.

Sites of Democratic Deliberation

The foregoing provides only the barest sketch of a deliberative conception of democracy, but it is sufficient, I hope, to motivate the significance of reasoned deliberation to the health of democracy. To this sketch, we can add a few points about the sites and ideal character of democratic deliberation. Three important sites of deliberation are worth distinguishing. The relevant features of deliberative virtue in these sites may be different in some respects.[3] First, there is deliberation that occurs in the context of election campaigns. It is in this context that citizens are likely to be most actively engaged in deliberation about the platforms of competing political parties. Since most people have limited time and energy to devote to deliberation, it is important that issues and positions are framed clearly and accessibly. Presentation of highly technical matters that are important to crafting legislation and regulations is generally not conducive to illuminating deliberation during campaigns. Instead, we can hope for deliberation that focuses on matters such as identification and diagnoses of current problems facing the electorate, proposed solutions to problems, and the principles and basic commitments that parties and candidates adopt and defend.

Second, there is deliberation that occurs amongst elected representatives in Parliament both on the floor of the House of Commons and via the work done in committees and in cabinet. Here there is greater room for debate and discussion about the details of legislation and one can expect that the informational basis on which debate and discussion takes place is richer and more complex than on the campaign trail. In general, we can expect parliamentarians to be more informed about policy matters than most ordinary citizens and to draw upon that information during deliberation.

Third, there is deliberation amongst civil servants about how best to develop and implement the policy directions provided to them by the government. In this setting, we can expect the development of policy to be guided by greater levels of technical and informational complexity, but we can also expect less robust debate and discussion about which objectives are appropriately pursued by government. As some scholars have pointed out, there are important and complex issues about the democratic accountability of decisions made by government bureaucracies, and some of these issues are linked to the nature of deliberation within the civil service.[4] However, in the rest of the paper, I will bracket these issues and focus on deliberation in the context of campaigns and Parliament.

Democratic deliberation of the sort that contributes to legitimacy involves the exchange of reasons. Many common elements of contemporary political discourse clearly do not contribute to deliberation in this sense. Insults, empty sloganeering, spin, scare mongering, and image-focused advertising aimed at making candidates for office appear either more or less attractive are best understood as attempts at manipulation rather than contributions to reasonable deliberation and rational persuasion. The practices of evading pertinent questions, making obfuscating remarks, and ignoring relevant evidence are also corrosive to democratic deliberation. If these all too familiar features of discourse undermine democratic deliberation, what are the features that enhance the deliberative character of political discourse? There are four features that are worth highlighting.

First, and perhaps most obviously, substantive content matters. The claims that participants in political debate advance must be intelligible and should be rationally connected to the overall political positions people wish to advance for consideration. Credible evidence, not mere opinion, should be supplied to support claims, and arguments should respect basic principles of logic. Advancing contradictory claims, employing blatantly fallacious arguments, and engaging in sophistry diminish the substantive content of discourse.

Second, although it is understandable and even sometimes appropriate for political argument to be heated and driven by passion, civility is an important virtue of political discourse. We can expect reasonable people in democratic communities to have strong disagreements about political issues, but we signal our respect for one another as equal participants in political community by speaking in a civil tongue. Mocking one's opponents or contemptuously deriding their views renders the exchange of reasons extremely difficult. One is not likely to be receptive to criticism, even if sound, if it is delivered in a manner that expresses disrespect.

Third, it is important not only that participants in political discourse give reasons but also that participants "take" reasons. In other words, they should be responsive to arguments made in political debate and they should be prepared to revise their positions in light of reasonable argument. The reflective component of deliberation requires citizens to acknowledge the fallibility of their judgment and to regulate their beliefs in relation to the evidence. A civil exchange of substantive arguments is not very deliberative if no one will contemplate revising their views in light of the exchange.

Finally, in light of the plurality of reasonable views that citizens hold, it is important for political discourse to be inclusive. A reasonable view that is (currently) popular only with a minority of people is not thereby a mistaken or implausible view. Marginalizing or sidelining unpopular positions is epistemically problematic since there may be wisdom in such perspectives, but it is also potentially alienating to those that hold them. Decent democratic deliberation should be reflective of pluralism in the democratic community.

It is important to note that democratic discourse displaying these features need not be dry, stiff, pedantic, or recherché. Fruitful exchanges of reasons can occur in many ways, and there is ample room within this conception of deliberation for spirited debate, partisanship, humour, and sharp criticism.

Electoral Systems and Deliberation

Ideally, we want an electoral system that incentivizes, as much as possible, political discourse that is civil, substantive, responsive to rational argument, and inclusive of the plurality of reasonable positions held by citizens on matters of political import. It is unlikely that there is any simple and straightforward relation between the design of electoral systems and the facilitation of these deliberative virtues. Many variables are likely to influence the deliberative character of a political community, and these factors will interact in complex ways. The factors shaping deliberation include the quality of democratic education, the conduct and character of the major media, political traditions, the personalities of prominent politicians and political pundits, the degree of conflict and disagreement between different groups, and the adequacy of opportunities for meaningful deliberation. So electoral reform will not be a deliberative panacea. Nonetheless, different electoral systems provide different incentives for the conduct of citizens, politicians, and the media, and the way people respond to these incentives can influence the deliberative character of a community. We can label these "deliberative incentives."

So how do FPP and PR affect deliberative incentives? In addressing this question, I will focus on two well-known contrasting features of FPP and PR. First, critics of FPP frequently emphasize the tendency of FPP in multiparty systems to produce "false majorities." In Canada, it is now common for a party that receives a modest plurality of votes to enjoy a substantial majority of seats in the House of Commons. By contrast, under PR, securing a parliamentary majority requires securing a majority of votes cast. Second, there is the phenomenon of the "wasted vote." The votes that go to losing candidates in an election under FPP have no effect on the representation of the parties in Parliament. So even parties that have reasonably high aggregate levels of support can find themselves without any representation in Parliament. Under PR, parties are ensured representation in relation to the percentage of votes they receive.

In considering the deliberative incentives associated with FPP and PR, I shall assume that political parties seek power. They aim at winning seats in Parliament, forming government, and implementing their platforms. If they do not succeed in winning seats or forming government, they still want to highlight the importance of issues and influence public policy.

Exchanging Reasons on the Campaign Trail

We can begin with some deliberative defects of FPP in relation to campaigns. The expectation that an election is likely to generate a false majority and the associated anxiety about wasted votes create various regrettable deliberative incentives. To begin with, for those parties that see themselves as having a credible chance to form government (in light of historical success and polling data), there is a reason to focus electoral efforts on mobilizing a base sufficiently large – say 35 per cent of the electorate – to secure a parliamentary majority. The need for any party to engage seriously with the concerns of a majority of citizens or to seek broad based consensus on important issues is thus weakened. Similarly, it often makes strategic sense for larger parties to offer exaggerated negative portrayals of their chief rival for government. Given that a mere plurality of votes is usually sufficient to form a majority government, parties do not need to moderate their political rhetoric in the expectation that after the election they will have to work closely and co-operatively with their rivals. Civility in political discourse is thus a likely casualty.

In recent elections, media coverage of campaigns and the advertising of political parties have tended to focus on party leaders, their daily activities, and their personalities. Linked to this is a strong tendency for a politics of personalization[5] that encourages various familiar forms of mudslinging about the character traits of party leaders. Personalization itself tends to come at the expense of substantive debate about the merits of different policy platforms. Parties who are deemed to have no chance of forming government and who thus struggle to garner valuable media attention have an incentive to engage in publicity stunts aimed more at generating controversy than advancing substantive deliberative discourse.

The expectation of a false majority also incentivizes a problematic narrowing of the range of positions that receive serious consideration during elections. Media discussion tends to focus on the views of parties deemed contenders for power. It is easy therefore to ignore the ideas of third- or fourth-placed parties or to assign them marginal status. Similarly, it is frequently in the interest of major parties to diminish the importance of smaller parties and to argue for their exclusion from significant political debates. Processes of reason-giving and reason-taking thereby suffer: one cannot seriously consider and respond to the reasons of a party that is simply ignored or assigned to the periphery of mainstream discussion.

In this context, citizens who may be inclined to support a smaller party are encouraged to shift their allegiances to a larger party, not because the larger party has substantively better ideas but because supporting a smaller party simply involves throwing one's vote away. Supporters of contending parties may also be inclined to express frustration or anger for citizens who are attracted to smaller parties on the grounds that voting for a smaller party rather than a larger party will have a spoiler effect that robs a larger party of a chance of forming government.

The adoption of PR cannot, on its own, radically transform the discursive character of election campaigns. But it does have some important deliberative advantages. Most obviously, by eliminating the expectation of false majorities, it encourages consideration of a broader range of views. Since smaller parties can be expected to play a role in minority or coalition governments, it makes sense to devote more sustained attention to their platforms. The expectation that different parties will have to work together cooperatively also provides an incentive for greater civility on the campaign trail. Rather than highlighting stark divergences in political outlook, many political parties will have reason to identify points of agreement and areas of possible compromise. The media will also have reason to offer broader and more sustained coverage of different issues and the range of views that command support in the community.

The search for compromise itself can encourage reason-giving and reason-taking amongst rivals. Rivals are more likely to listen attentively to one another and to aim at persuasion when imbalances of bargaining power are less dramatic. In a competitive multiparty state, it will be unlikely that any party will be in a position to impose its will on others, and this leaves room for productive, mutually respectful dialogue. Of course, in some political contexts, PR can elevate the bargaining power of smaller parties in ways that can distort campaign deliberation. The platform of a small, single-issue party may assume influence in politics that is grossly out of proportion to its actual deliberative significance. Such parties have an incentive to mobilize a base of supporters by focusing only on a very narrow set of issues. This kind of "targeting" may be encouraged by PR and it can disrupt balanced consideration of issues.[6] But targeting is not unique to PR and there may be mechanisms within PR to mitigate its adverse effects. Recognition and anticipation of targeting by small parties also provides an incentive for larger parties, who, political rhetoric aside, have greater ideological affinity with each other than with fringe parties, to reason together and find common ground.

Exchanging Reasons in Parliament

We hope that a meaningful exchange of reasons can occur not only on the campaign trail but in the legislature as well. But in many ways the regrettable deliberative features of FPP are more pronounced in Parliament than on the campaign trail. The tendency of FPP to produce false majorities is particularly problematic. At least during an election there are some incentives for contending parties to engage with each other in meaningful debates as they vie for support from the electorate. Smaller parties that do not win seats still have some voice. But if, as frequently happens, they are denied seats in Parliament, then their voice in legislative debates is silenced altogether. The denial of representation to smaller parties creates a deliberative deficit in the legislature.

Similarly, where one party commands a substantial majority (despite having only a plurality of votes), there is little incentive for the governing party to engage in respectful reason-giving and reason-taking with those with whom it disagrees. Having won the majority of seats, the governing party can impose its will simply by outvoting rather than out-arguing the opposition. The ability of a majority government to push through its legislative agenda as it sees fit discourages recognition and acknowledgment of reasons articulated by the opposition, even if such reasons resonate strongly with the majority of citizens. Although the opposition can, of course, raise substantive objections to a majority government's policies, the government has little incentive to take criticisms on board and to seek common ground that may be more reflective of the views of the citizenry as a whole.

The stranglehold on power that a majority government enjoys also encourages partisan incivility on behalf of both government members and opposition members of Parliament. The government is free to ignore and disparage the opposition since advancing its agenda does not depend significantly on opposition cooperation. The opposition for its part has reason to raise matters that embarrass the government and reason to deny it credit for successes for which it, from a reasonable point of view, deserves credit. We are frequently left with a Parliament that does not represent the full range of political views held by citizens and is dominated by partisan bickering and political posturing.

As with the campaign trail, PR is not likely to transform the deliberative character of Parliament completely, but it does deliver some positive deliberative incentives. First and most obviously, it addresses the problem of deliberative exclusion that plagues FPP. Citizens get to see the full range of views that command electoral support in the legislature. Democratically relevant political voices are not deprived a place in Parliament by the voting system. Deliberation of the sort suitable to a pluralistic democracy is thereby enhanced. Second, the tendency of PR in a multiparty state to generate minority and coalition governments is arguably a deliberative virtue. In order to form government, parties must engage in negotiation that involves finding common ground and compromise. Of course, under PR political negotiation may sometimes consist in rather cynical political horse trading that is far from politically reasonable or principled. But under PR there is a structural space for meaningful reason-giving and reason-taking that is typically absence in the false-majority world of FPP. Third, the fact that advancing a legislative agenda depends crucially on cooperation with one's political opponents provides an incentive for civility and mutual respect. Coalition members can see themselves as working productively together and are thereby less likely to fall prey to partisan rancour. It is harder to vilify those with whom you have worked closely, especially if the work has produced results that political rivals can endorse as a shared achievement. Even the fact that governments under PR are more easily defeated and are thus less secure in their hold of power can encourage an ethos conducive to deliberation. The expectation of shifting coalitions and allegiances encourages parliamentarians to be receptive to working with people with diverse political commitments.

Conclusion

I have suggested that improving the deliberative character of Canadian democracy is important because of the contribution the exchange of reasons makes to political legitimacy. It is thus very important to examine electoral reform in relation to its potential contribution to improved democratic deliberation. It would be naïve and simplistic to suppose that the adoption of some form of PR automatically yields huge deliberative dividends. Civil, substantive, inclusive, and responsive deliberation can be disrupted in many ways. Nonetheless, the deliberative incentives of PR are generally superior to those present in FPP. So from a deliberative point of view, we should be enthusiastic about electoral reform that delivers PR.

9

Can Proportional Representation Lead to Better Political System Performance?

Mark E. Warren

Canadian democracy is not in crisis. *The Economist*'s latest ranking of countries according to how democratic they are places us in seventh place, grouped roughly with small to medium population countries such as Australia, Finland, and Switzerland, and well above larger population countries such as the US, the UK, and Germany. Does this ranking mean that we should be satisfied with our current electoral system? We should not. And, indeed, we might take another cue from *The Economist*'s ranking: of the fifteen top ranked democracies, thirteen use proportional representation (PR). Of the other two, one is majoritarian: Australia, which uses the alternative voting (or preferential ballot) system. Within this group, only Canada uses a single-member plurality system (SMP), often called "first-past-the-post."

So even though we do well, this rough comparison suggests that we might do better. And it is possible that we can do better by adopting the kinds of electoral systems that the highest quality democracies use—PR in one of its many forms. The question I shall ask here is one not usually addressed in debates about electoral reform. Could adopting a new electoral system—PR in particular—increase political system capacities to develop the potentials with which Canada is so thoroughly blessed?

Broadly speaking, a country's ability to make the most of its resources, human and natural, has much to do with its government's capacities to act for the common good, and to do so wisely and effectively. In this respect, *The Economist*'s democracy ranking is probably not a good guide to challenges that go unmet and opportunities that are not developed. Yes, most of our institutions work well by global standards. Yet we also have potentials that go untapped—very likely, at least in part, owing to weak national political capacity. Some indicative challenges are these: Canada sits below the United States in the United Nations Human Development Index; and it sits at the bottom of the Organization for Economic Cooperation and Development (OECD) countries in innovation and labour productivity, signifying low levels of capital investment. We remain too heavily reliant on a resource-extraction economy, which masks underperformance in those sectors of the economy that will become increasingly important to our prosperity in the coming decades. We lack industrial policies that will be necessary to transition more fully to a knowledge-based economy. According to Commonwealth rankings, our health care system performs poorly and remains expensive relative to other universal systems—indeed, at or close to the bottom ranks of our peer comparators. Our wealth is somewhat more equally distributed than in the US, but the per capita GDP is about 20 per cent less. We have no national securities regulator, which probably costs some amount of capital formation and investment. We have extensive trade barriers between provinces, often greater than north-south trade barriers. We have failed to lead in environmental stewardship and sustainability, and we remain a laggard in reducing carbon emission. We have yet to find functional governance regimes that both respect and support First Nations. And, like many democracies, Canada has not been immune to stagnating rates of voting and popular disaffection from political elites. This in a country with a smart, diverse, civil, highly educated population; with attractive and dynamic urban centres; with a relatively high trust, high social capital society; and with an enviable abundance of natural resources and natural beauty. Canada does not do badly by its people by global measures; but it could better serve its people than it does, relative both to its peer group, and—more importantly—relative to our own enormous potentials.

So what does any of this have to do with the electoral system? I am certainly not going to argue that the gaps between our potentials and performance can all be blamed on our current electoral system. But it may be one key part of helping solve the puzzle of how to generate collective capacities that would allow us to address challenges and grasp opportunities. Importantly, it is something that can be changed with relative ease and low costs, and without much risk.

To make this case, we need to take a step back so we can think about electoral system change in the context of the key features of our political system. Electoral democracies have three general structural features.

First, there is the question of where powers are located: In particular, is the system unitary or federal? Canada is, of course, a confederation—a relatively weak form of federalism in which many key powers are held by the provinces.

Second, there is the constitutional system. In particular, there is the question of whether the system is one of separated powers, such as that of the US, or a unitary power system, such as that of the United Kingdom. Canada, of course, functionally unifies power in the House of Commons (despite formal bicameralism), and follows the British Westminster system of parliamentary supremacy.

Finally, there is the electoral system. How are citizens' interests, values, and preferences transmitted into the institutions of power? Canada's single-member plurality system magnifies the powers of pluralities, so much so that it can produce majority governments with around 38 per cent of the vote, and with as few as 24 per cent of eligible voters when our relatively low voter turnout is figured in. The electoral system tends to produce governments that have strong formal powers, but with weak electoral mandates within the context of a weak federation. The political hazards and lost opportunities are many. A government can make decisions, because it has the formal powers, while also lacking the political capital and legitimacy to make any kind of decision stick. The Harper government's attempt to force the Northern Gateway Pipeline is a case in point. Obvious win-win national projects, such as free trade among provinces or a national securities regulator, are vetoed by provinces, which are more likely to be held captive by strong local interests and industries than is the federal government. Deals such as the Charlottetown Accord are done through executive federalism, only to be undone by popular disaffection. Governments that are politically savvy find they must supplement their institutional powers with ad hoc consultations, as is the case with electoral reform itself. No federal government has been able to take leadership on energy or environmental issues (although the current government may have pieced together a coalition to make a start). And so on.

Structurally, the problem is this: we need a federal government with greater capacity to realize our national potentials. We can't get there by changing the terms of confederation, nor can we change the Westminster unified power system. But we *can* change the electoral system, and probably do so in a way that could, I believe, make these other two features of the political system work much better than they do. It is likely, for example, that our unified power system would actually be *more* powerful if the governments wielding power benefited from more inclusion and functioned more deliberatively – much like Canada's peer countries in *The Economist*'s democracy index.

In any democratic political system, power – understood as the collective capacity to do things – must be generated rather than imposed. The means for generating political power are inclusion, negotiation, and deliberation, combined with institutional capacities to decide and follow through. That is, a *democratic* political system generates power by empowering inclusiveness, enabling deliberations, and fostering negotiations, and then gathering these inputs and processes into the decision-making process. So the question is: Would electoral reform, proportional representation in particular, increase these capacities of our system unified federal power?

Let us look at each of these power-generating capacities, making some informed guesses about how proportional representation would affect each of them.

We usually think about *inclusion* in terms of voice, fairness, and responsiveness: a democracy should have mechanisms to listen and respond to its citizens. Electoral systems that make it more likely that a vote serves to empowerment a citizen and that weight votes more equally tend to be democratically more acceptable. On average, PR systems do a much better job in this dimension than SMP systems. But we can also think about this question in functional terms: *the ways in which electoral systems generate inclusions and exclusions determines where and how politics is conducted.* Our SMP system usually produces decisive majorities in Parliament, but it does so at the cost of moving much political activity, especially political conflict, out of the political system. Indeed, majorities are left with only the political tools of organized advocacy and opposition, the tools of the judicial review brought into existence by the Charter of Rights, and veto through provincial and municipal governments. So apparently clear and decisive majority governments are gained at the cost of externalizing politics into opposition, and generating political gridlock.

Could a PR system fix this problem? Because PR systems don't produce false majorities, an immediate effect would be to move much more politics into Parliament. It is likely that a PR system would lead to centre-left or centre-right coalition governments, as PR systems do in most of Europe. Parties would need to negotiate to form governments, and policies would reflect compromises among the governing parties. Such compromises would require tough bargaining after elections, and around each piece of legislation, but the results would be more likely to be broadly inclusive, more likely to reflect the preferences of majorities, and less likely to be vetoed by external opposition. In short, moving more politics into Parliament would likely increase its political capacities to do things on behalf of citizens.

What about the *deliberative* capacities of the political system? Generally speaking, democratic systems manage conflict and make decisions using the resources of talking and voting. Electoral systems are about voting, but systems of voting structure both the ways in which talk is incorporated into the political system and the kind of talk that takes place. The extent to which talking tends toward deliberation is important because this determines how "smart" a political system is—that is, its abilities to incorporate information and perspectives, its capacities to find positive-sum positions, and, more generally, the likelihood that it will develop good and well-informed policies.

When combined with SMP electoral systems, Westminster systems are among the least deliberative, and thus least smart, of the democratic systems. There are two effects that combine to produce this dumbing down of democracy. First, because the SMP electoral system tends to exclude many voices from representation, they move differing perspectives and interests out of the political system, generating epistemic losses. Second, because Westminster parliamentary systems unify power, it reduces the need for governments to deliberate. Once a government is formed, it needs only to make and defend decisions, while the role of opposition is simply to criticize. So rather than deliberation, what we get are highly scripted and highly oppositional debates, "gotcha" politics, and feigned outrages. If this is politics, it is no wonder that Canadians hate it.

We will not be changing the Westminster system, of course, but a PR electoral system is likely to change the way it operates. It would change the structural incentives so that deliberation becomes a more common practice. When governments are coalitions, their powers depend to a much greater degree on finding common ground in advance of decisions. It is not only that PR systems include more interests and perspectives, but also that the coalition governments that they generally produce require more negotiation and compromise, which means more deliberation. In short, PR would turn one of the most mistake-prone forms of government—one that depends, in an unhealthy way, on the brains, character, and ethics of the prime minister—into a more deliberative form of government. And it would do so simply by changing electoral inducements, and without touching constitutional fundamentals.

Finally, a word about decisiveness. Democracies not only need to include and deliberate; they need to have decision-making capacities so they can get things done. A democratic government is the mechanism through which a citizenry provides collective goods to itself. One of the often-claimed virtues of a Westminster system combined with an SMP electoral system is that is enables decisiveness. It exaggerates pluralities into majorities, and unifies the powers of government so that decisions can be taken without other political actors having much in the way of veto powers.

These powers often prove illusory, especially within the context of a weak federal system. Having the formal power to make a decision does not translate into workable powers of decision-making, particularly if the electoral basis of a government is narrow. Or, put slightly differently, relative to other electoral systems, an SMP electoral system does a poor job of creating the legitimacy necessary for a government to make decisions. Again, consider the example of the Northern Gateway Pipeline. Because of the Harper government's weak legitimacy, it could not translate its formal powers to make decisions into the effective power to do so. While a smart and inclusive prime minister can operate more inclusively and deliberatively – as the Trudeau government seems to be doing in the best cases – SMP electoral systems in a Westminster context provide few institutional incentives that generate power from the political resources of greater legitimacy. No healthy democratic system, however, should be so beholden to the leader of the governing party. Its legitimacy-generating qualities should be designed into its institutions.

In contrast, decisions that are broadly inclusive and properly deliberated will also benefit from greater legitimacy. And where there is more legitimacy, there are also more powers. PR systems push institutional incentives in these directions. Once a unified power system is combined with inclusiveness and deliberativeness, then the formal powers can operate as actual powers. It is probable that a PR system would transform our Westminster system from a relatively weak and mistake-prone system into a more capable, more legitimately powerful system. This kind of change might very well also help to compensate for the collective action deficits of our weak federal system. A federal government that can claim greater legitimacy is also one less subject to the downward levelling vetoes of the provinces in those policy areas where we need greater national-level direction.

In conclusion, the windows for institutional reform tend to be narrow. Canada's political system works well enough to mostly avoid broad and deep pressures for change. The pressure for reform, such as it is, was generated by a decade of plurality government that did not represent most Canadians. Our current Liberal government, though elected by a similar plurality of 39 per cent, nonetheless is much closer to representing a majority owing to the overlaps between its policy platforms and those of the New Democratic Party, producing what is, in effect, a true majority government. This circumstance is already reducing pressures for reform. This said, this opportunity for electoral reform should not be missed simply because the system, for the moment, has produced results that are acceptable to a majority of Canadians. Times change, and a democratic system should be designed so that it can weather changes, reliably producing governments that reflect broad majorities with capacities to act on behalf of Canadians. A PR system would help to get us there. It is a doable and relatively easy fix for the well-known deficits of a Westminster system operating within the context of a weak federation. It is also a relatively predictable fix: the broad experience of PR among our peer countries suggests that it would produce moderate, centrist coalitions. These kinds of governments would suit Canada's generally moderate political character very nicely. We can and should take this modest step forward. Although there are never any guarantees in politics, it is a very good bet that this kind of electoral reform would help to generate the political capacities we need to meet our challenges and realize our potentials.

10

What Is the Problem that Electoral Reform Will Solve?

Lydia Miljan

Electoral reform has recently been put on the agenda with the Liberal government's campaign pledge that 2015 would be the last election held under the first-past-the-post system (FPP). Despite the statement in the party platform that a Liberal government would embark on electoral reform, the government has not provided Canadians with a compelling rationale to undertake this exercise.[1] Typically, policy changes such as this are a result of a recognized policy problem, which is sometimes defined as "unrealized needs, values, or opportunities for improvement that may be pursued through public action."[2] Yet, as Ken Carty notes in his essay submitted for this collection, there doesn't seem to be any precipitating event behind this drive for policy change. This is problematic, both for the government moving ahead with electoral reform, and for Canadians who appear to be disinterested in the process.

A poll conducted in September 2016 found that 81 per cent of Canadians had no idea that the federal government had begun the process of public and parliamentary consultations on electoral reform. Moreover, the survey found that only 3 per cent of Canadians have been following the issue closely. I suggest that one of the reasons for this lack of knowledge, or interest, in the topic is that the government has not made the case for the need for electoral reform. Without a doubt, the people involved in providing testimony to the Special Committee on Electoral Reform have been actively engaged, as are those involved in this symposium, but it is simply not a burning issue for 97 per cent of the country.

For an issue to resonate with the public, it must be put on the public's agenda. Although all the federal parties in the last election mentioned electoral reform in their platforms, it was not a dominant part of any party's election bid. Moreover, it was mentioned only in passing during the first leaders' debate and given scant media attention throughout the campaign. Of the three English language debates, only one – the Maclean's debate – included any discussions of electoral reform.[3] And even though the Maclean's debate incorporated two segments on democracy, electoral reform was only a minor part of those segments. Of the over 20,000 words uttered during debate, only about 600 words, or roughly 3 per cent, of the total debate was about electoral reform. Much more time was spent debating Quebec separatism, the Fair Elections Act, and Senate reform, than on discussing any move away from FPP.

Media coverage of this issue proved to be scant as well. From when the writ dropped to election day on October 19, "electoral reform" was mentioned 851 times in print and online media. This may seem like a lot, but during the same period, "health care" was mentioned 31,979 times. This translates into more than thirty-five news stories on health care for every one story that mentioned electoral reform. Just because a party pledges reform of the electoral system in its platform does not necessarily ensure the issue becomes part of the public's agenda.

It is incumbent upon the government to convey to the public why FPP is a problem and why it believes there is urgency in changing it. To date, the government has provided little rationale for either. In this essay, I examine what problems the government seeks to solve in this endeavour and also speculate on whether this exercise can achieve the stated goal. I also examine the process by which these reforms have been undertaken. My analysis is informed by the recently published collection of essays that I edited, *Counting Votes: Essays on Electoral Reform*. In short, this paper argues that while periodic review of institutions can be positive, it should be done by comparing alternatives with the status quo. Only then can the committee, and Canadians, decide which electoral system best suits the unique interests and situation of the country.

Problem Definition

The Liberal government's commitment to electoral reform is predicated on two things: first, that FPP is outdated; and second, that FPP is the reason why "Canadians don't engage in or care about politics."[4] While it is true that Canadians have elected their national representatives using FPP since before Confederation, that fact alone should not be the only criterion to judge the legitimacy of the system. Most of our parliamentary traditions stem from the nineteenth century and many have served us well. Some examples: the principle of responsible government, the political party system, and the important role of opposition. All of these are institutions that we have used for generations. To state that something is old is not justification for concluding that it is out of date. In fact, as Patrice Dutil argues, our inherited electoral system is "part of the very fabric of the country's political culture."[5] It is a system of electing representatives that is used not only in federal elections, but in all provincial elections, too. While some provinces have attempted to reform their electoral systems over the last fifteen years, in each instance the public has rejected the reforms. Moreover, when provinces unilaterally changed their electoral systems in the early to mid-twentieth century, the reforms were reversed after only a few election cycles.[6]

Lack of Engagement

Far more vexing than the government's claim that the electoral system is outdated is its attempt to link the public's lack of engagement in political life with the electoral system. There are several problems with this assertion, not the least of which is that there is no evidence provided to confirm the statement in the first place. How does the government know that Canadians don't engage in politics? How does the government know that Canadians don't care about politics?

An indicator often used to measure lack of engagement is voter turnout. Over the last 150 years, Canadian voter turnout has averaged around 70 per cent. While the last decade saw voter turnout reach as low as 59 per cent (2008), the 2015 election saw a dramatic increase to 68 per cent, up seven percentage points from 2011.[7] Although the Liberal Party made its campaign commitment in the context of the 2011 campaign, the results of 2015 should give them reason to reassess their premise. As can be seen in figure 1, the average voter turnout worldwide in systems that have non-compulsory voting is 63 per cent. In all parliamentary elections around the world, voter turnout has been on the decline since the 1990s. Canadian voter turnout was well below both the global average and the OECD average throughout the 1990s and 2000s. However, the 2011 and 2015 elections saw Canadian turnout rise dramatically and exceed those averages.

Figure 1: Voter Turnout, Most Recent National Election (per cent)

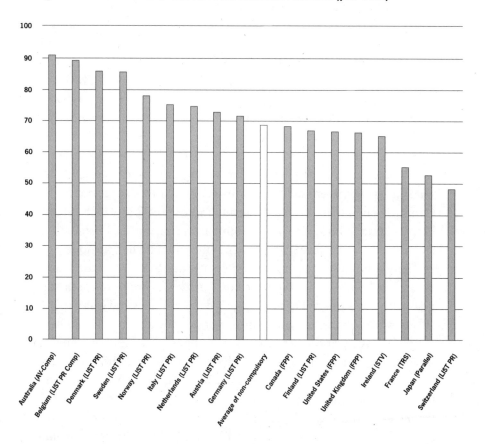

Source: International Institute for Democracy and Electoral Assistance (International IDEA)

Simply ranking Canada's voter turnout on a global basis is not the most illuminating way to measure the robustness of our democracy. Yet, a recent Conference Board report that compared Canada with seventeen peer countries ranks Canadian voter turnout as a "C" based on the 2011 election. While it is true that in both 2011 and the most recent election Canadian turnout was lower than countries such as Australia or Belgium, which have compulsory voting, it is not dissimilar to countries such as Germany, Finland, the United States, or the United Kingdom, which do not have compulsory voting.

In 1993, the Royal Commission on Electoral Reform and Party Financing (the Lortie Commission) tabled its recommendations. The first principle that guided the Lortie Commission was "the need to secure the democratic rights of voters."[8] With the then federal turnout of 73 per cent, the commission noted Canada ranked worse than 27 other democracies. It also warned that the country risked falling below the international average if measures were not taken to make voting more accessible. The Commission made several recommendations to remove the unjustified exclusion of some voters. These included improving voter registration, increasing mobile polls and absentee voting, and adjusting the times that Canadians could vote. Over the years, the government adopted many of the reforms suggested by the Commission to make voting easier and more accessible, which ostensibly was done to improve voter turnout and engagement. Despite these efforts, with each reform came lower, rather than higher, turnout.

There are many reasons why voters choose to exercise their franchise. Some may be as simple as convenience, as some research suggests. Other reasons might be changing demographics and generational effects, with subsequent generations not developing the habit as early as previous generations. As can be seen in figure 2, turnout over the last several decades demonstrates that each election is unique and the reasons for voting depend on many things, such as the frequency of the election, the issues, and whether it is a "change" election. The elections with the largest turnout were 1984 and 1988, with three-quarters of Canadians voting. Both elections saw Brian Mulroney bring in strong majority governments. While 1984 could certainly be described as a change election, 1988 was an election fought on the issue of free trade. In both cases, Canadians were engaged and demonstrated their passion for the issues by voting.

Figure 2: Federal Voter Turnout, 1980–2015

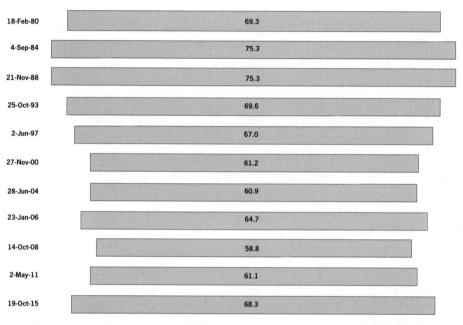

18-Feb-80	69.3
4-Sep-84	75.3
21-Nov-88	75.3
25-Oct-93	69.6
2-Jun-97	67.0
27-Nov-00	61.2
28-Jun-04	60.9
23-Jan-06	64.7
14-Oct-08	58.8
2-May-11	61.1
19-Oct-15	68.3

Source: Elections Canada

From the 1990s until the 2000s, voter turnout steadily declined. The dominance of the Liberal Party, and the split of the Conservatives during this time, could have reduced voter participation. In other words, while the outcome of those elections was not pre-determined, they were nonetheless rather easy victories for the Liberals. The frequent elections in the 2000s could also have contributed to the decline in turnout. Neither should we discount the possibility that the failure of Canadians to vote in the 2008 and 2011 elections had more to do with Liberal Party supporters sitting out elections than it had to do with overall public engagement.

Another plausible explanation for the decline in turnout is the increase in the number of political parties vying for representation in the House of Commons. What makes the Canadian experience unique is that it runs counter to academic theory on political parties and voter turnout. While many scholars suggest a strong link between the number of political parties and turnout, it was precisely when our party system expanded from three to five that voter turnout declined.[9]

The 2015 election demonstrates that a robust Liberal Party can engage its supporters. The success of the Liberals in 2015 had more to do with revitalizing Liberal support than taking votes away from the other parties. While the Conservatives lost 220,000 votes from 2011 to 2015, the Liberals gained over 4 million votes. About 1 million of those came from the NDP. The more dramatic number is the 1.6 million increase in supporters from the last time the Liberals won a majority government. This suggests that disenchanted Liberals came back to the party.

All this is to say that why Canadians choose to vote, or not to vote, varies with the circumstances of each election. Administrative changes to making voting easier simply have not resulted in increased voter turnout. To change the electoral system without examining the party system is short-sighted and is likely to be ineffective.

The Special Committee on Electoral Reform was charged with examining the electoral system within five guidelines:

1. Restore the effectiveness and legitimacy of voting, such as by reducing distortions and strengthening the link between voter intention and the electoral result;

2. Encourage greater engagement and participation in the democratic process, including by underrepresented groups;

3. Support accessibility and inclusiveness of all eligible voters, and avoid undue complexity in the voting process;

4. Safeguard the integrity of our voting process;

5. Preserve the accountability of local representation.[10]

While three of the guiding principles provide specifications on how an electoral system might be designed, the first two imply that there are problems with the current system.

The first guiding principle boldly claims that voting in Canada has become ineffective and illegitimate. This is astounding given that Freedom House ranks Canada as one of the freest countries in the world with an aggregate score of 99/100. Moreover, Canada scored the full 40 points on political rights. This category includes the electoral process, political pluralism and participation, and the functioning of government.

Legitimacy of voting speaks to whether a government has a mandate. This is a tricky position for the current government to place itself in. On the one hand, it is saying that in the most recent election, because the majority of Canadians did not vote for the Liberal Party in the popular vote, it does not have a full mandate. This despite the fact that it holds 54 per cent of the seats. Yet, this is the same government that argues it has a mandate to proceed with electoral reform without allowing the people a direct vote. As Patrice Dutil asks, "What is the point of promising consultations if the government has already made up its mind to proceed with making fundamental changes?"[11] Moreover, Dutil makes a compelling case that the government was not given a mandate to push ahead with electoral reform by an "arbitrary, hard deadline."

While the government's official documents on electoral reform make it appear that the country's electoral system no longer serves the interests of the Canadian electorate, remarks by Prime Minister Trudeau reveal the real motivation behind the reforms. In an interview with *Le Devoir* Trudeau said,

> Sous M. [Stephen] Harper, il y avait tellement de gens mécontents du gouvernement et de son approche que les gens disaient "ça prend une réforme électorale pour ne plus avoir de gouvernement qu'on n'aime pas". Or, sous le système actuel, ils ont maintenant un gouvernement avec lequel ils sont plus satisfaits. Et la motivation de vouloir changer le système électoral est moins percutante [ou moins criante].

> Translation: Under Stephen Harper, there were so many people unhappy with the government and their approach that people were

saying, "It will take electoral reform to no longer have a government we don't like." But under the current system, they now have a government they're more satisfied with and the motivation to change the electoral system is less compelling.[12]

This statement suggests that electoral reform was only a problem when the Liberals faced a humiliating defeat and were relegated to the third party in the House of Commons. Their desire for electoral change has more to do with what is good for the Liberal Party than what is good for the country. Given this revelation, the guiding principles and what they don't say have new meaning. In particular, the guiding principles place no value on regime change or a robust policy debate being facilitated by electoral reform.

Despite the fact that the prime minister has signaled that electoral reform may be put aside, the remainder of this paper will nonetheless examine the alternatives of Proportional Representation (PR) and the Alternative Vote (AV) against the status quo (FPP). This exercise will assess the systems on the guiding principles, with the additional principle of the probability that there will be a change in governments.

Proportional Representation

Both the New Democrat and Green parties have stated a preference for PR. The NDP platform categorically states that it wants to ensure "everyone's vote matters by bringing in proportional representation for elections."[13] The Green Party claims that the current system punishes voters in various ways because it does not reflect the popular vote. The party's campaign promise was clear. It intends to replace FPP with PR: "The Green Party of Canada believes that Canada must change, immediately, to a proportional voting system that fairly and directly translates all votes into representation in Parliament."[14]

Some researchers point out that electoral systems such as PR tend to have higher voter turnout than FPP.[15] Yet questions remain about the consistency of such correlations.[16] As figure 1 illustrates, there are six countries comparable to Canada that have PR and have better voter turnout than we do. However, Switzerland, a country with PR, has the lowest voter turnout of comparable countries at 48 per cent. Of those with FPP, Canada has the highest voter turnout in national elections. Canada also has a higher voter turnout than Ireland with its single transferable vote, or Finland with its PR system.

PR is often credited with increasing minority voices in government. It does that because smaller parties receive seats based on popular support. This also means that PR regimes have more parties. Thus, PR systems often have difficulty producing majority governments. To pass legislation, these systems often resort to coalition governments. While some find this to be ideal, it does undermine the legitimacy of the government as the coalition itself becomes a negotiation between political parties and the electorate loses a voice in those decisions. As John Pepall argues, PR systems give significant power to smaller parties as they often join coalition governments.[17] While their interests may be reflected in the new government, it is nonetheless a minority position and this can undermine the democratic will of the electorate.

The need to increase minority participation is something that the Organization for Security and Co-operation in Europe (OSCE) noted in its needs assessment mission as something that should be improved in Canada. While the organization acknowledged that Aboriginal and minority representation grew from 10 per cent to 16.8 per cent in the last election, it was still short of the 23.4 per cent share of the visible minority community in the total population.[18] Proponents of PR argue that representation of minorities and women will be strengthened with a changed electoral system.

Nonetheless, Canadians have been able to make gains for women and visible minorities under the existing FPP system. In particular, the 2015 federal election marked a significant improvement in the representation of women in the House of Commons. Both the NDP and the Liberals made a concerted effort to encourage women to seek and win their party's nominations. Consequently, women comprise 26 per cent of the legislature, up from 24.6 per cent in the previous election. It should be noted that the representation of women in elected office is not only influenced by the electoral system. The problem starts much earlier than on election day: women are less likely to have their name on the ballot than men. However, when women are on the ballot and their party wins government, they compete well against men in the election.

For example, in 2011, female candidates who ran for the Conservatives had a 41 per cent success rate. In 2015, the women who ran for the Liberals had a 47.6 per cent success rate.[19] Nonetheless, women's representation at the federal level is woefully short of their proportion in the population and of the rate set by the UN to establish effectiveness.

Proportional representation systems are often said to provide much better representation of women and visible minorities than majority/plurality electoral systems. However, as Karen Bird notes, while PR systems tend to increase the representation of women, it may not necessarily work the same way for ethnic minorities.[20] Electoral theory suggests that an FPP electoral system has lower voter turnouts because there is a tendency for these systems to have fewer political parties than PR or other systems. Thus, the public has fewer choices and this suppresses interest. However, more recent research suggests that the added complexity of PR systems suppresses voter turnout among the less educated. So, while in aggregate it appears that PR systems have higher voter turnout, that turnout is disproportionally weighted in favour of those with high levels of education and a high interest in politics. Changing electoral systems toward PR may violate the third guiding principle of supporting the inclusiveness of all voters.

Alternative Vote

One problem in a country as large and regionally diverse as Canada is that changing the electoral system to make it appear more legitimate does not necessarily mean that there will be no distortion in the outcome. The difference between the percentage of popular support and the percentage of seats in the legislature has more to do with the party system in Canada than it has to do with the electoral system.

One way to fulfill the guiding principle of reducing distortions and strengthening the link between voter intention and the electoral result is to adopt an alternative vote (AV) system, as is the case in Australia. The system is the one for which the prime minister himself has stated a preference. One problem with this system is that it doesn't change the first preference of voters; it only enables voters who selected less popular candidates to have their second (and subsequent) choices counted until a majority is reached. In this form of election, smaller parties wield greater power because they can instruct their voters about strategic voting decisions, which gives them greater influence in the formation of coalition governments.

The other problem with the AV system is that it would give an unfair advantage to the Liberal Party of Canada. This violates the guiding principle of safeguarding the integrity of the voting system. To determine whether AV does indeed give one party an advantage over the others, Taylor Jackson and I conducted simulations of Canadian federal elections from 1997 to 2015 to see if there was an inherent bias in the outcomes of those elections, favouring one political party over the others.[21] We found that in all elections, the party that increased its number of seats was the Liberals. The Conservatives would have received fewer seats in all elections under AV as compared with FPP, and an AV system would have cost the party its minority government in 2006 and its majority in 2011. The NDP's electoral fortunes would have been reduced in the 1997–2004 elections, but would have increased in all subsequent campaigns.

No doubt had we been operating under an existing AV electoral system, the parties would have employed strategies and decisions to compensate for the change in the way governments are chosen, and any one of these elections would have been affected by those changes. Some have suggested that under an AV system, parties would have changed their policy platforms to appeal more to the centre. This argument assumes that voters place a higher value on consensus than conflict. While that value might appear laudable, it negates the purpose of a vigorous liberal democracy. For there to be policy change, there needs to be a spirited opposition to the government. Parties who adjust their platforms only for vote gains run the risk of avoiding policy renewal and dissent in order to secure seats. While this practice exists in the current FPP system, it could be amplified if Canada were to adopt an AV system that gives an unfair advantage to one party over the others.

The complexity – or simplicity – of the voting process is something that is an integral part of the electoral system. Of the various electoral systems available, most would concede that in terms of casting a ballot and counting the vote, FPP is the simplest. The marking of an X next to a candidate's name and associated party is well established in the current system. Both PR and AV increase the complexity of the voting system, which would disproportionately affect the participation of less sophisticated voters.

Fiscal Consequences

Many have noted that there is no perfect electoral system. Each system has its benefits and its drawbacks. While we often think about elections in terms of representation, one area that is often neglected in the discussion is policy outcomes, especially fiscal policy. Moving away from FPP will not only affect who serves in government, but also the power structure itself, and the resulting impact on fiscal policy. One of the drawbacks with systems that result in coalition governments, such as PR, is that they lead to higher government spending and government debt. As Persson and his associates note, PR systems end up with a more fragmented party system, which tends to produce coalition governments. They found that between 1960 and 1998, 63 per cent of plurality/majority systems, such as AV or FPP, ended up with a single-party government, compared with only 17 per cent of PR systems.[22] PR systems encourage smaller parties, and consequently there is an increase in the number of parties running in those electoral systems as compared to plurality/majority systems. More parties result in more cases of coalition governments. From 2000 to 2015, countries using PR electoral systems were over five times more likely to have coalition governments than countries with plurality/majoritarian systems.[23]

There are policy consequences to increasing the number of parties in a government. Several economists have found that both minority governments and coalition governments have higher budget deficits compared with majority governments.[24] There are several reasons for this phenomenon. First, minority governments require additional negotiation between parties, and to ensure stability, the major parties often trade off fiscal responsibility for staying in government. Second, smaller parties can exert pressure on the government to increase spending in their preferred policy areas. Third, because the chance of coalitions in the future is also high, there is a smaller probability that any one party is held accountable for the increased spending and subsequent debt and deficit. Therefore, the cycles of debts and deficits are higher in these systems than in systems where one party takes owner-ship of fiscal policy.

There is no perfect electoral system. Each of the main systems has its benefits and its drawbacks. As this essay has shown, while flawed, FPP has served Canadians well. The guiding principles established for the Special Committee on Electoral Reform place the committee in an impossible position. No single electoral system will be able to achieve all the goals asked of it. To have Parliament mirror the Canadian public will result in a much larger Parliament and may come at the expense of local representation. When smaller political parties get more power, it may come at the expense of the will of the people, or even fiscal respon-sibility. Given that the reasons for electoral reform have not been prop-erly articulated by the current federal government, it is paramount that any proposed changes to the system go beyond consultation with inter-ested parties and include the electorate in a direct vote.

PART THREE

Issues and Alternatives

The Electoral System and Parliament's Diversity Problem: In Defense of the Wrongfully Accused

Erin Tolley

Advocates of electoral reform have leaned heavily on research that asserts an association between proportional electoral systems and increased demographic diversity in elected bodies. The evidence is alluring, but contestable. I argue that the relationship between proportional electoral systems and the representation of diversity is not absolute. Moreover, it has conflated the representation of women with that of racial minorities and Indigenous peoples, where arguments for proportional representation are less compelling. Finally, I suggest that advocates of electoral reform have not sufficiently attended to the potential unintended consequences of a shift to a new voting system. I take these unknowns seriously and provide a cautionary tale about the effects of electoral reform on the representation of diversity. I argue that the representation of diversity could be improved under our current electoral system, which advocates of electoral reform have largely ignored.

Underpinning my argument is the assertion that the electoral system is not the principal barrier to increased demographic representation in the House of Commons. Rather, it is the failure of parties to identify and recruit diverse candidates, and the acquiescence of voters in accepting that the most suitable candidates for office must just happen to be middle-aged, heterosexual, able-bodied, white men. We have long had the ability to increase diversity in our elected bodies, but quite simply have opted not to. This suggests that the problem is not simply one of institutional constraints, but also a deficit in our normative commitment to equality and diversity.

Representation and the Unintended Consequences of Electoral Reform

Hanna Pitkin's 1972 classic, *The Concept of Representation*, details several ways in which we can think about the notion of representation. I will focus on two: descriptive representation and substantive representation. Descriptive conceptions of representation focus on the congruity between elected bodies and the broader population. The key question when thinking about descriptive representation is whether those elected to office share the characteristics of those they represent. Although descriptive representation is important because the mere presence of diversity in elected bodies can strengthen citizens' perceptions of the inclusiveness or legitimacy of those bodies, the so-called "politics of presence" is only one way of understanding representation.[1] Pitkin thus points to a second conception of representation that acknowledges the actions of representatives. The central preoccupation here is whether legislators act in a manner that reflects the interests and wishes of their constituents. Pitkin herself did not chart the relationship between descriptive and substantive representation; for her, the main concern was to encourage linguistic precision and conceptual clarity when the term "representation" is invoked. I take up this preoccupation.

When advocates of electoral reform discuss representational effects, they are typically referring to descriptive representation. Fair Vote Canada has widely circulated a bar graph that depicts the percentage of women officeholders in countries with different electoral systems. The organization's preferred interpretation of the graph is that women are better represented under proportional representation. This may be true in a descriptive sense, although even there the evidence is not so clear-cut, but with respect to substantive representation, the evidence is absolutely mixed. To the extent that women and minorities may be more substantively represented under a particular electoral system, it is almost impossible to determine that the outcome is a function of voting rules.

Those who study policy representation – a form of substantive representation – ask whether the policy agenda aligns with public preferences. Much of this literature suggests that policy representation is higher under proportional electoral systems, not so much because of the mechanism of proportionality but instead because government formation under such systems typically requires the building of a coalition. As a result, governments in proportional systems will exhibit an ideological orientation that is closer to the average voter.[2] Others question this evidence in part because of measurement error, but also because most studies look only at representation in the immediate aftermath of an election, without examining how governments respond to public opinion in between elections.[3]

There is in fact some reason to expect policy representation to be higher in plurality or majority systems because such systems more clearly link voters and representatives; this may lead to greater accountability and responsiveness.[4] Additionally, given that smaller and more fringe parties tend to develop in proportional systems, representation may skew toward extreme positions, which could in fact be detrimental to immigrants and minorities.[5] Looking specifically at policy representation in Canada, it seems that governments do pursue policies that respond to public preferences. Although policy representation is somewhat weaker in Canada than in either the United States or the United Kingdom, all three countries vote using first-past-the-post so if Canada has a policy representation problem, the electoral system is not the only cause.[6]

Hoping to combine "the best of both worlds," many who have intervened in the debate around electoral reform have advocated a mixed-member system in which some legislators would be chosen using our existing single-member district simple plurality system, while others would be selected using list proportional representation. Although this combination of features does have its advantages, mixed-member systems can make it more difficult for voters to assign policy responsibility, which may create a space for elected officials to shirk that duty. Despite this, list PR systems have the potential to increase the numerical representation of women and minorities because in such systems parties put forward a list of rank-order candidates. That creates an incentive to place women and minorities near the top of the list not only to increase the party's broad appeal, but also to avoid accusations of racism and sexism. This is an attractive feature of list PR although, as I argue below, public shaming could be achieved under SMP. It is also worth noting that most advocates of electoral reform have focused on this positive aspect of mixed-member systems without according sufficient attention to the potentially negative consequences. What do these negative consequences entail?

A major drawback of mixed-member systems is that they create two types of representatives: those who are elected in districts to represent a set of constituents, and those who are elected from the list. The comparative evidence suggests that in mixed systems, women tend to fare better on the list than they do in the districts. For example, in Germany's 1990 election, 28 per cent of PR seats went to women, compared to just 12 per cent of the district seats. In Australia in that same year, women made up 25 per cent of PR seats, but just 7 per cent of the district seats. Finally, in New Zealand, the 2005 election saw 43 per cent of PR seats going to women, but less than half of that (20 per cent) going to women in the districts.[7] When women are effectively shut out of the districts, it reinforces the perception that women cannot win unless they are the beneficiaries of some sort of electoral engineering, which in this case is the list. Such an outcome allows problematic assumptions about women's electoral acumen to persist.[8]

A second unintended consequence of mixed electoral systems is that list candidates could be shouldered with the burden of representing demographic or "special" interests since they do not have specifically designated geographic constituents. This could be positive for substantive representation in that list candidates would be free to act as trustees for a variety of interests, but it may also hamstring or limit these candidates and leave them with less time to pursue other issues. It should be underscored that most representatives have policy concerns that extend well beyond their race or gender: they want to make an impact outside of the "special interests" ghetto. Even under Canada's current electoral system, women and minority members of Parliament note they are often viewed as representatives of their demographic group and are asked even by non-constituents to advance these interests.[9] This representational burden is typically not placed on white or male members of

Parliament. A mixed-member system would institutionalize the expectations for substantive representation that are already disproportionately placed on women and minorities because it would cluster these individuals into the list seats. Representatives who are unanchored by geography are likely to be viewed by parties and citizens as a natural conduit for activism on women and minority issues. Some research suggests that although women legislators understand the representation of women's interests to be one of their duties, male legislators do not view this as one of the roles of their female colleagues,[10] meaning that women legislators are doing representational work for which they receive little credit. A mixed-member system has the potential to exacerbate this compensatory deficit.

In thinking about the relationship between a country's electoral system and the representation of diversity, much more attention needs to be given to the inter-relationships between the components of the electoral system, and to the impact of electoral system design on politics more generally. As I point out below, electoral reform could alter the numerical representation of particular groups, but it might not or it might do so only marginally. Although some have suggested that even a small uptick in the numerical representation of women and other groups would be desirable, that perspective ignores the potential effects on other aspects of representation. Changes to the electoral system may have unintended consequences, including the representational effects described above, but also broader concerns about stability, consistency, and the link between voters and representatives, which are enumerated elsewhere in this volume.

Electoral Systems and the Representation of Diversity

Conventional wisdom frequently asserts that Canada has a representational deficit. For example, following the 2015 federal election, the proportion of women in the House of Commons stood at 26 per cent, just a one-point increase from the previous election and only half-way to the 52 per cent of women who make up the general population. How do racial minorities and Indigenous peoples fare? Racial minorities' numerical presence in Parliament has increased substantially in the past two decades. Racial minority members of Parliament now make up 14 per cent of the House of Commons, compared to 19 per cent of the population. However, within the population count, there are a number of non-citizens who are not eligible to vote or hold office. Therefore, a more appropriate comparator is the proportion of racial minorities within the population of Canadian citizens. In this group, 15 per cent have racial minority backgrounds, which is almost at par with the presence of racial minorities in the House of Commons. It is hard to argue that on numerical grounds, racial minorities are in the aggregate underrepresented. The same is true for Indigenous Canadians who made significant gains in the 2015 election and now make up about 3 per cent of the House of Commons, which is only slightly below the 4 per cent of the population of who have Indigenous origins.

Numerically speaking, underrepresentation is therefore clear when we look at the presence of women in Parliament, but much less apparent among racial minorities and Indigenous peoples. For the latter two groups, the representational deficit is not really one related to numbers since both groups have achieved an aggregate legislative presence that rivals their proportion of the Canadian population. Rather, the concern here is with respect to substantive representation and issues of voice and influence. It is also clear that there is considerable variability in the numerical representation of particular segments of these populations. Within the racial minority category, South Asian Canadians – and particularly Sikh Canadians – have achieved significant electoral success in federal politics, but the proportionate presence of Black Canadians has been much lower. This underscores that the focus on aggregate numerical representation – a tactic employed by proponents of proportional representation – conceals important gaps in representation.

Would electoral reform correct the imbalance? Although evidence suggests that more women are elected under proportional systems, the relationship is not absolute. For example, there are countries with proportional electoral systems where the proportion of women legislators barely deviates from the level that has been achieved in Canada under SMP. This is the case in Poland and Israel, which both use proportional representation and have legislatures where women make up 27 per cent of the members. Ireland uses the single transferable vote, and yet only 22 per cent of lower house members are women. In other countries with proportional representation, the number of women legislators is surprisingly low. In Uruguay and Hungary, both of which use proportional representation, the proportion of women in the lower house is just 16 per cent and 10 per cent, respectively.[11]

Moreover, although many of the countries that elect larger numbers of women do have proportional electoral systems, there are countries with non-proportional systems where the proportion of women legislators actually exceeds the level achieved in some PR countries. This is the case in Ethiopia, a fledgling democracy to be sure, but one that uses a plurality system and in 2015 elected a legislature where 38 per cent of members are women. Although we likely do not want to emulate Ethiopia's approach to democracy, it provides a counterpoint to the inaccurate claim that a proportional electoral formula is a necessary or even sufficient condition for more diverse elected bodies.

An additional shortcoming of cross-country comparisons of representational diversity is they are taken at a single point in time and do not account for the wide variability in representation within the same country or across countries with similar electoral systems. Roberts and colleagues argue that much of the evidence on the link between proportional electoral systems and the increased representation of diversity derives from studies with serious methodological flaws. They caution against cross-country comparisons that can only weakly account for varying cultural norms and that thus conceal whether the mechanism causing positive representational effects is in fact the system's proportionality.[12] For example, the Nordic countries all use proportional representation and have achieved high levels of numerical representation for women, but these countries also have significant measures in place to increase gender equity, which could foster a climate that supports the election of women.[13] As I argue below, in the absence of a strong normative commitment to representational equality, institutional changes are unlikely to have a significant impact on the numerical representation of women and minorities.

We can also look at cases where the electoral system was changed in a country – moving from plurality to more proportional – to determine whether the reform had an unequivocal effect on women's representation. Although these comparisons are somewhat simplistic, they are instructive. In France, which experimented with proportional representation for a single election in 1986, there was absolutely no effect on women's numerical representation. Even New Zealand, which adopted a mixed member proportional system in 1996 and is frequently touted by advocates hoping to "prove" that there is a relationship between electoral reform and the representation of diversity, provides a less than compelling case. While the proportion of women in elected office did increase after New Zealand adopted a new voting system, the direction and magnitude of the change was consistent with the country's overall trend toward electing more women.[14] In other words, the uptick in women's representation in New Zealand was not a function of the change in voting system, but simply an extension of an already existing trend that likely would have continued irrespective of electoral reform. Given that women's representation in Canada's House of Commons has been relatively stagnant over the past four election cycles, it is not clear that we would realize the same positive effects were we to reform our electoral system.

Even in countries with upper and lower legislative houses that have substantially different electoral rules but where cultural differences can be controlled for, the expected effects of electoral systems on women's representation are inconsistent. This suggests that electoral laws are interacting with other factors or social structures to either augment or depress women's representation. On the basis of this and other evidence, Roberts and colleagues conclude that "although a switch to a more proportional electoral system may improve women's representation in some cases, the effect is sometimes absent or even negative and when present is usually not large."[15]

Paxton, Hughes, and Painter provide one of the most extensive analyses of the effects of proportional electoral systems on women's representation. They looked at more than one hundred countries over a twenty-five-year period and suggest that women's representation is 2.5 per cent higher under proportional representation than under other systems. Although their study included both established and developing democracies, the results are not entirely transferable to a Canadian context.[16] While Richard E. Matland suggests that women's representation will rise nearly 16 per cent under proportional representation,

Rob Salmond highlights a number of methodological problems with this analysis and points out that none of France, Italy, Japan, or New Zealand – countries that all made substantial changes to their electoral systems – realized an increase of this magnitude.[17]

Aiming to correct what he saw as shortcomings in some of the existing studies, which he suspected over-estimated the impact of proportional representation on women's representation, Salmond looked at twenty-one advanced industrial democracies over a fifty-year period. He found that a shift from a single-member district simple plurality configuration to a system of proportional representation with high district magnitude led to an increase in the proportion of women legislators; the size of the increase varied between 1.5 per cent and 7 per cent.[18] Using the high end of this estimate would bring the proportion of women in Canada's House of Commons to just 32 per cent, which is well below proportionality. Although such a bump is not insignificant, when we focus only on numerical representation, we ignore the other consequences that could result from changes to the electoral system.

An additional problem with the research on the relationship between electoral systems on the representation of diversity is that nearly all of it focuses on women. Many seem to assume that the benefits of proportional representation for women candidates will naturally extend to racial minorities, Indigenous peoples, and other traditionally marginalized groups. The limited data we do have casts serious doubt on this conclusion. Indeed, as was noted earlier, under SMP, the numerical representation of racial minorities and Indigenous peoples in Canada has reached near parity. This is in part because Canada's electoral geography tends to advantage groups with significant residential concentrations. Racial minorities and Indigenous peoples are clustered into a relatively small number of electoral districts with significant co-ethnic concentrations, a feature that racial minority and Indigenous candidates can translate into electoral gain. This advantage of a single-member district simple plurality system is not present in countries that use proportional representation, where racial minorities and Indigenous peoples seem to fare less well.

Take Denmark and Norway, for instance. These are countries that both use proportional representation and where women's numerical representation is comparatively high, but they have rather dismal records when it comes to electing legislators with non-Western origins. In the Danish Folketinget, 2.2 per cent of representatives have minority backgrounds, compared to 6.4 per cent of the Danish population, meaning minorities have achieved barely a third of what would be their proportionate representation. The situation is worse in Norway, where less than 1 per cent of legislators have non-Western origins, compared to 5.6 per cent of the population.[19] In Australia, which uses preferential balloting to elect members of its House of Representatives, just 2 per cent of legislators have non-European origins, compared to 10 per cent of the population.[20] Although the country has an important Aboriginal population, only two Indigenous MPs have ever been elected to the House of Representatives, the first in 2010. These examples illustrate two things: First, the advantages of proportional representation for women might not extend to minorities and Indigenous peoples, and second, a country's electoral system does not, on its own, determine the demographic composition of its legislative bodies.

The word "system" is significant because it signals that the component parts of an election do not exist in isolation. These pieces include the electoral formula, district magnitude, ballot composition, and the existence of mechanisms such as quotas that either encourage or require the nomination or election of individuals from identified groups. Indeed, while the electoral formula – plurality, majoritarian, or proportional – has received the lion's share of attention, there is some evidence that women achieve higher levels of numerical representation in countries with proportional representation not because of the electoral formula but because of higher district magnitudes.[21] This is because single-member districts are a zero-sum proposition. For women or minorities to win a nomination, they must displace a man or someone from the majority population. That forces parties to make choices that they do not have to make in systems with multi-member districts. Increasing district magnitude would address that problem and provide additional avenues for parties to nominate women and minority candidates.

Even though there is little evidence voters discriminate against women and minority candidates, in the case of women, in particular, party selectorates fear they might.[22] This is because party elites have ingrained – and often flawed – ideas about who makes the best candidate. When party selectorates are forced to make a single choice for a candidate, these biases may lead them to favour male candidates, particularly in competitive ridings.[23] In discussions about electoral reform, there is an almost singular focus on the electoral formula. Very little has been said about the power of political parties.

Political Parties and the Representation of Diversity

In the Canadian system, candidate recruitment and selection is highly decentralized, with local electoral district associations overseeing the entire nomination process, with very limited intervention from the central party. When local elites prioritize the selection of diverse candidates, those efforts have tended to bear fruit. The New Democratic Party encourages local electoral districts to identify and support so-called equity-seeking candidates, and that party has consistently nominated some of the most diverse candidates. Meanwhile, when the president of a local electoral district is a woman, or there is an established history of nominating women candidates, female candidates are more likely.[24] Even still, the proportion of women candidates has always fallen below the presence of women in the population. In my current research, I am interviewing party elites about their efforts to nominate more diverse candidates. Even those who appear committed to the ideal admit they struggle with time pressures and a lack of tangible supports needed to encourage women and minorities to enter the political arena. There is also evidence that party elites associate electoral success with stereotypically masculine traits and that they are more likely to encourage men to seek office than women.[25] When parties do seek out non-prototypical candidates to run, in the case of women, there is some evidence that they continue to nominate them in less competitive electoral districts.[26]

The nomination of racial minority and Indigenous candidates provides an important counterpoint. Here, there is evidence that parties have in recent years made a strong and concerted effort to nominate such candidates in electoral districts that they believe they can win (and not coincidentally, often, those with significant racial minority or Indigenous populations). From the perspective of numerical representation, the results of these efforts have been positive: more racial minority and Indigenous candidates have been elected, with significant gains made in 2015. This underscores that when parties make a concerted effort to nominate diverse candidates in competitive ridings, elected bodies themselves become more diverse. This happened without any change to the electoral system: it is purely a function of parties' willingness to do so.

Bill C-237, a private member's bill introduced by New Democratic MP Kennedy Stewart in 2015, was a golden opportunity for parties to affirm their commitment to the nomination of more women candidates. The bill proposed to amend the Canada Elections Act to include a financial penalty for parties who put forward candidate slates with more than a 10 per cent difference in the number of men and women. Parties who did not nominate a sufficient number of women would see their electoral expense reimbursements reduced by 0.25 per cent for each percentage point by which they deviated from the 10 per cent threshold. If the provision were applied to the 2015 election, the NDP would not be penalized, while the Liberals and Conservatives would have stood to lose more than $1 million. The bill was imperfect. Financial penalties pertained only to candidate gender, and parties would still be free to nominate women candidates in less competitive ridings, but it would put in place a tangible measure to increase representational diversity and to punish parties that did not comply. This would send a clear signal about a country's normative commitment to equity. The importance of these normative commitments are, as I argue below, often overlooked in discussions about electoral reform. Tellingly, Bill C-237 was defeated at second reading in October 2016, with most Liberals and Conservatives voting against it.

Institutional Change and the Commitment to Equity

The lack of diversity among elected officials is not a natural outgrowth of the electoral system. When voters demand more diverse candidates, and parties make an effort to nominate them, the representation of diversity is more robust. Despite having the power to do so, political parties have not taken advantage of this opportunity. Their failure to act is not because they have been hamstrung by first-past-the-post, as some advocates would have us believe, but quite simply because they have chosen not to. I argue that parties' inactivity on this front this reflects a weak normative commitment to diversity in elected bodies. This is important because absent a strong equity norm, institutional change is unlikely to result in elected bodies that proportionately reflect the broader population.

Mona Lena Krook underscores this point when she distinguishes between systemic, practical, and normative institutions. She argues that to achieve gender equity, systemic changes must be accompanied by normative changes. The key point is that electoral systems do not operate in isolation.[27] In order to understand how institutional changes – such as a shift to proportional representation – will influence candidate selection and the composition of the legislature, one must take into account the cultural context in which those changes are occurring. Although academics and the media have drawn attention to the absence of diversity in Canada's elected institutions, voters have rarely demanded action, and political parties have either ignored or only weakly pursued the relatively minor institutional and practical changes that could be invoked to address numerical underrepresentation. Cynics might say that advocates for electoral reform have really only drawn attention to the representation of diversity because it provides a convenient means for touting the benefits of proportional representation. I am not convinced this commitment is sincere; if it were, the discussion of representation would be much more robust and far less simplistic.

Some party elites actively limit the definition of equity to strict equality of opportunity. In that sense, they would argue, Canada has met this objective in that there are no formal barriers that prevent women from attaining elected office. This understanding of equity norms conceals gendered differences in outcome. Electoral reform alone is unlikely to overcome this. A normative commitment to equitable outcomes is what ultimately will result in elected institutions that mirror the characteristics of the broader population.

How does one encourage a change in cultural norms? Some argue that proportional systems encourage a normative shift because they allow voters to identify parties that have put forward lists with very few women and minority candidates. Even in proportional systems, however, if there is only a weak normative commitment to equality, parties may be tempted to rank women and minority candidates in less advantageous positions on the list. The argument also often presumes that it is only under proportional systems that such a norm can develop or flourish. Under non-proportional systems, formal measures might set quotas for the nomination of candidates from identified groups, or impose financial penalties on parties that do not put forward equitable candidate slates. Parties could also be required to document the number of women, minorities, and Indigenous peoples they have nominated and to publicize the strategies they have pursued to encourage individuals from these groups to run. Just like party lists in proportional systems, these latter two measures engender an environment where it is culturally unacceptable for parties to put forward homogeneous candidate slates.

Conclusion

My objective here was not to argue that proportional representation and increased legislative diversity are entirely unrelated. That kind of reasoning is foolhardy. Much of the evidence suggests that proportional representation can have positive effects, particularly on the representation of women. But this does not mean a shift to proportional representation is the only way to achieve more diversity in Parliament. Indeed, the evidence is mixed. Any observer who draws a straight-line relationship between proportional representation and diversity in elected bodies is willfully ignoring not just the counter-examples, but also the relatively marginal effects on numerical representation. Proportional representation on its own will not lead to a House of Commons where 50 per cent of MPs are women. It is not even clear such a change would have any effect on the legislature's demographic composition.

Our current electoral system is imperfect, and much has been written about its shortcomings. I will not enumerate these here. However, I am cautious about discarding a system that has resulted in stable and continuous government for a period of nearly 150 years. This is a system that has discouraged the development of the kind of extremist, anti-immigrant parties that have developed elsewhere. Indeed, when Canadian parties have waded even ankle-deep into this pool – witness early iterations of Reform or the muted xenophobia of the

2015 Conservative Party – they have been punished electorally. No such party has ever formed a government in Canada. Moreover, while the numerical representation of women has been less than admirable under SMP, racial minorities and Indigenous peoples have representation in the House of Commons that is almost at parity. What might result under a new system is unclear.

I would advocate more serious discussion about the unintended consequences of electoral reform, and a more measured analysis of proportional representation's perceived advantages. I would also urge reformers to look more closely at what can be achieved under our current system. To the extent that the current system has failed, not all of its shortcomings are a function of the electoral formula. Instead, I would place the blame squarely at the feet of political parties, which have failed to adopt even moderate reforms to their own candidate recruitment practices. In the face of their weak normative commitment to equality, the promise of a representative Parliament has not yet been realized.

12

Indigenous Representation, Self-Determination, and Electoral Reform

Melissa S. Williams

I. The Importance of Indigenous Representation in the Electoral Reform Agenda

Canada is at a crossroads in coming to terms with its long history of colonial domination, as reflected both in the work of the Truth and Reconciliation Commission, concluded in 2015,[1] and in the current government's own express commitment to "reset" Canada's relationship with Indigenous people. In the words of Prime Minister Trudeau, "It is time for a renewed, nation-to-nation relationship with First Nations peoples, one that understands that the constitutionally guaranteed rights of First Nations in Canada are not an inconvenience but rather a sacred obligation."[2] Reform of the electoral system is a major change to the political order, and it will inevitably affect the ways in which Indigenous interests are (or are not) represented in the electoral and legislative process. Canada cannot undertake such a change while also honouring its commitment to renewing its relationship with Indigenous people unless electoral reform actively engages Indigenous publics and solicits their support.

Indigenous people have been chronically underrepresented in Canada's parliamentary system. Until the 2015 federal elections, there had been only thirty-four Indigenous members of Parliament in the entire history of Canada since Confederation, and only fifteen Indigenous senators.[3] Following the unprecedented mobilization of Indigenous voters by Idle No More's "Rock the Vote" campaign, together with Assembly of First Nations chief Perry Bellegarde's pleas for Indigenous people to vote,[4] voter turnout in the last election reached a record high. Whereas the turnout on reserves had been 47.4 per cent of eligible voters in the 2011 election, it reached 61.5 per cent in 2015. Although this rate of participation was still lower than overall voter turnout in 2015 (68.3 per cent), it came closer than ever before.[5] The result was a striking increase in the number of Indigenous MPs, for a total of ten.[6] This may be close to the upper limit of what is achievable under the existing single-member plurality (SMP) electoral system, and yet it still constitutes less than 3 per cent of the total number of MPs, whereas Indigenous people comprise at least 4.3 per cent of the population.[7]

The underrepresentation of Indigenous people in Parliament is of particular concern because of the unique position of Indigenous peoples within Canada's legal order, combined with the long history of colonial domination and ongoing patterns of deep inequality. Aboriginal people are the only group that is governed according to laws different from those governing the rest of the population, beginning with the deeply problematic and colonial Indian Act. Although living under separate orders of law would be consistent with a decolonized "nation-to-nation" relationship, in which Indigenous people governed themselves in accordance with their own legal traditions, we are far from achieving that aspiration.

As matters stand, the federal government exercises jurisdiction over Indigenous people in policy domains that are within provincial jurisdiction for non-Indigenous Canadians, including such fundamental matters as education, health, child welfare, housing, and water. The federal government's enduring failure to provide basic social protections for Indigenous people on a par with what non-Indigenous Canadians enjoy is nothing short of scandalous.

Earlier this year, the Canadian Human Rights Tribunal ruled that Canada discriminates against Indigenous children by providing less per-child funding for on-reserve child welfare services than is allocated by the provinces for children living off-reserve, even though on-reserve needs are greater.[8] Children living on reserves are allocated 30 per cent less funding for their educations than children living under provincial jurisdiction.[9] A recent study shows that the educational achievement gap between Indigenous and non-Indigenous students is widening, not narrowing.[10] Although the federal government regulates water quality across Canada, these standards are not applied to reserves. Over one hundred reserves are or have recently been under boil-water advisories, in some cases for many years. Over 150,000 Indigenous people are affected by unsafe water conditions, including children who are suffering health consequences.[11] These gross inequalities make clear that the existing system of political representation is failing to protect the most basic interests and well-being of Indigenous people.

Another reason why electoral reform should give prominence to Indigenous underrepresentation is that non-Indigenous Canadians would support such efforts. A recent Environics survey showed that a plurality of Canadians (46 per cent) unequivocally support more representation for Indigenous people in governing institutions, and another 29 per cent support it conditionally. Only 16 per cent of Canadians stated that they oppose enhanced Indigenous representation.[12] In a different survey focused exclusively on Canadian public opinion concerning Indigenous people, a significant majority favoured ensuring Aboriginal representation at every First Ministers' meeting (76 per cent), requiring at least one Aboriginal minister in federal cabinet (73 per cent), and establishing a parliamentary committee of Indigenous representatives to review all legislation from an Indigenous perspective (63 per cent). A near-majority (49 per cent) supported the creation of a new Aboriginal political party in Canada.[13] There is every reason to believe, then, that a majority of Canadians would welcome greater attention to Indigenous representation in the current electoral reform process.

Given these factors, one might expect that the electoral reform agenda that is now under way would pay special attention to the issue. Indeed, Maryam Monsef, the minister of democratic institutions, noted in the early days of the House of Commons Special Committee on Electoral Reform that engaging underrepresented groups, including Indigenous people, is "a key purpose of electoral reform."[14] Yet, strikingly, the otherwise commendable cross-country consultations of the Committee have made no visible effort to reach out specifically to Indigenous communities. A review of the available transcripts of the Committee's consultations does reveal that the issue has arisen repeatedly as one of the forms of underrepresentation that motivates proponents of proportional representation (PR). In some instances, witnesses have commended New Zealand's mixed-member proportional (MMP) system, not only for its effectiveness in increasing the number of women and minorities in parliament, but also for its method of securing Māori representation through a system of reserved seats.[15] Some witnesses have also invoked previous Canadian proposals to entrench Indigenous representation in the federal parliamentary system, notably those of the Royal Commission on Electoral Reform and Party Financing (the "Lortie Commission," 1991), the Royal Commission on Aboriginal Peoples (RCAP, 1996), and the Law Commission of Canada's report on electoral reform (2004).[16] Georges Erasmus, who had served as co-chair of the Royal Commission on Aboriginal Peoples, spoke at an open microphone at the Committee's hearings in Yellowknife; he had not been specifically invited to speak about Indigenous representation. "At the time when [RCAP] reported," he said, "which was twenty years ago ..., we had maybe fewer than twenty members who had ever been elected in Canada up to that time. Obviously, we're doing better; in this House I notice we have quite a few more members, but it's still not really enough. So I recommend that you look at ... our report and see if you can garner anything out of it that's useful to you." Erasmus also recommended that the Committee review the recommendations of the Lortie Commisssion.[17]

Notwithstanding all the good reasons for putting Indigenous representation on the electoral reform agenda, there has not been a widespread mobilization of Indigenous people to bring that about. To be sure, there have been some Indigenous voices calling for greater attention to the issue, as the example of Georges Erasmus demonstrates. James Arreak, the chief executive officer of Nunavut Tunngavik Inc., told the Committee that "each of Canada's three Aboriginal peoples should have direct representation in a reformed House of Commons," citing New Zealand's system of reserved seats as a possible model. "We know what it looks like to be on the outside looking in to the electoral system," he said. "We have experienced colonialism with all its attendant problems."[18] Last year's successful efforts to increase Indigenous voter turnout also demonstrate that many clearly do see participation in electoral institutions as an important means of protecting Indigenous interests.

But precisely because of the Indian Act system and other features of the colonial state in Canada, some Indigenous people do not identify with mainstream political institutions and do not believe that it does or can represent them. This stance is rooted in the history of the Canadian state's relation to Indigenous people. Prior to 1960, a First Nations person could become enfranchised only by relinquishing his or her status as "Indian" under the Indian Act. Inclusion in the political process was, explicitly, a policy of cultural assimilation. It was not until 1960 that the federal government extended the right to vote to all First Nations persons without loss of status, and that was done unilaterally, without consulting Indigenous people as to whether they wanted the franchise.

This history, combined with the failure of the Canadian state to protect the fundamental interests of Indigenous people, goes a long way to explaining their relatively low turnout rates: Canadian institutions lack legitimacy in the eyes of many Indigenous people.[19] As leading Indigenous scholar Pam Palmater has put it, "Every federal and provincial government that has ever been in power has failed to address ... urgent social issues, let alone recognize Aboriginal title or Aboriginal and treaty rights. Voting in the oppressor's regime has, not surprisingly, failed to end oppression."[20] Further, many see participation in mainstream electoral processes as contradictory to the aspiration to Indigenous self-determination and a nation-to-nation relationship between Indigenous peoples and Canada.[21] Against this backdrop, it is understandable that there has not been a massive Indigenous mobilization around electoral reform.

The fact that there is disagreement among Indigenous people about the value of participating in Canadian political institutions does not justify the absence of Indigenous underrepresentation from the electoral reform agenda. To the contrary, given the Canadian state's systematic failures, the underrepresentation of Indigenous people is a matter of far greater moral urgency than any other defect in our representative institutions. But this defect cannot and should not be addressed without seriously engaging Indigenous people about the changes that, in their judgment, would make the representative system more legitimate.

II. Mechanisms for Indigenous Representation (PR Is Not Enough)

As noted earlier, the problem of Indigenous underrepresentation is not new, and several learned commissions have recommended institutional reforms aimed at addressing it. Let me briefly canvass some of the most prominent.

A. NEW ZEALAND

I begin with the case of New Zealand, which is often invoked as a possible model for Canadian reform both because of its provisions for Indigenous (Māori) representation and because New Zealanders opted in 1993 to switch from an SMP to an MMP system. In New Zealand's system of Indigenous representation, legislative seats are reserved for candidates chosen by Māori voters who have opted into a separate Māori voters' roll.

The map of Māori districts is superimposed on the district map for the general electorate. Prior to reform, New Zealand had four Māori districts. Since the adoption of MMP, the number of Māori seats has been apportioned to the number of voters who choose to be listed on the Māori roll. The number of Māori people who have opted for the Māori roll grew from 40 per cent in 1991 to 58 per cent in 2006, falling to 55 per cent in the most recent enumeration in 2013.[22] The number of Māori electorates has grown from five to seven since electoral reform. The Māori Party was formed in 2004, increasing pressure on other parties to add Māori candidates to their lists, with the result that the percentage of seats held by Māori MPs now exceeds the percentage of Māori people in the New Zealand population as a whole (15 per cent).[23] Studies have shown that the increased representation of Māoris translates into legitimacy gains for parliament[24] and enhanced representation for Māori interests,[25] and that representatives elected from Māori districts do a better job of representing Māori interests than those elected from general districts.[26] In 2011, New Zealanders voted in a national referendum to retain the MMP system.[27]

B. THE LORTIE COMMISSION

In 1991, Canada's Royal Commission on Electoral Reform and Party Financing (the "Lortie Commission") recommended a remedy to Indigenous underrepresentation that bore some similarities to the pre-reform New Zealand model (without the PR component). It proposed that separate single-member Indigenous districts be superimposed upon the map of general electoral ridings and Indigenous voters be given the option to vote in those districts or in the general districts. The boundaries of these Aboriginal Electoral Districts would fall within provincial boundaries and be apportioned according the electoral quotient (the number of electors per legislative seat) within each province, with some allowance for the modest overrepresentation of Indigenous voters in recognition of their permanent minority status. In this way, special Indigenous districts could be created without necessitating constitutional amendment. Because the small number of Indigenous people in each of the Atlantic provinces would have fallen short of the electoral quotient, the Commission proposed that a single Aboriginal district be drawn for that region, though this would require constitutional amendment. The Lortie Commission was clear that its recommendations were offered as a starting point for discussions between federal and provincial leaders and Indigenous leaders, and were not intended for unilateral adoption by the Government of Canada.[28]

C. THE CHARLOTTETOWN ACCORD

The Charlottetown Accord, which was defeated in a nation-wide referendum in 1992, would have secured a major increase in Indigenous representation in both houses of Parliament while also recognizing Indigenous peoples' inherent right of self-government. Although it left the details for later negotiation, it provided that the Lortie Commission's recommendations for increased Indigenous representation in the House of Commons serve as a starting-point for consultations with "representatives of the Aboriginal peoples of Canada."[29] It further provided for guaranteed Aboriginal representation in a reformed Senate, suggesting that a double majority of both Aboriginal and non-Aboriginal senators would be required to pass legislation affecting fundamental Indigenous interests.[30] These institutions would exist alongside constitutionally entrenched powers of Indigenous autonomy as a third order of government, together with federal and provincial governments.[31]

D. THE ROYAL COMMISSION ON ABORIGINAL PEOPLES

In 1996, the Royal Commission on Aboriginal Peoples took the view that enhanced Indigenous representation within existing institutions might be in tension with a nation-to-nation relationship between Indigenous peoples and Canada. Instead, RCAP proposed the establishment of an Aboriginal parliament that would initially serve in an advisory capacity to Parliament. This was proposed as an interim measure that would not require constitutional amendment. Over time, they envisioned the transformation of this assembly into a third body in the parliamentary system, a House of First Peoples. Modeled in part on the Saami parliaments of Scandinavia, the House of First Peoples would (in contrast to Saami parliaments) be empowered to propose and vote on legislation.[32] The RCAP made explicit that the Aboriginal parliament would not displace Indigenous peoples' right of self-determination or the establishment of a nation-to-nation relationship between Canada and Indigenous peoples:

> Rather, it is an additional institution for enhancing the representation of Aboriginal peoples within Canadian federalism. The design of the institution, however, must provide for more than symbolic representation. At the centre of our proposal for an Aboriginal parliament is the principle that the renewed relationship between Canada and Aboriginal peoples is a nation-to-nation relationship that supports the inherent right of Aboriginal self-government. The proposed powers and responsibilities of an Aboriginal parliament reflect this principle and provide the basis for an effective role for Aboriginal nations in the decision-making processes of the Parliament of Canada.[33]

E. LAW COMMISSION OF CANADA

Finally, in 2004, the Law Commission of Canada recommended that Parliament draft legislation to create an MMP electoral system. As part of that system, and in harmony with the recommendations of the Lortie Commission and New Zealand's system of reserved seats, it proposed the possibility of creating special Aboriginal Electoral Districts to enhance Indigenous representation.

Beyond these proposed changes to the electoral system, the Law Commission recommended a number of additional measures to enhance Indigenous representation, including quotas for Indigenous candidates on party lists, appointing Indigenous MPs to cabinet positions, and strategies to encourage Indigenous voter participation and recruitment to electoral office. Like the Lortie Commission, the Law Commission emphasized the importance of consultations with First Nations, Métis, and Inuit peoples as a necessary condition of moving forward with measures to enhance Indigenous representation in the federal parliamentary system.[34]

Despite the significant differences between them, these various options for strengthening Indigenous representation at the federal level share one key point in common: they all recognize that adopting a system of proportional representation would not suffice to address the ills of Indigenous underrepresentation. Most systems of proportional representation would likely yield increases to the number of Indigenous MPs as compared with the current SMP system. But this would be insufficient to secure the representation of Indigenous interests, even if the number of Indigenous MPs were proportional to the Indigenous population. The most important factor is that without a direct electoral connection between a representative and his or her Indigenous constituents, constituents have no means for holding their representatives accountable for advancing their interests in legislative debates. Representatives elected from constituencies with large numbers of non-Indigenous voters lack the incentive to give particular weight to the interests of their Indigenous constituents. Representatives elected from party lists owe their primary allegiance to their parties: where party agendas are contrary to Indigenous interests, representatives will be constrained to toe the party line. To use the language that is common in the theoretical literature, *descriptive* representation (the presence of a group within the legislature) does not necessarily translate into *substantive* representation (advocacy for the group's distinctive interests).[35]

All of the proposals canvassed here recognize this feature of legislators' behaviour by building in an electoral connection to their proposals for Indigenous representation. For this reason, the current state of discussion as reflected in testimony before the Special Committee, which tends to discuss Indigenous underrepresentation as if it were continuous with the underrepresentation of women and visible minorities, is severely lacking.

III. Does Indigenous Representation in Parliament Conflict with a Nation-to-Nation Relationship?

As suggested earlier, one of the reasons for a lack of Indigenous mobilization around the electoral reform agenda might be that many Indigenous people perceive a tension between participation in shared Canadian institutions and the realization of Indigenous self-determination and a nation-to-nation relationship between Canada and Indigenous peoples. Indeed, as we have seen, this was central to the rationale RCAP offered for demurring to the Lortie Commission recommendations and proposing, instead, the creation of a House of First Peoples at the federal level. The relationship between rights of self-determination and participation in common institutions is not a question that is appropriate for a non-Indigenous scholar, or any non-Indigenous agent, to resolve. It is a question that Indigenous people must answer for themselves. Nonetheless, there are reasons why we should not assume that these two pathways to Indigenous empowerment are mutually exclusive. I offer some of those reasons here because it is important that possible tensions between self-determination and representation in common institutions not be used as an excuse for the failure to engage Indigenous people regarding the electoral reform agenda.

The principal reason why a nation-to-nation relationship is not incompatible with enhanced Indigenous representation in common institutions is that even in a fully realized system of Indigenous self-determination within Canada's borders, federal legislation will affect Indigenous communities in ways that are not immediately evident to non-Indigenous legislators. Many such issues, such as environmental regulation – or deregulation, as in the case of the legislation that sparked the Idle No More movement – have a profound impact on Indigenous communities but are diffuse, not confinable to negotiations between federal and provincial governments and individual Indigenous peoples or communities. To put the point simply, Indigenous and non-Indigenous people live together on a common territory, and this coexistence and interdependence require an order of shared rule even though they must also be reconciled with Indigenous rights of self-determination.[36] If the laws that govern the zones of interdependence are made by a parliament that lacks significant Indigenous representation, as historically they have been, they will likely reproduce familiar patterns of colonial domination. As Ovide Mercredi, former grand chief of the Assembly of First Nations, stated to the Lortie Commission, "There is no inconsistency in Canada recognizing our collective rights of self-government and us still getting involved and maintaining our involvement in the political life of the state, which means getting involved in federal elections."[37] Further, though many Indigenous and non-Indigenous scholars and leaders agree that the Indian Act must be dismantled, the legislation that will replace it should not be fashioned without the active and empowered participation of Indigenous representatives.[38]

We need not resolve all the complexities of honouring, establishing, and renewing a treaty-based, nation-to-nation relationship between Canada and Indigenous peoples in order to arrive at the judgment that Indigenous underrepresentation in Parliament is a severe defect in our constitutional order. Should that defect be addressed in the short run, at least partially, through reforms along the lines recommended by the Lortie Commission or the New Zealand model? Should such reforms be tied to a longer-term solution, such as the House of First Peoples recommended by RCAP? Whatever one's answers to those questions, they can have no legitimate resolution without a serious and well-designed consultation with Indigenous people.

IV. What Mode of Consultation?

What sort of consultation with Indigenous people should the Special Committee on Electoral recommend in its forthcoming report? At least three pathways, not mutually exclusive, suggest themselves.

The first would begin from the principle of a nation-to-nation relationship by formally approaching existing bodies of elected Indigenous representatives: the Assembly of First Nations, the Métis National Council, and the Inuit Tapiriit Kanatami. Respect for nation-to-nation protocol would require that the request for these bodies' participation in discussions of Indigenous parliamentary representation should come from the highest level, that is, from the Prime Minister's Office.

But just as consulting parliamentarians on electoral reform would not likely be viewed as adequate by Canadian citizens – hence the Special Committee's cross-country tour – many Indigenous people might not believe that consulting elected bodies of Indigenous leaders would be an adequate gauge of their opinions. The consultation process with Indigenous people should at least run parallel to the one established for non-Indigenous Canadians. Community consultations focused on both rural and urban Indigenous communities, and inviting input from Indigenous governments and civil society organizations, would be the closest analogue to the consultations the Committee has already carried out.

A third, more ambitious process, modeled on the citizens' assemblies established in British Columbia and Ontario in recent years, would recognize the *sui generis* character of Indigenous people in Canada's constitutional order by creating two parallel assemblies: a Canadian Citizens' Assembly and an Indigenous Assembly.[39] These assemblies would be constituted through a random sampling to ensure good cross-sectional diversity among their members. Members of the assemblies would be compensated to enable them to develop a clear and well-informed judgment about the institutional alternatives, much as jurors are compensated for the time they spend hearing trial evidence and deliberating. A final stage would engage both the Indigenous and the non-Indigenous assemblies in joint deliberation aimed at generating a consensus proposal for electoral reform that does justice to both Indigenous and non-Indigenous perspectives, interests and opinions. Perhaps their final recommendations could, as in the British Columbia and Ontario cases, be put to a referendum, where a double majority of both Indigenous and non-Indigenous voters would be required to validate a proposed change.

Such a process would take careful design and considerable time to implement well. It could not be rushed. But the experience of British Columbia and Ontario demonstrates that such a process is not impossible, and would generate invaluable knowledge that could be brought to bear. Indeed, the minister of democratic institutions, like several members of the Special Committee, expressed openness to the idea of a Canada-wide citizens' assembly earlier this year.[40]

There is no doubt that opening up the question of Indigenous underrepresentation will complicate the already-complex challenge of electoral reform. But the window of opportunity to undertake serious electoral reform opens only rarely. If Canadians are serious about "resetting" the relationship with Indigenous people, we should not miss this chance to address the most serious failing of our electoral system.

13

Addressing Representational Deficits in Canadian Legislatures

Angelia Wagner and Elisabeth Gidengil

Introduction

Canadian legislatures need politicians from all walks of life in order to effectively tackle the problems facing a multicultural society in the twenty-first century. Women and men in general have different life experiences, resulting from women's presumed responsibility for reproductive activities such as childcare. These gendered life experiences are further shaped by the varying cultural, social, and economic effects of other aspects of their identities such as ethnicity, sexuality, and class. The result is that different groups of women and men have specific policy needs.[1] If government policies are to be effective at addressing the issues confronting society today, members of these various communities must not only be allowed but must also be encouraged to bring their insights to the policy-making process.[2] It is unfair, to say the least, to impose government policy on women, visible minorities, Indigenous peoples, and lesbian, gay, bisexual, and transgender (LGBT) individuals without them being equally involved in drafting it.

Moreover, the legitimacy of the political system is threatened when its elected representatives are consistently chosen from an unrepresentative candidate pool.[3] Citizens who do not see members of their social group holding political power are unlikely to have confidence in, or support, the decisions emanating from the country's political institutions. Yet the lion's share of the individuals who gather in Canadian legislatures on any given day are strikingly similar. The typical politician continues to be male – and, in particular, a white, heterosexual male from a profession such as law or business.[4] Understanding why more women, visible minorities, Indigenous peoples, and LGBT individuals do not run or are not elected to our legislatures is important in order to address representational deficits.

Representational Deficits

The diversity gap – or the difference in the proportional representation of Canadians in relation to characteristics such as gender, ethnicity, and sexuality – becomes apparent when we examine the composition of those individuals most recently elected to Parliament. While women's representation reached a record high after the 2015 federal election, it is hardly a cause for celebration. Figures collected by the Inter-Parliamentary Union rank Canada sixty-fourth in the world when it comes to the percentage of women in the lower house. Only 26 per cent of MPs in the forty-second Parliament are women. Between 1984 and 1997, women's representation in the House of Commons jumped more than 15 points, but since then the figure has increased by less than 6 points. If not quite stalled, women's representation is only inching upwards. At this rate, it will take decades to achieve a gender-balanced legislature.

Visible minority representation also reached a record high in 2015: forty-seven visible minority MPs were elected, compared to only twenty-eight in 2011.[5] They comprise 14 per cent of the MPs in the forty-second Parliament. Given their population numbers, visible minorities might appear to be close to achieving descriptive representation. However, a closer look reveals a less rosy picture. Visible minority women achieved no representational gains. Only fifteen visible minority MPs are women. Moreover, the predominance of MPs of South Asian or Chinese ancestry means that many visible minority communities lack representation. Canada's forty-second Parliament also includes ten Indigenous MPs.[6] Once again, this is a record high, up from the seven Indigenous MPs elected in 2011. Nonetheless, First Nations, Inuit, and Métis individuals remain underrepresented relative to their population numbers, and only three Indigenous MPs are female. LGBT Canadians are also numerically underrepresented in Parliament. Only six self-declared LGBT candidates were elected in 2015, the same number as in the previous Parliament.[7] They account for a mere 1.8 per cent of MPs. Only one of the LGBT MPs is female and none belong to a visible minority.

Is the Electoral System to Blame?

Canada's first-past-the-post single-member electoral system is widely blamed for these representational deficits. A variety of reasons have been suggested. First, this type of system turns the nomination process into a zero-sum game.[8] This makes it impossible to accommodate competing interests, and so the preferred candidate of the most powerful intra-party faction will win the nomination. Second, electoral volatility tends to be greater in winner-take-all systems. This makes it more difficult to determine which seats are safe and increases the perceived risk associated with nominating candidates that do not fit the white, male, heterosexual norm.[9] Third, the electoral system impedes what Richard Matland and Donley Studlar have termed "microcontagion."[10] Microcontagion happens at the local district level: one party nominates a female candidate, say, and its competitors respond by nominating female candidates of their own. Matland and Studlar attribute the lack of microcontagion in Canada to the fact that the political costs of responding to contagion pressures are higher in a single-member system because it may entail displacing a powerful incumbent. Meanwhile, the electoral costs are much lower, especially in safe seats, because a loss of votes will not necessarily mean a loss of seats. Finally, it is much more difficult to implement affirmative action measures or to impose quotas than it is in proportional systems that use party lists.[11] This problem is exacerbated by the decentralized nature of the nomination process and the national party leadership's lack of control over the process. In proportional systems, by contrast, it is not only easier for political parties to accommodate a wider range of intra-party forces, but there is also an incentive to offer more diverse slates in order to maximize their vote share. Moreover, party lists make the underrepresentation of women and at least some racialized minorities more visible to the electorate.[12]

At the same time, we should not overstate the drawbacks of the current system and the virtues of alternative systems. Women, for example, have made much more substantial representational gains in British Columbia and Ontario, where they currently make up 36 per cent of the members of the provincial legislatures, and yet both provinces use the same first-past-the-post single-member system. Moreover, there are countries using proportional representation that have lower levels of female representation than Canada, including Ireland, Greece, and many post-communist countries. It also bears emphasis that the benefits associated with proportional systems are conditional. In principle, women and other underrepresented population groups are more likely to be elected when district magnitude – or the number of representatives to be elected – is high because it takes a smaller share of the vote to get elected.[13] However, larger district magnitude only enhances women's representation if women have mobilized effectively and attained a degree of influence within a party.[14] This finding is likely to generalize to other underrepresented groups.

A case could be made that the electoral system has actually facilitated greater representation for visible minorities and some First Nations. This is because the system works to the advantage of groups that are geographically concentrated. Indeed, on the basis of a comparative study of visible minority representation in Canada, Denmark, and France, Karen Bird concludes that the electoral system has encouraged Canada's political parties to nominate more visible minority candidates in order to attract votes in ridings that are densely populated with visible minority voters.[15] In 2015, for example, 69 per cent of the major party candidates were visible minorities in the thirty-three ridings where visible minorities make up more than half of the population. In fifteen of these ridings, all of the candidates for the three major parties belonged to a visible minority.[16] Visible minorities made up 45 per cent of the population, on average, in the ridings that elected visible minority MPs in 2015.[17] Similarly, Indigenous peoples made up 33 per cent of the population in the ten ridings where Indigenous MPs were elected.[18] That said, this leaves visible minorities living in white-majority ridings and Indigenous peoples living in ridings with smaller Indigenous populations underrepresented.

What Role Does Malapportionment Play?

An important, but less discussed, barrier to electing a more representative Parliament is the overrepresentation of rural areas. The allocation of seats in the House departs significantly from the principle of one person/one vote. First, the least urbanized provinces receive more seats than their share of Canada's population warrants. Secondly, the allocation of seats within provinces allows a riding's population to vary by as much as 25 per cent above or below the provincial electoral quotient,[19] or even more if there are "exceptional circumstances." One of the main reasons for permitting so much variation is Canada's sheer geographical size. If seats were allocated strictly on the basis of population, ridings in sparsely populated rural regions would cover vast distances. In addition to ensuring that ridings remain a manageable size, boundaries also have to be set in ways that ensure representation of "communities of interest."

The systematic underrepresentation of city dwellers hampers women's representation because women are much more likely to be candidates and to get elected in urban areas.[20] Urban areas are likely to have a larger pool of women with the requisite educational qualifications and professional credentials to run for elected office. Moreover, urban women are more likely to benefit from the support of organized women's groups and to have access to larger fundraising networks.[21] As long as women remain less likely to win nominations and run successfully in rural ridings, the system of allocating seats will remain an impediment to electing more women. Similar arguments can be made with respect to visible minority and LGBT individuals. The majority of visible minority MPs elected in 2015 ran in Canada's largest cities. Twenty of the forty-seven MPs represent ridings in the Greater Toronto Area; another six represent ridings in the Greater Vancouver area.[22] It is easy to understand why. Visible minority candidates in ridings with large visible minority populations can draw on their social networks and connections with community organizations to fund and staff their nomination campaigns and then run for Parliament.[23] LGBT candidates are also more likely to run in ridings in major cities, though not necessarily in ridings with large LGBT populations.[24]

The way that seats are allocated has a particularly negative effect on the representation of visible minorities because it dilutes their voting power.[25] Michael Pal and Sujit Choudhry have argued that electoral boundary commissions could address this problem by broadening the interpretation of "communities of interest" to include visible minorities.[26] They also suggest that federal legislation could be amended to limit the permissible deviation from the principle of one person/one vote, as the United Kingdom has done.

Are Party Gatekeepers the Problem?

Analyses of representational deficits concur that party gatekeepers play a critical role when it comes to impeding or advancing the candidacies of members of underrepresented groups. Several considerations are at play when local party associations select candidates. First, party gatekeepers typically want to reduce electoral risk, especially in a context of electoral volatility.[27] They may perceive candidates who are female, nonwhite, or LGBT to be too risky. However, there is little or no evidence to suggest that voters are biased against women,[28] visible minority,[29] or LGBT candidates.[30] Indeed, if anything, female candidates may have a slight electoral advantage over their male counterparts.[31]

It has also been suggested that party gatekeepers are more likely to seek out and support candidates who are like themselves.[32] The fact that women are more likely to be selected when the riding president is a woman lends weight to this argument.[33] The problem, of course, is that men, and more particularly, white men, are more likely to be riding presidents. They are not necessarily actively discriminating against aspiring candidates from underrepresented groups. The biases in the recruitment and nomination process tend to be subtle. Party gatekeepers are apt to recruit candidates through established networks, and this works to limit candidacies from non-traditional sources.

At the same time, it is important to acknowledge that the nomination process can actually enhance the chances of visible minority candidates being selected. As noted above, the political parties have strategic incentives to nominate visible minority candidates in ridings with large visible minority populations. Meanwhile, nominees in these ridings try to boost their chances by signing up new party members. This is facilitated by their social networks and associational ties and by the fact that non-citizens who are permanent residents can join the party and vote for their preferred nominee.[34] While this has undoubtedly helped to elect more visible minority MPs, it still leaves visible minorities in less diverse ridings underrepresented.

The concentration of visible minority candidates in ridings with a large visible minority population may help to explain why there is little evidence overall that these candidates are disproportionately nominated to run as "sacrificial lambs" in ridings that their party has little or no chance of winning.[35] The story is different for female candidates. Women are more likely to be nominated to run in lost-cause ridings than in safe seats or competitive ridings.[36] Nonetheless, their success rates are not markedly lower than men's. In 2015, for example, there was only a three-point difference in the success rates of male and female candidates. This points to an understudied aspect of representational deficits. The problem is that not enough women are seeking elected office. Linda Trimble and Jane Arscott have stated the matter bluntly: "Very simply, women cannot win office if they do not run."[37] The same is true of other underrepresented groups.

It Takes a Candidate[38]

Addressing representational deficits therefore requires more women, Indigenous peoples, visible minorities, and LGBT individuals to embark on the lengthy and challenging process of becoming a political candidate. They need to decide that politics is a viable, and desirable, career option. Candidates typically arrive at this decision after carefully considering a range of factors relevant to their personal circumstances. Angelia Wagner's ongoing research on the Canadian context, and other analyses of the factors shaping political candidacy, have revealed a number of factors shaping the willingness of underrepresented groups to become candidates.

Are Family Obligations a Constraint?

A person's willingness – and ability – to put in the necessary time and effort for a political career is shaped by their age, marital situation, and family responsibilities. A strong belief in many cultures that women are "naturally" suited to be wives and mothers means they are expected to be the primary caregivers for children and to prioritize these roles over any others. Many women therefore delay their entry into politics until their children are in school or grown,[39] suggesting childbearing is an important restraint on women's political ambitions, especially at a younger age. Parenthood generally does not have the same effect on men, but this conclusion is likely based on a presumption of heterosexuality. The sexual division of labour is not easily replicated when both parents are of the same sex. Childcare responsibilities could dampen the political aspirations of gay fathers but not necessarily those of lesbian mothers. Gender norms can also vary among social groups. Indigenous societies, for example, place equal importance on the roles performed by women and men, and expect women to be actively involved in the political affairs of their communities.[40]

Still, some women might try to reconcile their domestic roles with their political aspirations by running for municipal office. The close proximity of town hall in comparison to provincial or federal legislatures, as well as the part-time nature of many municipal councils, could reduce the conflict between work and family.[41] But women are not the only ones who dwell on family issues when weighing the pros and cons of running for elected office. Preliminary research findings suggest some men also want to find a way to balance their political ambitions with their personal lives. Efforts are already underway to make legislatures more family friendly.[42] The Alberta government, for example, plans to introduce changes to provincial legislation to improve parental leave for MLAs.[43] Such reforms would benefit politicians regardless of their gender, sexuality, Indigeneity, or ethnicity.

Spousal support has also been found to weigh heavily in some women's decision regarding a career in politics.[44] Ongoing research indicates this factor continues to play a role in shaping women's political ambitions, as it does for some men's aspirations. One reason why spousal support appears to be so important to women and men today is the potential for their political activities to affect the lives of their loved ones, both personally and professionally. Louise Carbert asserts that the family is a corporate unit in Atlantic Canada, where "every success or failure, every compliment or slur reflects on the entire family."[45] A person's political activities can have serious consequences for themselves and/or extended family members if people boycott their businesses or choose not to hire them because of political disagreements. While circumstances specific to Atlantic Canada could make it a greater threat in that region, the potential for a public backlash to extend to family members matters to individuals from across the country and from different social backgrounds.

Variations in Confidence and Ambition

A long-standing interest in politics is key to political ambition. Individuals need to be drawn to politics in the first place, and this interest is typically fostered in childhood.[46] Parents play an important role in shaping their children's orientation to politics, whether it be through discussing politics and current affairs at the dinner table or by being actively involved in politics themselves. Political socialization is especially important in fostering women's political ambitions. Studies have found that women who have a politically active mother are much more likely to become politically involved themselves than those women who did not, while fathers exert no such influence.[47] Family also likely plays a role in sparking the political participation of visible minorities, Indigenous peoples, and LGBT individuals. Yet preliminary research findings suggest not everyone who becomes a candidate can point to their families as stimulating their political interest. Some individuals first get drawn into politics in high school or university, getting involved in school elections as maybe a volunteer or candidate. Other youths might become friends with people who are active in party politics and join in at first for social reasons.

Another factor shaping an individual's willingness to become a candidate for elected office is self-confidence. Men typically express far greater confidence in their abilities than do women,[48] though this might be due to differences in women and men's definition of "qualified."[49] A woman's class position does little to negate these gendered differences: both affluent and poor women are less likely than similarly situated men to view themselves as politically competent.[50] Whatever boost in confidence women might get from greater financial resources has declined since 1965, while the negative effects of financial scarcity have only increased. Yet gendered expressions of self-confidence might vary among ethnic groups. One study found that white women are "more likely to downplay their confidence in their leadership abilities and deny their desire to run for political office" while black and Latino women do not.[51] We therefore need to be careful not to give the notion of confidence too much weight in the decision-making calculus to become a candidate. Ongoing research suggests some individuals decide to become candidates despite not possessing all of the qualities they believe are desirable or necessary in a politician. Some likely gain confidence in themselves as a result of the candidate experience.

When women do express interest in becoming candidates, they are far less likely than men to set their sights on elective offices at higher levels of government.[52] Most women, and many men, contemplate a bid for local office. Once in local office, fewer women politicians than men politicians demonstrate a desire to run for higher office.[53] The role of ethnicity in progressive ambition is less settled, with studies producing conflicting results.[54] The idea of progressive ambition, popular in American research, appears to have little relevance in the Canadian context. Preliminary research findings indicate that many Canadians are driven by their policy preferences when deciding which type of office to seek. If the policy domain that interests them the most falls under the jurisdiction of the federal government, for example, they prefer to seek federal office. They often have little desire to pursue elected office at another level unless that government addresses some key aspect of their policy interests.

Finding the Right Party

As we noted above, political parties play an important role in recruiting individuals to become candidates. But ongoing research indicates that more attention needs to be paid to the extent to which ideological misalignment between potential candidates and political parties depresses political ambition. Some individuals might choose not to run for elected office because none of the major parties adequately represent their political views or their preferred party shifts its position over time, often in response to the preferences of a new leader. Individuals might not want to submit to party discipline, and the dictates of message control in particular, unless their views closely align with those of the party and, especially, the party's leader. Otherwise they risk censure. They could also jeopardize their political ambitions within the party and their ability to pursue their policy goals within the legislature. People's perceptions of politics in general, and politicians in particular, could also affect their willingness to run.[55] Differences in opinion exist among ethnic groups, with non-white youths holding more positive views of politicians than did white youths during Barack Obama's tenure as the American president.[56]

Is Money a Barrier?

Investigations into the factors limiting women's electoral success have often focused on campaign financing.[57] Women have historically had a harder time than men in raising enough money to mount a competitive campaign.[58] In response, Canadian political parties created internal funds to support their female candidates while American activists founded political action committees.[59] Campaign finance reforms have also attempted to create a more level playing field, banning contributions from corporations and unions, limiting the amount of personal donations, and placing caps on campaign expenditures.[60] One consequence appears to be that campaign financing is less of a concern to potential candidates than issues around employment. Preliminary research findings indicate that, depending upon where they work or what job they hold, some individuals have to take a leave of absence as soon as they publicly declare interest in becoming a candidate or, at the very least, as soon as the election writ is dropped. Those lost wages can be a considerable burden, especially for working-class individuals. Other individuals might have to quit their jobs completely because the norms of their profession demand a non-partisan stance or political non-involvement. Journalism is one such example. Potential candidates also have to consider what will happen to their careers once their partisanship is known, regardless of whether or not they win the election. Candidates who are self-employed might lose out on government contracts. Politicians are also barred from engaging in certain kinds of professional activity for a period of time after leaving public office.[61] Ongoing research suggests these concerns likely weigh on the minds of women and men when contemplating a bid for elected office, regardless of their Indigeneity, ethnicity, or sexuality.

The Spectre of Public Scrutiny

Feminist scholars have long viewed journalists as key gatekeepers to elected office. They argue that journalists can shape electoral viability by drawing upon stereotypes when describing the candidacies of women, Indigenous peoples, LGBT individuals, and visible minorities, creating the impression that individuals who do not conform to the white, heterosexual male norm do not belong in political life.[62] But recent analyses suggest that discriminatory news coverage is not a major barrier to office for members of underrepresented groups.[63] Even if individuals expect such coverage, preliminary findings indicate it is not usually enough to discourage them from pursuing their political ambitions. What is of greater concern is media invisibility, or a lack of news coverage of their campaigns.[64] A candidate's electoral viability depends, in part, on the ability to attract news coverage during an election. Media skills are therefore vital for anyone who wants to mount a competitive campaign.

In contrast to the news media, social media has emerged as a concern for potential candidates over the last ten years. Preliminary findings suggest avid users of Internet-based applications such as Facebook and Twitter could hesitate to run out of a concern that opponents might dredge up old posts to discredit their candidacies. Problematic posts could range from inappropriate comments with a sexist, racist, or homophobic bent to political statements that contradict the current party line or are viewed as politically extreme. LGBT individuals could be particularly vulnerable to social media controversies if online sites contain photographs of them that mainstream society might find uncomfortable. Social media controversies can not only derail a person's candidacy, but they can also affect that person's reputation long after the election is over. Another aspect of public scrutiny is the feeling of being exposed. Some individuals may choose not to run because they do not want to be subjected to the intense scrutiny they see directed at current politicians or they do not want their lives to become the subject of public discussion. In an era of increased political polarization and negative politics, individuals must therefore consider both the short- and long-term impact of public attention when deciding whether or not to become candidates for elected office.

Conclusions

Changing the federal electoral system could help alleviate representational deficits in Canada's Parliament, but it would not be enough to achieve the descriptive representation of women, Indigenous peoples, visible minorities, or LGBT individuals in the House of Commons. The barriers to political candidacy and electoral success are numerous and complex, in part because their impact varies from one social group to another. Addressing representational deficits therefore requires actions on several fronts.

First, we need to find new ways to encourage more women, LGBT individuals, Indigenous peoples, and visible minorities to develop an interest in and aptitude for politics at a younger age. Civic education curriculums should be strengthened at the high school level in every province and territory, and special initiatives developed for university students. Additional programs could be designed for and to meet the needs of specific groups, such as visible minority girls, LGBT youths, or Indigenous boys, so they not only develop self-confidence but also learn the skills necessary to become effective political leaders.

Second, recruitment efforts might be more effective if they also focused on specific levels of government. The Federation of Canadian Municipalities has been active on this front for at least a decade through its Women in Local Government program, which has a youth component. This initiative could be replicated for provincial and federal offices. Alternatively, general-purpose campaign schools might consider including information sessions on each level of government, educating potential candidates about what the municipal, provincial, and federal governments do, their respective policy domains, and the expectations of elected leaders at each level. This training would not only help candidates choose which office to seek and craft a platform but also better prepare them for their public duties should they get elected.

Third, resolving family-related challenges requires the active involvement of spouses and family members. Organizations keen to improve the diversity of elected representatives should hold information sessions for spouses, children, and parents to prepare them for what lies ahead as their loved one seeks office. As it stands, awareness campaigns typically focus on the needs of potential candidates.

Fourth, political parties need to substantively incorporate the interests, needs, and insights of women, visible minorities, Indigenous peoples, and LGBT individuals in both their internal operations and policy platforms in order to attract more candidates from underrepresented groups. Minority candidates do not want to be treated as tokens – just there to make their party look progressive without an accompanying change in policy.

Finally, individuals exploring a run for elected office should have early access to training on how to handle public scrutiny and manage media relations. This includes sessions on the nature of public scrutiny, its purpose, and its potential consequences, as well as the steps individuals can take to deal with public evaluations of their personal lives, professional activities, and political comments or policy stances. Intensive media training targeting the specific needs of different groups of women and men is also vital to help these candidates deal with journalists and make the most of these relationships over the course of an election and a political career. Moreover, efforts need to be made to help potential candidates cultivate these skills over several years and not in the weeks before an election. Developing confidence in one's political abilities takes time.

In summary, addressing the representational deficits in Canadian legislatures is a complex task. Measures such as these would assist women, Indigenous peoples, visible minorities, and LGBT individuals to develop the requisite confidence, leadership abilities, and campaign skills to mount a competitive bid for elected office.

PART FOUR

How Should We Decide?

Public Consultation on Electoral Reform Through Referenda or Plebiscite: Recent Experience in British Columbia

Keith Archer

Introduction

This volume explores the topic of electoral reform at the federal level in Canada, a reform agenda introduced by the government elected in October 2015. It may seem odd that a chief electoral officer of British Columbia would have much to say about such a reform initiative, since it has no direct bearing on my responsibilities in BC. The federalization of election administration means that Elections Canada administers federal electoral events, and my agency, Elections BC, administers provincial electoral events in my province. Furthermore, we do so using legislation that is unique to our separate jurisdictions.

However, one of the questions that has arisen over the course of the federal electoral reform discussions is the matter of whether there should be a referendum to solicit popular sentiment on the topic. Elections BC recently administered two referendums on electoral reform, in 2005 and in 2009. In addition, we also administered another referendum in 2011 (on the harmonized sales tax), and a further plebiscite in 2015 (on transportation and transit options in Metro Vancouver). My comments, therefore, draw upon the experience of Elections BC in administering these public consultation processes to highlight a number of issues that may arise in administering such an event at the federal level.

What an Electoral Administrator Can, and Can't, Contribute

Procedures used to elect members of our legislative assemblies (federal as well as provincial and territorial) have a significant impact on the character of the legislative process, and indeed on the very nature of representation. Consequently, they deserve serious reflection. Let me begin by setting out the terms of reference for my comments. As Chief Electoral Officer for British Columbia, my obligation is to administer electoral processes, including associated political financing requirements in British Columbia, according to the Election Act, the Recall and Initiative Act, the Referendum Act, and the Local Elections Campaign Financing Act. Indeed, section 12 of the Election Act contains a specific provision, which states that the chief electoral officer has a duty to ensure that the Act is enforced.[1] Since the electoral system is specified in the Election Act, and of course British Columbia uses the single-member plurality (SMP) system used federally as well, then I have a duty to administer electoral processes based on that system.

As an electoral administrator, my role is to ensure that whatever electoral system is used in my jurisdiction, it is administered to the highest professional standards, ensuring that all eligible voters can fairly and effectively exercise their franchise. How those votes are aggregated to produce legislative seats is a matter of political choice, and not simply an administrative matter, which belongs, quite rightly, in the political sphere of legislators. Therefore, unlike other contributors to this volume, my remarks do not make pronouncements on the merits of one electoral system over another. My office would as readily administer a general election using any number of alternative electoral systems, such a proportional, or mixed-member proportional, or run-off systems, among others, as it would under SMP. That is the role of my office.

An additional question that arises in discussions of electoral reform, and one that has been raised in the current discussion of reforming the federal electoral system, is the following: Where there is an interest in considering changing the electoral system, what process should be used either to affirm the status quo, or to select an alternative electoral system? To put a sharper focus to this, the question is often raised as to whether changing the fundamental rules of the electoral process requires some level of public consultation. If so, should that consultation involve some type of public input process, such as the one undertaken by the federal parliamentary committee on electoral reform that has been conducting hearings across the country? Or should it involve more and perhaps different public input, for example through the administration of a plebiscite or a referendum on the issue?

In my jurisdiction, the Election Act is silent on this topic, which means of course that from a legal perspective, the standard legislative rules apply. One changes the Election Act through the normal legislative process of passing another act of Parliament and obtaining royal assent. One might take the view that a constitutional convention exists, whereby additional consultation is required by virtue of some previous precedents. However, ascertaining the status of constitutional conventions is not the purview of a chief electoral officer, and therefore I have no view on the matter. My authorities derive from statute, not from constitutional convention.

Therefore, since the Election Act is silent on the topic of whether public consultation is required prior to amending the Election Act, then as chief electoral officer I am not in a position to comment on the requirement of any form of public consultation. The decisions on whether and how to engage the public in a consultation on electoral reform is a matter for government and the legislative assembly, and is not one of the duties or responsibilities of a chief electoral officer. Therefore, I have no comments on the merits of public consultation. Now that I've outlined what I won't be discussing, and my reasons for doing so, let me turn to the thing I am prepared to discuss – namely, once the government and legislature have decided to consult the public through a referendum or plebiscite, what is involved in doing so.

First, it is useful to distinguish between referendums and plebiscites. A referendum is a question put to the electorate (or a portion thereof) that asks voters to express their views on the question. The result of a referendum normally is binding on the government. A plebiscite also is a question put to the electorate (or a portion thereof) that asks voters to express their views on the question. The result of a plebiscite normally is non-binding on the government.

Those are the simple "black and white" definitions, but of course the world is often characterized by shades of grey. Thus, for example,

Elections BC administered a plebiscite on transportation and transit options in the lower mainland (greater Vancouver) area in 2015, and the minister responsible for transportation indicated that the government would consider itself bound by the outcome of the vote. Therefore, although plebiscites are normally non-binding, a government may choose to be bound by the result.

Or, as another example, Elections BC administered referendums on electoral reform in conjunction with the general elections in 2005 and in 2009. The elections returned the same party to power in both instances, and the government abided by the referendum result. The BC Referendum Act specifically states that should a referendum pass the standard threshold (of 50 per cent plus one vote), then the result is binding on the government that initiated the referendum.[2] What would have happened, however, had another party won either of those elections? Since they had not initiated the referendum, would they be legally bound by the result? Although this question was moot in the 2005 and 2009 referendums in BC, it is a question that inevitably will arise when a referendum is held in conjunction with a general election.

Elections BC has administered three referendums and a plebiscite since 2005. I will draw upon those experiences to highlight a number of issues that may arise in considering whether a referendum or plebiscite may be used in the course of the current examination of electoral reform at the federal level.

Why Use a Referendum or Plebiscite?

Referendums and plebiscites are discretionary instruments of public consultation. In British Columbia, the government is not legally required to use either a referendum or plebiscite in policy development. Rather, referendums and plebiscites are used when government "considers that an expression of public opinion is desirable."[3] Two of the referendums conducted in BC in the past eleven years were on the question of electoral reform. The other referendum was on a proposal to rescind the HST and to return to a tax structure that included a GST and PST. And a plebiscite was held in Metro Vancouver on transportation and transit options. Each of these consultations had a different origin, or triggering event.

The 2005 referendum on electoral reform flowed from the recommendations of a citizens' assembly on the topic. The Citizens' Assembly on Electoral Reform was created in 2003, but its origins can be traced to the outcome of the 1996 provincial election, in which the NDP won a majority government with thirty-nine (of seventy-five) seats on the basis of 39.5 per cent of the popular vote, whereas the BC Liberals won only thirty-three seats (and became the official opposition) after receiving 41.8 per cent of the votes.[4] The BC Liberal government elected in 2001 had committed to establish a citizens' assembly and furthermore committed that if the citizens' assembly recommended changing the electoral system, and recommended a single alternative, that it would consult the electorate through a referendum, which would be held in conjunction with the 2005 general election.[5] Thus, in short, the Election Act did not require Elections BC to administer a referendum on electoral reform in 2005. Instead, the decision to hold a referendum was a political decision, made by the government of the day.

The 2009 referendum on electoral reform was held because the government recognized, following the vote in 2005, that the electorate was unaware of the electoral districts that would be in use under the proposed alternative electoral system – BC-STV.[6] Therefore, in fall 2005 and following the defeat of the referendum earlier that year, the government tasked the BC Electoral Boundaries Commission with proposing new electoral districts using both SMP and BC-STV, and the Commission did so in its report in 2008. The Commission's report proposed twenty BC-STV electoral districts in contrast to the eighty-five SMP electoral districts (included in the report's Appendix 4).[7] It was these district configurations that provided context for the 2009 referendum. The government once again directed Elections BC to administer a referendum on electoral reform, and once again, the referendum question failed.

The 2011 referendum on the HST began under the Recall and Initiative Act, legislation that is unique to BC. When the HST initiative had run its course to the extent that a province-wide vote on the HST was required, the government shifted the vote from an initiative vote to a referendum vote. Therefore, the decision to hold an initiative vote on the HST (which varies from the manner in which a referendum is administered) began through a petition that was initiated by citizens, rather than by government.[8] Subsequently, the vote on the topic was administered as a referendum due to a government decision, but it was the initiation of the process by a citizen petition that sets its origin apart.

In 2015, Elections BC administered a plebiscite vote to about half of the registered electors in BC, when it was directed to administer a plebiscite to eligible voters in metropolitan Vancouver. The 2015 plebiscite came about because a new source of funding was being proposed by the Metro Vancouver Mayors' Council to fund transportation and transit in the Metro area.[9] The provincial government had committed that any such new funding would be subject to public consultation, and the plebiscite option was chosen.

The discretionary character of referendums and plebiscites means that the starting points for the administration of these events may vary. Recent experience in BC has shown that referendums and plebiscites can be initiated due to election commitments of government, or they may be used to solicit public opinion when further information is available, such as in response to new electoral districts proposed by an electoral boundaries commission. They can also be used in response to calls for public votes through the initiative process by citizens, or in response to other political stakeholders, as was the case with the Mayors' Council and the transportation and transit plebiscite. The decision to proceed, and the rules for doing so, continues to rest with government.

What Is the Voting Threshold or Decision Rule?

The Referendum Act in BC states that if more than 50 per cent of the validly cast ballots vote the same way on a question, the result is binding on the government that initiated the referendum.[10] However, the legislative assembly can change this threshold by passing new legislation, as was done for the 2005 and 2009 referendums on electoral reform.[11] Recent experience in BC has shown a number of voting thresholds in operation. For the 2005 and 2009 referendums on electoral reform, the voting thresholds involved what can be described as double supermajorities. There were two thresholds: first, at least 60 per cent of valid votes had to cast the vote "yes"; and second, in at least 60 per cent of electoral districts, more than 50 per cent of valid votes had to cast the vote "yes."[12]

In 2005, the referendum question nearly passed this dual threshold. Of the total votes cast, 57.7 per cent were in favour of adopting BC-STV. Furthermore, in seventy-seven of seventy-nine electoral districts, over 50 per cent of votes were in favour of BC-STV.[13] Therefore, in the 2005 referendum, the second threshold was met, but the first threshold was not met, and consequently the referendum question failed.

In 2009, in contrast, support for BC-STV was much less pronounced in the referendum. Only 39.1 per cent of total valid votes were cast for BC-STV (which of course was less than the required 60 per cent), and more than half the voters in only eight electoral districts supported BC-STV.[14] Therefore, neither threshold was met. Consequently, the result was not binding on government, and the electoral system was not changed. It may be useful to speculate on why a similar referendum question, asked to the same electorate, would produce such markedly divergent results when held just four years apart. Such speculation, however, is more appropriate to political analysts than to electoral administrators, and therefore I will leave it to others.

For the 2011 HST referendum and the 2015 transportation and transit plebiscite, a simple majority of votes was required for the question to be passed. This was achieved in the former and was not achieved in the latter. As a result, the HST referendum led government to rescind the HST legislation, and to revert to a combination of GST and PST. In the case of the transportation and transit plebiscite, its defeat resulted in the Mayors' Council's transportation and transit plan being put aside.

It is noteworthy that different thresholds were used for the different consultation processes that have been used recently in BC. In keeping with the discretionary character of both referendums and plebiscites, there is considerable latitude for government to establish the threshold for success at the outset of a consultation process. Some might be inclined to suggest that the experience of 2005 and 2009, when government established a super-majoritarian threshold for changing the electoral system, may have created a precedent for future referendums on electoral reform in BC. Others, however, may point to the fact that the use of the 50 per cent plus one rule in the two most recent consultations has produced a competing precedent. For the election administration body, this matter is best left to those in the political and judicial domains to resolve. We take our instruction from both the legislation and associated regulations in force for each electoral event.

How Are Electors Informed About the Process?

Electoral events at the federal and provincial levels involve candidates offering differing perspectives and agendas, and political parties helping to communicate the message of their group. Over time, rules have been established for the financing of electoral competition, including rules of disclosure, and in some instances limits on expenditures and contributions. Similar questions arise with referendums and plebiscites. Are there formally registered proponent and opponent groups, are there limits on what each group can spend in advertising, is there a particular public education role for the election agency, are there disclosure requirements, and are there limits on contributions? A variety of rules have been used in recent experience in BC.

In 2005, legislation did not provide for the establishment of yes and no groups. However, advertisers were required to register, include identification statements on advertising, and submit financial reports. There were no spending limits or public spending for advertising sponsors. A total of three individuals and five groups registered, with expenditures ranging from $998 to $46,441.[15] In addition, a Referendum Information Office was established by government to provide neutral information.

In 2009, there was a registered yes side and a registered no side, with each receiving $500,000 in public funding. Each side could also accept private funding. Total expenditures for the no side were $508,145, and for the yes side were $849,841.[16] In addition, there was a publicly funded Referendum Information Office.

For the HST referendum in 2011, the provincial government appointed an independent Referendum Funding Decision Maker, and allocated $1.7 million for public education on the referendum. The funding was allocated between yes and no groups ($500,000), to a public dialogues fund ($500,000), and to the production of a guide ($700,000).[17]

For the transportation and transit plebiscite, there was no disclosure requirement, no formal registration as yes and no groups, and no public funding.

Therefore, unlike general elections, which have consistent and highly regular requirements for raising and spending money and disclosing their spending, referendums have been more variable in both their spending provisions and their disclosure requirements.

How Are the Ballots Cast?

Balloting in a referendum or plebiscite can occur either in conjunction with or separate from a general election, and can be done through either in-person paper balloting or an alternative balloting method, such as postal voting or telephone and internet voting. BC used paper balloting in conjunction with general elections for the referendums in 2005 and 2009. This has been described as using a "thin layer" on top of the general administrative procedures for the elections. The cost of using this method is very modest, but of course there is limited flexibility regarding the date of administering the vote. BC has experienced high turnout in relation to general election turnout using this method – in other words, almost all voters who cast a vote in the general election also cast a vote in the referendum. In 2005, Elections BC's total event costs were $22.9 million for the general election, or $8.05 per registered voter. The additional costs for the referendum were $1.06 million, or $0.37 per registered voter.[18] Similarly, for the 2009 general election, total costs were $35,260,610, which results in a cost of $11.77 per registered voter. The additional costs for administering the referendum in 2009 were $2,121,526, or an additional $0.71 per registered voter.[19]

BC also has successfully used postal voting methods for referendums and for the recent plebiscite, and this method has produced similar levels of turnout as in-person paper balloting. For the HST referendum, conducted as a mail ballot, turnout was 52.7 per cent.[20] For the transportation and transit plebiscite, which also used mail balloting, turnout was 48.6 per cent.[21] For the HST referendum, the voting period extended from the beginning of initial mail-out of the voting packages on June 13, 2011, to the deadline for returning completed ballots on August 5, 2011, a period of nearly eight weeks. All returned ballots were processed and counted manually at a single processing facility. Results were announced on August 26. The cost for administering this mail-in ballot was $8.07 million, or $2.63 per registered voter.[22]

For the transportation and transit plebiscite in 2015, a number of administrative changes were introduced. Ballot counting was conducted in a centralized facility, and the counting was completed with optical scanning technology. The cost of administering the event was $5.4 million, or $3.44 per registered voter.[23] The higher per-voter costs were due, in part, to the establishment of eight plebiscite service offices that were open throughout the region for the final six weeks of voting, and the smaller number of eligible voters in Metro Vancouver compared to a province-wide vote.

An alternative voting system for referendums could be telephone or internet voting, or some combination of both of these. British Columbia has not used either telephone voting or internet voting as voting options in any of the public votes that we administer. In 2014, in response to a request from the Attorney General and Minister of Justice, I chaired an independent panel on internet voting that submitted a report to the BC legislative assembly. The report[24] had four principal recommendations. First, the panel advised the province against using internet voting as a widespread option for public elections at either the provincial or the local government level. The panel held that the risks, and in particular security risks associated with fraudulent voting, were far greater than any possible benefit that such a change would produce. Although it recommended against universal internet voting, the panel held the view that providing internet voting options on a more limited basis, such as for voters with various mobility challenges or other disabilities, may provide useful testbeds for piloting internet voting.

Second, the panel recommended that the province establish a technical committee to review, and possibility to certify electronic voting systems that may be used in the province. The panel also proposed that BC take a collaborative and cooperative approach between the provincial and local levels of government, to ensure that the benefits of a technical committee be felt at all levels within the province. And finally, the panel recommended a set of principles be adhered to in all cases in which alternative voting processes, such as internet voting, are used. On the basis of the report of the independent panel on internet voting, it is my view that it is premature to conduct electoral events, such as a referendum or a plebiscite, using internet voting in BC.

Conclusion

As noted in Ken Carty's article for this collection, electoral reform is back on the federal agenda, this time a result of an election promise made by the governing party. Although it is clear at this time that this initiative has involved some public engagement, particularly through the parliamentary committee on electoral reform, it is not certain whether other instruments of public consultation, such as a referendum or a plebiscite, will be used. British Columbia's recent experience suggests that should the government choose to use a referendum or plebiscite, it continues to have considerable latitude in determining the character of the input received on matters such as the threshold for success, the provision of information on the voting options and procedures, and the format of balloting, including whether it would be conducted as a stand-alone event or held in conjunction with a general election. With referendum and plebiscite votes, it surely is the case that the devil is in the details. Specific administrative rules and procedures go a long way in determining what the government hears when the public is asked about its views on a matter of policy.

15

Should We Have a Referendum?

Dominique Leydet

Calls in favour of a referendum over electoral reform are based on two main arguments. Firstly, some claim that any significant change to the way Canadians vote is similar to changing the constitution and cannot be treated like ordinary legislation. To be legitimate, such fundamental changes, it is argued, must receive the express consent of a majority of citizens. Secondly, support for a referendum is often based on a critical assessment of the capacity of elected representatives to rise above partisan interests and reform the electoral system in accordance with the common interest. To check the parties' self-interested behaviour, it is necessary to appeal to the nation itself through a referendum. If the first argument formulates a positive reason to support a referendum, the second argument is essentially negative: the referendum is described as a means to restrain partisan representatives. The two arguments are compatible and are often used in conjunction, but they remain distinct and I will discuss each in turn.

* * *

The first argument rests on the claim that altering the method of voting is a fundamental change to the democratic rules of the game. Even if it does not involve the formal amendment of the constitution, it should be understood as a change of a similar magnitude, requiring the deeper form of democratic legitimacy that stems from the direct expression of popular consent. The claim is less about constitutional law per se than it is about democratic legitimacy. The argument's major premise, which I accept here, states that there are fundamental issues that need the direct endorsement of a majority of citizens in order to achieve democratic legitimacy. The minor premise simply states that electoral reform is an issue of that kind. Well, is it?

Let's start by identifying instances of the kind of decisions that, in the mind of many people, do require the nation's consent to be legitimately adopted. I submit that the most likely candidates are issues like secession or similar kinds of regime change. Should Quebec become an independent state? Should Australia become a Republic? Should the United Kingdom remain a member of the European Union or leave the European Union? This is because we understand intuitively that these issues touch upon the very core of the constitution and should not be decided by officials alone, even if they are elected. These are fundamental decisions that establish the very "identity of the constitution," or in other words, decisions that structure or define the political and social regime of a country.[1] To be authoritative, decisions that are understood as "constituent acts," or *actes constituants*," have to be based on the express consent of the people themselves. As such, they differ from actions that modify some constitutional provisions without changing the substance of the constitution.[2]

Suppose we accept this view. We now have to decide whether abandoning first-past-the-post (FPP) is a change of that kind. I don't think so. Though no one would deny the importance of changing the voting system, adopting a version of the single transferable vote (STV) or mixed-member proportional (MMP) system at the federal level would not alter the constitution's core in the same way that Quebec's secession or Canada's transformation into a unitary state would. By switching from FPP to a form of proportional representation, we would be modifying a structural element of our democratic system, a move that would affect the politics of our country in very concrete ways. But we would not be transforming the substance of the constitution. Changing the voting system of a polity represents a change that is closer in kind to something like the reform of the civil code in the justice system. It is a significant change (or set of changes) that affects the lives of citizens in concrete ways. It touches on matters of basic principle while also involving very technical issues. It certainly calls for a deliberate and careful process involving broad and extensive consultations with different sectors of the society, but it does not alter the core of the system and, consequently, need not be explicitly endorsed by a majority of citizens to achieve legitimacy.

But why, then, do we hear forceful calls in favour of a referendum when it comes to electoral reform? And why do these calls seem to find a positive echo in the population itself?[3] After all, and unless I am mistaken, no one ever suggested that the revised civil code of Quebec be submitted to the citizens in a referendum when it was finally adopted in 1991. To answer this question, we need to move to the second, negative argument in support of a referendum.

* * *

What is it about electoral reform that leads people to call for a referendum? What is the problem to which a referendum is supposed to be the solution? The answer is not hard to find. There is a widespread feeling that the parties dominating Parliament are not well placed to reform the voting system because they have vested interests to protect. In other words, partisan legislators are interested agents that cannot be trusted to reform the system in a way that answers to the common interest.

This argument from partiality is compounded, in countries with FPP, by the fact that a party can secure a majority of seats in the legislature and form a majority government even though it has received the support of only a minority of voters. This enables a single party to change the rules of the democratic game as it sees fit, without having to seriously heed other voices. Here the lack of effective institutional restraint on government action aggravates the problem of partiality. A referendum may appear, in this context, as the solution to the problem of partisan control over the process of electoral reform. It is a means to restrain the power of partisan government by appealing to the nation, described as standing above the parties. As Vernon Bogdanor aptly puts it, the referendum is called upon to act as a "*democratic* check upon the excesses of popular government."[4]

This was the view, Bogdanor tells us, defended by Dicey in the context of his campaign against Home Rule. Though he is now mainly remembered as the great apologist of parliamentary sovereignty, Dicey advocated the referendum as "the only check on the predominance of party which is at the same time democratic and conservative."[5] The referendum appeared to Dicey as the only restraint or shield that could be strong enough – because of its democratic nature – to break the power that comes with majority status and that enables the party forming the government to ram pivotal pieces of legislation through Parliament with little opposition. Notice that the electorate's role is framed in this context in negative terms and that the referendum appears as "an instrument of protection and not of change."[6]

This, I think, is at the core of the arguments made by the Conservatives in their campaign in favour of a referendum over electoral reform. Recall the statements made in late December of 2015 by Rona Ambrose, interim leader of the Conservative Party: "If the Liberals want to make a fundamental change to our country's voting system, the process must not be dominated by one political party's interests"; "[the] Liberal committee scheme is simply a vehicle through which they can impose their own pre-determined agenda without any meaningful way to restrain them" [... .] "It is arrogant of the Liberals to believe that they are entitled to make a change of this magnitude to our democracy without bringing it directly to the people first."[7]

As initially proposed by the Liberal government, the process of electoral reform fully deserved the Conservatives' critique. Thanks to the present electoral system, the Liberals enjoy a strong majority in the House of Commons (with 183 MPs out of a total of 338 MPs), though the party received only 39.47 per cent of votes in the last election. And the composition of the All-Party Parliamentary Committee, in the first version proposed by the Liberals in May 2016, was meant to reflect the House of Commons' partisan make up. The Committee was supposed to have ten full members: six Liberals, three Conservatives, and one NDP with the Bloc Québécois and the Green Party having one member each, but with observer status only.[8] Given that the Liberals would have had a clear majority in the Committee, as they do in the House of Commons, the process could be fairly described as narrowly partisan. The Liberals would have had the ability to push through their preferred version of electoral reform with very little restraint. One can understand, in this context, the call in favour of a referendum. Advocating for the right of all Canadians to express their view on the Liberal proposal of electoral reform was a call to give the nation, standing above the parties, the ability to veto the eventual result of a tainted process.

Notice that the referendum appears as a solution to a specific aspect of the problem: the ability of the party in power to impose its own proposal with little constraint. Holding a referendum would introduce a veto point at the very end of the process. But notice also that it makes little sense to present the referendum as a solution to the problem of partiality itself since it has no direct impact over the substance of what is proposed. It gives the nation the opportunity to reject a proposal once it has been formulated; it does not secure the integrity of the process that produces the proposal. In other words, if the key problem is the suspicion that the reform proposal will cater to the partial interests of partisan legislators, then holding a referendum is not the solution. Holding a referendum might be part of the solution, but perhaps we should be calling for a different process.

Indeed, in the last wave of attempts to reform electoral systems in Canada, there was a clear move to make the process as non-partisan as possible. As Louis Massicotte has noted: "The widely accepted view that parliamentarians should not be involved in electoral boundary changes has been extended to the electoral system itself."[9] This explains why recent attempts at reform have followed either one of two basic models: the independent commission, on the one hand, and the citizens' assembly, on the other.[10] The provinces of Prince Edward Island (2003–2005) and New Brunswick (2005) chose versions of the first model while British Columbia (2004–2005) and Ontario (2006–2007) broke new ground in adopting the second. These two models insulate, as much as possible, the process of elaborating reform from the influence of elected representatives.[11]

This shared objective may also explain the decision to submit any proposal for reform coming out of those processes to a referendum before it is formally adopted.[12] However, the referendum appears in this context as the solution to a very different problem than the one presented by a partisan process. If un-elected commissioners or citizen representatives are responsible for the formulation of a reform proposal, one may want to secure the democratic legitimacy of that proposal while keeping the parties and elected representatives on the sidelines. And an obvious solution to that question is to hold a referendum.[13] But this has very little to do with the situation we are facing today and to which I now return.

* * *

On June 7, 2016, the motion to establish an All-Party Committee on Electoral reform was finally adopted in the House of Commons. It included a significant change to the parameters of the initial problem. The Liberal government, under pressure by the opposition parties, accepted the NDP's suggestion to modify the composition of the Committee. By subtracting one Liberal member, adding one NDP member, and giving voting rights to the Green Party and Bloc Québécois members of the Committee, the Liberal government had in fact accepted to give up control over a crucial stage of the process.[14] Given the Committee's new composition, any proposal that it were to submit to the House of Commons would had to have received the support of more than one party. This transforms the nature of the process from narrowly partisan to inter-partisan. The question now becomes whether this modification weakens the negative argument in favour of a referendum and, if so, to what extent.

If the problem is a lack of restraint on the power held by the party enjoying a majority in the legislature, then having to secure the support of at least one other major party in order to proceed introduces a significant constraint on that party's actions. Moreover, whether the proposal was supported by the Liberals and by the NDP, or, alternatively, by the Liberals and the Conservatives or (as was eventually the case) by the Conservatives and the NDP, in any case it meant that parties representing a majority of voters supported the proposed reform.[15] The

specific issue raised by the weak democratic legitimacy of party government based on FPP (affording a majority of seats in the legislature to a
party that has received the support of only a minority of electors) has
been bypassed. One may then plausibly argue that, in a representative
democracy, where citizens entrust their political authority to elected
representatives, a proposal supported by parties representing a majority of electors has "good enough" democratic credentials and need not
be submitted to the citizens through a referendum.

In short, in the case of an inter-partisan process of reform, the main
rationales in support of a referendum that we have seen in the preceding section seem less relevant. On the one hand, the need for significant cross-party support acts like a constraint on the self-interested
behaviour of the party in power. On the other hand, since those in
charge of the inter-partisan process are elected legislators, the need to
hold a referendum in order to give democratic legitimacy to the proposed reform is not as pressing as it may appear to be in the case of an
independent, non-partisan process.

But there are two questions that we need to answer before coming to such a conclusion. Firstly, does the need to get the support of
another major party constitute enough of a restraint on the action of
the party in power to make the use of a referendum as a democratic
check unnecessary? Secondly, even if we are satisfied that a referendum
is not required to give democratic legitimacy to electoral reform in the
case of an inter-partisan process, should we not recognize that holding
one would strengthen legitimacy? If so, we should perhaps conclude
that, though holding a referendum is not necessary, it would be best to
hold one. I will discuss each issue in turn.

*   *   *

The requirement of having some cross-party support means that
any reform proposal that made it past the Committee stage would
not simply express the narrow self-interest of the party in power. Is
that enough? Were the Liberals and the NDP Committee members to
strike an agreement over electoral reform, the Conservatives would

presumably claim that the proposal expressed an interest shared by two parties at the expense of the country's overarching interest. As it happened, the NDP and the Tories struck an agreement, and the Liberals, predictably, accused the two parties of playing politics with the electoral system. (And they were right.)

To move the discussion forward, it may be useful to compare the present process in Canada with the provisions proposed by the New Zealand Royal Commission on Electoral Reform. In its 1986 report, the Commission asked whether it should be possible to alter "the whole of the electoral system" [...] "by simple majority in the House of Representatives, that is effectively by the political party in power? Or should there be some restraint on that ordinary process?"[16]

The Commission answered that restraint was indeed needed and recommended that specific provisions of the Electoral Act – the so called "reserved provisions," which include the method of voting – should be protected from the ordinary legislative process: their repeal or amendment should be supported either by three-quarter of all members of the legislature or by a majority of voters in a referendum.[17]

The 75 per cent rule sets the bar for a legitimate inter-partisan process much higher than the present process in Canada. In practical terms, the threshold would not be reached even if a proposal attracted the support of the Liberals, the NDP, the Bloc Québécois, and the Green MPs. In fact, it could only be reached if the Liberals and the Conservatives agreed on a reform proposal.[18] But notice that even such a strict rule is no guarantee against the possibility of parties getting together to serve their own partial interest against that of their competitors. In theory, it would be possible for the two larger parties – the Liberals and the Conservatives – to agree on a proposal that would negatively affect the electoral prospects of the smaller parties (including the NDP).

But, of course, this would go against the intention behind the 75 per cent requirement. As the New Zealand Royal Commission explains in its report, the rationale behind the rule is that a cross-party *consensus* – that includes all the major parties in the legislature – is the only acceptable alternative to a referendum when it comes to altering the reserved provisions of the Electoral Act.[19] In the Canadian context, it would mean that the support of the Liberal, Conservative, and NDP members of Parliament would be required to make a referendum unnecessary. This constitutes a severe constraint, and one has to wonder whether the veto point it introduces would be actually harder to overcome than winning a referendum.

But that may be exactly the point. The requirement of a cross-party *consensus* means that any proposal that satisfies it is likely to be uncontroversial. In that case, there is no need to call on the people to exercise their collective voice. If we look at the history of electoral reform in New Zealand since the first introduction of the 75 per cent requirement in the 1956 Electoral Law, we see that the changes made to the reserved provisions using that requirement were largely uncontroversial. In 1965, for instance, the Electoral Amendment Act stabilized the representation of the South Island to twenty-five seats against the background of a growing disparity between the population of the two islands, and in 1969, the voting age was changed from twenty-one to twenty, etc.[20] It would be highly unrealistic to expect something as difficult and controversial as reforming the method of voting to achieve consensus among all major parties.

If this is right, then the 75 per cent requirement seems misguided. It is either too weak or too strict. Though it seems very demanding, it is too weak to eliminate the risk that the party in power may bargain with other parties in order to impose a shared partial interest against that of competitors.[21] If we read it as requiring a consensus among all the major parties, then it will appear as too strict, condemning the process of reform to failure. So there is not much to be gained, and actually much to be lost, in accepting something like the 75 per cent requirement. If an inter-partisan process to reform the electoral system is to have any significant chance at succeeding, then we must hold on to the notion that a sufficient level of cross-party support must be attained if the reform proposal is supported by parties representing a majority of voters.

* * *

Let me retrace my steps briefly. In the preceding sections, I have argued that holding a referendum is not necessary to secure the democratic legitimacy of electoral reform. Firstly, though changing the way we vote is an important modification of the democratic system, it does not affect the core of the constitution. It is not part of the small set of cases where getting the direct consent of citizens is required. Secondly, I have shown that the force of the negative argument supporting a referendum rests on two claims: (a) that partisan legislators cannot be entrusted with the task of reforming the electoral system because they are in a conflict of interest; (b) that this problem is compounded in countries that have a FPP system. Here the fear is that the party in power, though supported by only a minority of voters, can ram through a proposal of radical change that is tailored to its own selfish interest. In my discussion, I have shown that if partiality is the problem, then the answer cannot be a referendum; it should be a different process, one from which elected representatives are kept at arm's length. If the crucial problem is the ability of the party in power to impose a narrowly partisan reform, then a referendum (which appeals directly to the nation as a whole) does appear as a way to check such abuse of popular government. Since the present process has lost its narrowly partisan character and has become inter-partisan, resorting to the people's veto power is not required.

But, if a referendum is not required, isn't it still desirable? Suppose for a moment that the Liberals and the NDP agree on a proposal for reform, one to which the Conservatives object. Wouldn't it be better to give the Conservatives the opportunity to take their case to the people directly? If the proposal survived the test of the referendum, then the legitimacy of the new electoral system could only be stronger. I think that this is certainly an important consideration. But notice that if we agree that a referendum is not required, then the judgment as to its desirability should be understood as an "all things considered" judgment. In other words, we need to balance the considerations in favour of holding a referendum with those that militate against it.

At the beginning of the paper, I argued that changing the way we vote represents a significant change to our democratic system, a change of a similar order of magnitude as reforming the civil code in the justice system. It touches on matters of basic principle while also involving very technical issues. Given our constitutional arrangements, electoral reform will also have to include discussions with the provinces. The seriousness and complexity of the tasks involved certainly call for a deliberate and careful process that includes broad and extensive consultations. I want to suggest that, in principle at least, the legislative process is more likely to afford such deliberate and careful examination of the issues than a referendum would.

Parliamentary procedure involves successive readings of a proposed legislation in both chambers of Parliament. It secures the possibility of moving amendments and also of holding further consultations, giving elected representatives more opportunities to reflect, discuss, negotiate, modify, and modify yet again the different elements of a complex package. This process opens different entry points at which the opposition, interested groups in civil society, and experts can express their positions, alerting and informing the public through the media. Though citizens have no formal say in the process, they exercise an indirect influence through the different channels that make up public opinion.

In contrast, a referendum campaign, because it is constructed around a yes and a no camp, leads to polarization, forcing citizens and groups to choose sides. It closes off possibilities of compromises between advocates of different positions. In other words, while the referendum formally extends collective deliberation to include every citizen, it does not secure the conditions for the careful examination of different alternatives. Holding a referendum presupposes that the political debate has matured enough so that the binary choice offered to voters is well considered and deliberate, and that the two options can be presented clearly to citizens. I don't think that the debate over electoral reform in Canada has attained that level of maturity. There is no clear idea of what the alternative to FPP should be, there have been as yet no discussions with the provinces, and so on. Under these conditions, and given the time constraints imposed by the government, to rush the process forward to hold a referendum would probably be the best way to abort the debate over electoral reform altogether and for a long time. If our elected representatives are sincere in their desire to engage Canadians over electoral reform, then they should commit themselves, first and foremost, to holding a serious and constructive debate through the different avenues provided by the parliamentary process.

16

A Modest Case for Constitutional Limits on Electoral Reform in Canada

Hoi L. Kong

The topic of this collection, *Should We Change How We Vote?*, is fascinating. The topic of my paper is decidedly less so. And even within the general body of writing on this subject, my paper is relatively boring. Some contributions to this conversation in the press adopt a provocative stance, particularly in their titles. Yet much constitutional law cannot be easily captured by bold or unqualified statements. Constitutional debates are often conducted over fine differences, and contending positions give nuanced readings of texts, concepts, and practices. I believe the constitutional dimensions of electoral reform are marked by uncertainty, and so the analysis that follows will, in its subtle shadings, be deliberately unprovocative. I will structure my arguments as responses to one unqualified claim about the absence of constitutional limits on electoral reform in Canada and to a second such claim, which states that a constitutional convention obliges Parliament to hold a referendum before enacting electoral reform. I will offer carefully qualified answers to each of these claims. I will examine, in turn, constitutional text, a constitutional doctrine, and a constitutional convention, each of which bears on the issue of whether federal reform of the electoral system is subject to constitutional constraints.

I: A Response to the Claim that Electoral Reform Is a Political, Not Constitutional, Matter

Let us begin with one bold statement about electoral reform,[1] which claims that it is a political, not constitutional, matter. The challenge in responding to this assertion is to identify which constitutional interests may give rise to restrictions on Parliament's ability to act unilaterally. In the next section, I will canvass the most obviously applicable constitutional provisions.[2]

A. CONSTRAINTS IMPOSED BY CONSTITUTIONAL TEXT

The electoral system is mentioned in the Constitution Act, 1867.[3] As Yasmin Dawood and Michael Pal have noted, sections 40 and 41 expressly address electoral districts and electoral laws, but both sections qualify the relevant rules with the proviso "Until the Parliament of Canada otherwise provides." Dawood and Pal disagree about the significance of this qualification, with the former claiming that these sections do not represent a meaningful constitutional limit on Parliament, since the proviso explicitly envisages unilateral parliamentary action.[4] I do not intend to enter into this debate, but rather to direct my attention to sections 51A and 52 of the Constitution Act, 1867.[5]

These two sections give rise to constitutional limits on Parliament's power to engage in electoral reform, despite the fact that they do not explicitly mention this power. Section 41(b) of the Constitution Act, 1982,[6] refers to section 51A's mention of the minimum number of members of the House of Commons that can represent a given province. Section 41(b) states that any amendment in relation to "the right of a province to a number of members in the House of Commons not less than the number of Senators by which the province is entitled to be represented at the time this Part comes into force" requires the consent of the Senate and House of Commons, and the legislative assembly of each province. Therefore, it would be unconstitutional for Parliament to attempt to alter unilaterally the electoral system in a way that would reduce any province's members in the House of Commons to a number below this threshold.

Consider next section 52 of the Constitution Act, 1867, which states that "The Number of Members of the House of Commons may be from

Time to Time increased by the Parliament of Canada, provided the proportionate Representation of the Provinces prescribed by this Act is not thereby disturbed." This section is referred to by section 42(1)(a) of the Constitution Act, 1982, which states that any proposed change to "the principle of proportionate representation of the provinces in the House of Commons prescribed by the Constitution" requires a constitutional amendment that complies with the formula set out in section 38(1). If Parliament were to enact electoral reform that affected this principle, it would require "resolutions of the legislative assemblies of at least two-thirds of the provinces that have, in the aggregate, according to the then latest general census, at least fifty per cent of the population of the provinces."

From this brief overview of the relevant constitutional provisions, we can see that there are constitutional limits on Parliament's ability to undertake electoral reform. At least to the extent that the above provisions are engaged, electoral reform is a constitutional matter. One might claim that no plausible electoral reform proposal would confront these textual limits. Yet it is not immediately obvious what alternatives to our current first-past-the-post system would be captured by, in particular, the section 42(1)(a) amending formula. It may be possible to design proportional representation or mixed electoral systems that satisfy the principle of proportionate provincial representation,[7] but any such design would have to be worked out carefully. The simple fact that such attention to detail would be necessary suggests that the claim that electoral reform is a political, not constitutional, matter needs to be qualified.

B. CONSTRAINTS IMPOSED BY CONSTITUTIONAL DOCTRINE

If the above constraints on electoral reform can be read with relative ease from the face of the constitutional text, other limits require an engagement with constitutional doctrine. The starting point for the present analysis is the *Reference re Senate Reform*.[8] There, the Supreme Court of Canada reasoned that the constitution should be interpreted in light of its "constitutional architecture." According to the Court, this doctrinal concept implies that "the Constitution must be interpreted with a view to discerning the structure of government that it seeks to implement. The assumptions that underlie the text and the manner in which the constitutional provisions are intended to interact with one another must inform our interpretation, understanding and application of the text."[9]

In *Reference re Senate Reform*, the Court appealed to the concept of constitutional architecture in order to identify which amending formula should apply to some proposed changes to the Senate. For present purposes, it is sufficient to note that the Court appealed to constitutional text and history in order to give specific content to the idea of constitutional architecture, and concluded that the section 38 amending procedure (not including section 38(2)) applied to proposed legislative changes to the tenure of senators.[10] The Court reasoned from these constitutional sources that any proposed changes affecting the Senate's "fundamental nature and role engage the interests of stakeholders in our constitutional design – i.e., the federal government and the provinces – and cannot be achieved by Parliament acting alone."[11]

The steps the Court followed in its analysis are significant for present purposes because they can apply by analogy to at least some proposed changes to the electoral system. Let us trace those steps. First, the Court noted that any change to senatorial tenure would alter section 29 of the Constitution Act, 1867, which specifies that a Senator "shall ... hold his place in the Senate until he attains the age of seventy-five years."[12] Second, the Court rejected a claim that the section 44 amending formula would apply to a proposed amendment to section 29. The Court came to this conclusion, despite the fact that (1) senatorial tenure is not expressly mentioned in either section the 41 or 42 amending formula, and (2) section 44 states that "[s]ubject to sections 41 and 42, Parliament may exclusively make laws amending the constitution in relation to the Senate."[13] Third, the Court appealed to constitutional history when it referred to statements made by then Minister of Justice Jean Chrétien in 1980 before the Special Joint Committee of the Senate and the House of Commons on the Constitution of Canada. According to the Court, Minister Chrétien argued that "significant Senate reform which engages the interests of the provinces could only be achieved with their consent."[14] Fourth, the Court reasoned that the Senate is a "core component of the Canadian federal structure of government"[15] and stated that the proposed amendment would affect its fundamental nature, as a chamber of sober second thought. Because any such change would necessarily engage the interests of the provinces as stakeholders in the constitutional design, the Court concluded that section 38 (not including section 38(2)) was the applicable amending formula.[16]

Let us turn now to apply elements of this architectural analysis to any proposed electoral reform that would affect section 37 of the Constitution Act, 1867. The Court in the *Reference re Senate Reform* provided a gloss on this section when it reasoned that it "expressly provides that members of the lower chamber – the House of Commons – 'shall be elected' by the population of the various provinces."[17] For our purposes, section 37 is significant precisely because it requires that the members of the House of Commons be elected by their respective provinces' populations. Any proposed electoral reform, therefore, that would affect this requirement would amount to an amendment to section 37, much in the same way as the proposed changes to senatorial tenure that were at issue in the *Reference re Senate Reform* would have entailed an amendment to section 29. This section 37 requirement of a connection between a member of the House of Commons and his or her provincial electorate, is (like senatorial tenure) nowhere mentioned in either section 41 or section 42 of the Constitution Act, 1982. As a consequence, one might claim that an amendment to section 37 would be covered by section 44, which, as we saw above, is subject to sections 41 and 42, and empowers "Parliament to exclusively make laws amending the Constitution of Canada in relation to … the House of Commons." In order to answer this claim, we can continue to follow the steps traced by the Court in *Reference re Senate Reform*, and turn from constitutional text toward constitutional history.

On February 14, 1865, during debates in the Parliament of the Province of Canada about Confederation, Sir Narcisse Fortunat Belleau made clear the significance of the ties between the electorate of Lower Canada and the members that would represent it in a federal legislature. He argued:

Suppose it were proposed to adopt a law in the Federal Legislature calculated to injure Lower Canada, our 65 representatives in the

House of Commons discuss the law, and decide that they oppose
it; they at once communicate with members of Government representing Lower Canada, and inform them that they cannot accept the
measure, and that if it be passed, they will coalesce with the minority,
which always exists under responsible government, and that they will
overthrow the Ministry.[18]

We can infer from this statement about the importance of provincial
representation that the tie between members of Parliament and their
provincial constituencies was understood at Confederation to be fundamental to the very nature of the House of Commons, which, like the
Senate, is a core component of the federal structure of government.[19]
Moreover, recall that in the *Reference re Senate Reform*, the Court stated
that any change to the fundamental nature of such a core institution
would necessarily engage the interests of the provinces as stakeholders
in Canadian constitutional design. The argument for such an interest is
stronger in the case of the House of Commons than it is for the Senate.
Pal has noted that some have challenged the Supreme Court of Canada's claim that term limits would "seriously affect the Senate."[20] Even if
one does not share these critics' specific reservations, it is not immediately obvious what the particular provincial interest in maintaining
senatorial tenure is.

By contrast, in the present case, any proposed change to the relationship between members of the House of Commons and their provincial
electorates would, as the quotation from Belleau reminds us, *directly*
engage the interests of the provinces. From the foregoing analysis of
constitutional text and history, and by application of the Court's architectural reasoning in the *Reference re Senate Reform*, we can conclude
that if Parliament were to propose any such change to the electoral
system, it would be subject to the section 38 amending formula (not
including section 38(2)).

Note that here, as in our analysis above of section 42(1)(a), the precise
scope of the constitutional constraint is unclear. Any system in which a
number of seats in the House of Commons were allocated in proportion
to the total number of national votes that parties received would on its
face seem to sever the electoral link between a member of Parliament and

the provincial populace. Determining whether a specific proposal would fall afoul of this constitutional constraint would require careful analysis. And it is this very requirement of attentiveness to detail that challenges any simple, though provocative, claim that changes to the electoral system are a political, and not a constitutional, matter.

II: A Response to the Claim that Since Everyone Should Get a Say in Electoral Reform that Affects Everyone, the Federal Electoral System Can Only Be Changed Following a Referendum

In the preceding Part, we appealed to constitutional text and constitutional doctrine in order to answer the bold claim that if Parliament were to change the electoral system, it would not be subject to constitutional constraints. We saw that this claim needed to be qualified and that the qualifications flowed from careful and nuanced readings of constitutional sources. Let us turn now to respond to a second unqualified statement, which asserts that electoral reform affects all Canadians and that a referendum is therefore constitutionally required. Consider the second part of the assertion. There is no express constitutional text or constitutional doctrine to which we can appeal to establish that there is a judicially enforceable constitutional rule that applies. If there is a relevant constitutional rule, it must take the form of a constitutional convention.

The *Reference Re: Resolution to Amend the Constitution (Patriation Reference)*[21] remains the canonical discussion of conventions in Canadian constitutional law. There, the Supreme Court noted that government action that breached a convention would be unconstitutional, even though there would be no judicially enforceable remedy.[22] The Court further set out three questions to ask in order to determine whether a constitutional convention exists: "first, what are the precedents; secondly, did the actors in the precedents believe that they were bound by a rule; and thirdly is there a reason for the rule?"[23]

A. IS THERE A CONSTITUTIONAL CONVENTION?

Let us turn now to apply this test to the question of whether there is a constitutional convention requiring Parliament to hold a referendum on any proposed change to the federal electoral system. The touchstone for such an analysis is Patrice Dutil's excellent paper "The Imperative of a Referendum."[24] Dutil concludes that all three questions of the test can be answered in the affirmative. He writes: "It has been, quite simply, the established practice – the very definition of convention – to consult voters about changes to the way representatives are elected."[25] Dutil's description of referendums on electoral reform that have been held in Canadian provinces and elsewhere in the Commonwealth, and his documentation of political actors' motivations, is most impressive. My analysis will focus on the third question as it applies to the present discussion. I will assess whether there is a reason that would justify a conventional rule requiring that a referendum be held before Parliament enacts any significant electoral reform. I will apply the reasoning of the Supreme Court in the *Patriation Reference* to the issue of electoral reform, and conclude that there is no such convention.

The Court in the *Patriation Reference* considered the federal government's claim that it could amend provincial legislative powers unilaterally. The Court rejected that claim and found that the rationale for the convention requiring provincial consent was the "federal principle," which it derived from the preamble to the Constitution Act, 1867, and the case law.[26] It concluded: "The federal principle cannot be reconciled with a state of affairs where the modification of provincial legislative powers could be obtained by the unilateral action of the federal authorities."[27] The Court seemed to hold that a departure from the precedents would be necessarily inconsistent with the relevant constitutional rationale. This is a stringent standard. If it were applied to the case of a proposed conventional rule that federal electoral reform can only be undertaken pursuant to a referendum, we would need to demonstrate that any change to the electoral system, without a referendum, would be inconsistent with an applicable constitutional principle.

In order to broach this issue, it is worth quoting Dutil's response to the third question of the *Patriation Reference* test:

[T]he answer lies in the preamble of the Canadian constitution. Canada adopted a Westminster system of Parliament that in turn created a balance of power between the Crown, the Houses of

Parliament, and the Courts. The electoral system was a fundamental part of that bargain, based on conventions. It follows that any change to that equilibrium would be constitutional (in nature).[28]

I believe that Dutil has made two errors here. First, the question in the *Patriation Reference* is whether there is a specific rationale that supports the proposed practice and justifies its being considered a constitutional rule. For the purposes of this analysis, the simple fact that a constitutional bargain exists is not relevant; we must be able to derive from it a specific reason or principle that is analogous to the federal principle in the *Patriation Reference*, and determine whether that reason or principle supports the claim that the practice of holding referendums about federal electoral reform is constitutionally required. Second, Dutil asserts that a convention exists and claims that any change that departed from it would be unconstitutional. But the objective of the third part of the *Patriation Reference* analysis is to discern whether there is a reason that justifies a given practice, such that it and its attendant rule could be considered to be a constitutional convention. That reason must be identified and its relevance defended. It is not sufficient to assert the existence of a (pre-existing) constitutional convention and claim that its very existence is a reason in favour of a practice being considered to be a convention.

If Dutil's analysis is not convincing, how might we proceed? I suggest that we begin with the standard that the Court in the *Patriation Reference* set. Recall that the Court reasoned that a departure from the practice of receiving provincial consent would be incompatible with the federal principle, which the court identified as the relevant rationale for the constitutional convention. Would it be possible to argue (as Dutil seems to) that all changes to the federal electoral system, if undertaken without a referendum, would be similarly inconsistent with some constitutional rationale? In Part I of this paper, we saw that the Constitution Act, 1982, amending formulas would apply to at least some potential changes to the Canadian electoral system. These are entrenched, formal constitutional rules and none of them mentions a referendum. Therefore, an alteration of the federal electoral system that complied with them, and that did not involve a referendum, would be constitutionally authorized. It follows, then, that if changes to the federal electoral system were made pursuant to the relevant formulas, and even if such modifications were to affect all Canadians, no constitutional convention would plausibly require that a referendum be held and no rationale could justify such a convention.

Moreover, the precedents that were invoked in the *Patriation Reference* all involved Parliament, and the applicable constitutional convention constrained that federal body. By contrast, the Canadian precedents invoked by Dutil in the context of his discussion of electoral reform are all provincial. It may be that the provinces, operating in their own constitutional contexts, are bound by a convention that requires them to hold a referendum before reforming their electoral systems. Yet the provinces are not held to the same constitutional limits as Parliament, and therefore a convention that is binding on them and a reason justifying such a convention would not necessarily apply to Parliament.

B. UNRESOLVED QUESTIONS

Even if one were to accept the arguments just advanced, there are still some unresolved questions. First, is there a constitutional convention that would require a referendum for proposed federal changes to the electoral system that do not engage any of the constitutional amending formulas analyzed in Part I? Second, although the *Patriation Reference* Court answered "yes" to all three questions about whether a constitutional convention existed in that case, could a constitutional convention be established in the present context, even in the absence of a supporting reason? I do not engage those questions here. I only highlight them to show that the constitutional arguments at play require nuance and subtlety and resist simple assertions about the existence and nature of constitutional limits on Parliament's ability to pursue electoral reform.

Conclusion

In this paper, I have sought to identify the nature and scope of some constitutional limits on Parliament's ability to change unilaterally the federal electoral system. I have traded in the currency of constitutional arguments and I hope to have shown that here, as in all situations of constitutional uncertainty, participants in debate should be alive to nuance and resist the temptation to issue categorical statements. I conclude by noting that the controversies over electoral reform in Canada extend well beyond the domain of constitutional law. The arguments in this paper are limited to that sphere, but I have very much benefited from listening to and reading my colleagues in other disciplines who have shed light on the political, moral, and empirical dimensions of electoral reform. I am grateful to them and the organizers of this conference.

17

Which Procedure for Deciding Election Procedures?

Arash Abizadeh

Some electoral rules foster wide participation, others dampen it. Some encourage close ties between representatives and their local riding, others don't. Some rules encourage strategic voting, others discourage it. Some enhance the power of party leaders, others diminish it. Some foster smaller parties, others don't. Above all, elections determine who forms government, and different electoral rules favour different candidates or parties. In short, different electoral rules cause different political outcomes. But they also embody and express different norms and values. Elections in which women, the underprivileged, or ethnic minorities cannot participate fail to embody a norm of impartiality and typically fail to express equal respect for those excluded. So we can evaluate electoral rules in at least two ways: instrumentally, in terms of the outcomes they cause, and constitutively, in terms of the values and norms they embody or express.[1]

My first thesis is that we should evaluate electoral rules not just instrumentally and constitutively, but also *genetically*. We should evaluate electoral rules in terms of the procedure by which they are selected—their genesis or origin. For reasons similar to why we care about the outcomes that elections cause and the values they embody, we should care about how the electoral rules are decided. We care about the instrumental and constitutive features of electoral rules because elections are a key part of representative governments' answer to the fundamental problem of politics: When people have conflicts of interest and disagreements over the norms and policies to which they should be subject, who should decide? We care about electoral rules above all because elections regulate who wields political power over us—who decides the laws that collectively bind us and the policies we live under. We want electoral rules to help select competent and reliable representatives, foster peace and just laws and outcomes, resolve conflicts and disagreements fairly and impartially, and express respect for all subjects as equals. For the same reason, we should want the procedure by which the electoral rules themselves are selected to produce fair, rational, and beneficial electoral rules, fairly and impartially resolve disagreements about which electoral rules to adopt, and express respect for all subjects as equals. A corollary: the democratic legitimacy of electoral outcomes depends not just on the instrumental and constitutive features of electoral rules, but also on how those rules were chosen.

Here's the snag: the answer we typically give to the problem of conflict and disagreement is wholly inadequate here. Our typical answer is that we should resolve conflicts and disagreements by authorizing elected representatives to decide. But here we want to decide how to select and authorize those very representatives. Letting the politicians who won the last round of elections decide future election rules is manifestly unfair: it's like letting the team who won the last playoff game decide the rules for the next game. There's an obvious conflict of interest: electoral rules determine who forms government, and different rules favour different candidates. This is why, when office-seeking politicians contemplate electoral reform, a question looms large in their minds: "How will any changes affect my (party's) prospects of winning future elections?" Not only is such a procedure unfair to challengers, it is also predisposed to produce bad electoral rules – ones tracking vested partisan interests, rather than the public interest. When my six-year-old races his younger sister, his preferred rule is this: whatever happens, he wins. But even he understands that it would be unfair to let him decide the rules of the game.

The problem of partiality is not solved by having an "all-party" committee decide future electoral rules. In one sense, the winner of an election is the party that gained a majority. But in another sense, the winners are all the individual candidates—from any party—who won a seat in parliament. An all-party committee of politicians is still composed of representatives with a vested interest in the electoral rules. Even balancing these vested interests against each other will not track the public interest: an all-party committee will reflect the biases of incumbent representatives. (Imagine if a party—the Greens, let's say—has considerable popular support but, given the existing electoral rules, cannot elect any MPs. And imagine if a commission including all incumbent parties chooses rules designed to keep them out of the House of Commons.) Even filling the committee with non-politicians does not itself solve the problem of partiality: the question is how these non-politicians are to be selected. If they are selected by politicians, they may very well do so for reasons motivated by their vested interests.

Democratic tradition offers one potential solution to these problems: a referendum. The idea here is to appeal to a referendum as an external check on the partisan, partial vested interests of incumbent politicians, to prevent them from deciding the rules that are supposed to govern their own selection. But referenda face several major shortcomings in this context. First, a referendum is a decision device; it is not a procedure for deliberating about the alternatives, and it can't be used to determine the alternatives from which voters can choose. Second, its epistemic and instrumental merits are doubtful in this context: few Canadians care much about electoral reform, and fewer still will cuddle up with a treatise on voting systems this Sunday evening. A referendum might be a big waste of money in which few vote and fewer still care to learn about the pros and cons of alternative electoral systems. Third, for these reasons, it may also be heavily biased toward the status quo.

So what should be done? Just as in the case of electoral rules themselves, we need a procedure that has both instrumental and constitutive features. We need a competent, impartial, and fair procedure—a neutral body, unbeholden to politicians, that will reasonably evaluate the alternatives. How could we select electoral rules in a way that satisfies these criteria?

Fortunately, democratic tradition has another answer, and it's a solution that fits the bill. Up until the eighteenth century, democracy was primarily associated not with elections, but with sortition—the random selection of political officers. Sortition was a staple of Athenian democracy. All Athenian citizens had a right to participate in the popular Assembly (*ekklēsia*), but membership in other key political institutions was determined by lot—including the people's courts (*dikastēria*), the Council (*boulē*) of magistrates, and, in the fourth century BCE, legislative commissions (*nomothetai*).[2] A number of representative governments still follow this model for selecting juries.

My second thesis is that electoral rules should be decided by a randomly selected citizen assembly.[3] The idea is this: randomly select a few thousand Canadians, ask if they are willing to serve, and, from those saying yes, randomly select a couple of hundred to serve on an assembly empowered to determine federal election rules. (The random selection could also be stratified by existing federal ridings; for example, one or two individuals could be randomly selected from each riding.)

Putting regular citizens in charge may initially seem crazy—for instrumental reasons. What if a racist, sexist, xenophobic man spewing hatred, cheering sexual assault, and inciting others to violence were randomly selected to the citizen assembly? Of course this is possible. But random selection does not have a monopoly on the Donald Trump problem. Elections face the same problem. Elections as we know them regularly elect racist, sexist, xenophobic men to office. So do other selection devices. So the problem is general; it's not peculiar to sortition. The premise of democracy from its inception in Athens has been that, if an assembly is large enough, then the extremists will be counterbalanced by other, moderating forces in the assembly.

The more pertinent question: Wouldn't citizens with no special experience or expertise make incompetent decisions? Not necessarily. It's well known to social scientists that, under the right conditions, there is intelligence in numbers. The decisions of an assembly of regular but diverse individuals are often more intelligent than decisions by a lone genius or expert.[4] Again, this insight seems to have been part of the genius of Athenian democracy.[5] And in Canada we have relevant experience with this. We've twice had citizen assemblies mandated to propose a project of electoral reform, once in BC and another in Ontario. Political scientists have studied these experiments, and both were in many respects a great success.[6] Once our fellow citizens received expert advice (about voting systems) and consulted the public, they became well informed, and their deliberations and decision-making were extremely competent and reasonable. It's true that in one respect the BC and Ontario assemblies "failed." Each recommended a reform ultimately rejected by referendum. (In BC, 57 per cent voted in favour, but the government had set a 60 per cent threshold.) These failures are presumably why the federal government has chosen not to pursue electoral reform by repeating the BC and Ontario experiments. But my thesis is that electoral rules should be determined on an ongoing basis by a randomly selected citizen assembly without resorting to ratification by referendum.

This raises a potential objection: letting a randomly selected citizen assembly decide, without ratification by a referendum or elected representatives, means that the procedure fails to secure the consent of the people for its own election rules. Sortition is manifestly not a way in which represented individuals consent: they consent neither to their representatives nor, even indirectly, to what the latter decide. The objection is ideologically powerful because, ever since the eighteenth century, (a) consent has come to be thought of as the only way to legitimize political power, (b) voting has come to be thought of as a way of expressing consent to political outcomes, and (c) democracy has come to be associated with the consent of the people via elected representatives. These are fairly recent ideological developments in the history of democratic ideology. They arose in part from fusing together democratic theory with modern social-contract theory. This is in part why after the eighteenth century, democracy came to be associated with elections rather than sortition.[7] But as recent philosophical analysis has demonstrated, equating voting and democracy with consent is nothing more than ideological claptrap.[8]

The normative appeal of consent lies in its promise to reconcile obligations with the individual's own will and autonomy. Here's the thought: even if an obligation requires me to do things I presently do not wish to do, it is nevertheless not an alien imposition on my will if I have consented to it, i.e., if I have intentionally and voluntarily taken it on myself. This is what consenting is: intentionally and voluntarily taking on obligations, or waving one's rights, by voluntarily undertaking (or omitting) actions that one intends others to understand as expressions of one's voluntary intention to take on obligations or wave one's rights. One way to consent to political rule is by explicitly doing so: articulating in language one's intention to take on the obligation to abide by one's rulers. Another way is by expressing one's intention tacitly, without explicitly spelling out one's intention.

Contrary to prevalent democratic ideology, elections do not in general secure people's consent to electoral outcomes. Consider someone who voted for the losing candidates in federal elections. She didn't explicitly consent to the winners' rule. Did she, in virtue of taking part in the election, tacitly consent? Not typically. She may have merely intended to try to help her preferred candidate get elected, without any intention of taking on obligations to the actual winners. Even someone who voted for the winners may have no intention to consent. People vote for many reasons. Of course it is possible that some people do intend to express their consent to abide by the rule of whoever wins. But others simply intend to influence the outcome, without intending to obligate themselves to it. Sometimes they might find all the candidates unpalatable, and their intention in voting is wholly strategic: to help prevent the worst alternative, but not to legitimize the elections or their outcomes. Perhaps they vote even though they think the elections are fraudulent and illegitimate.[9]

The same can said about referenda. Not everyone who votes in a referendum intends to express her intention to obligate herself to respect the alternative she rejects should it prevail. Even if she votes for the winning alternative, she may do so without intending to consent to it: she may simply intend to help defeat an even worse alternative as a stopgap measure, before fighting for an option not on the ballot. Voting in an election or referendum is primarily a way of expressing an intention to influence the outcome one way or another, not a method of expressing an intention to take on obligations or wave one's rights. Elections are primarily a means not for individuals to consent, but to exercise *power* over political outcomes.

Rather than a regime that secures the consent of the people, representative democracy is a regime that seeks (a) to render political outcomes responsive to the opinions and interests of the represented

(b) in an impartial way that respects their equality and freedom, and hence (c) legitimates or helps secure public confidence in political institutions. Letting a randomly selected citizen assembly decide the rules for electing representatives meets these requirements. The assembly would not only be competent, it would be representative of Canadians;[10] because it would be representative, it would be responsive to the interests and viewpoints that Canadians have in general. It would not suffer a conflict of interest; and it would not be beholden to politicians. Because sortition selects representatives without appeal to reasons, it is entirely impartial between different potentially conflicting interests, treats each individual as an equal insofar as each has the same prospect of being selected, and is sanitized from the corrupting influence of money or partisan power.[11] Precisely because assembly members would have the incentives to properly inform themselves and deliberate about the relative merits of the alternatives, their decision would be much more informed than a decision by referendum.[12]

Precisely for these reasons, Canadians would view the decisions of a citizen assembly as legitimate. That's the other lesson from BC and Ontario. The more voters knew about the assembly—how its members were chosen, its freedom from partisan influence, etc.—the more likely they were to vote for its recommendation even when they didn't know much about voting systems.[13] They didn't need to know about voting systems: they trusted the assembly, rightly assuming that its decisions reflected what they themselves might have decided if they had taken the time to study the matter.

A citizen assembly can avoid the pitfalls of referenda and of letting politicians decide. We could even ultimately supplement binding decisions by a citizen assembly with a referendum *after* the decision has already been implemented—as New Zealand did—to ratify or reject it once citizens have already had a chance to see the reforms in action. The point would not be to secure the proverbial consent of the people, but to canvass a wider diversity of informed opinion—the opinion of everyone who has experienced the relative merits of living under both the old and new systems.

Not only should we let a citizen assembly decide current reform, we should establish it as an enduring institution mandated to set electoral rules on an ongoing basis. There is no perfect electoral system, and the effects of alternative electoral rules in any particular political society are somewhat unpredictable. We may learn new things. Circumstances might change. What works today may not work tomorrow. If electoral reform is carried out as a once in a lifetime event, we raise the stakes and make these problems intractable. We need to be able to correct mistakes easily. Just as we need an ongoing, permanent solution for drawing constituency boundaries—a solution outside the regular game of partisan politics—so too do we need a permanent solution to potentially ongoing electoral reform. A randomly selected citizen assembly provides that solution.

Notes

Introduction

1. *Liberal Party of Canada, Real Change: A Fair and Open Government,* accessed on Dec. 15, 2016, at https://www.liberal.ca/files/2015/06/a-fair-and-open-government.pdf.
2. The lone voice in the wilderness here was Carleton professor Philippe Lagassé. http://www.macleans.ca/politics/ottawa/in-defence-of-the-liberals-electoral-reform-survey/.

1. Evaluating How We Vote – Again

1. This is an old problem. Four Canadian prime ministers, beginning with Laurier in 1896, came to office with fewer votes than their principal opponent, and it has happened in virtually all the provinces at least once.
2. See P. Fournier et al., *When Citizens Decide: Lessons from Citizen Assemblies on Electoral Reform* (Oxford: Oxford University Press, 2011).
3. Of the five parties sponsoring electoral reform projects, only the Quebec Liberals did not want to leave the issue to a referendum. The party had no enthusiasm for more referendums. It opposed holding them on the issue of provincial independence and was bogged down by its own promises of municipal de-amalgamation referendums that led to eighty-nine of them in June of 2004.
4. Matthew Shugart discusses this tension in terms of politicians' act-contingent motivations and outcome-contingent realities in his "Inherent and Contingent Factors in Reform Initiation in Plurality Systems," in *To Keep or to Change First Past the Post: The Politics of Electoral Reform,* ed. André Blais (Oxford: Oxford University Press, 2008).

5. Ironically, the New Brunswick government was defeated when its Liberal opponent won with a smaller vote share – another case of a "wrong winner."
6. M. Shugart & M. Wattenberg, *Mixed-Member Electoral Systems: The Best of Both Worlds?* (Oxford: Oxford University Press, 2001).
7. Confidential interview, spring 2004.
8. The Law Commission of Canada issued its own national MMP plan in 2004 under the title "Voting Counts: Electoral Reform for Canada."
9. On the Ontario campaign see L. Stephenson and B. Tanguay, "Ontario's Referendum on Proportional Representation: Why Citizens Said No," *IRPP Choices* 15:10 (2009). J. Lee provides an account of the PEI event in "The Prince Edward Island Plebiscite on Electoral Reform," *Canadian Parliamentary Review* 29, no. 1 (2006).
10. Academics have long pointed to the possibilities of using MMP in Canada. See W.P. Irvine's *Does Canada Need a New Electoral System*, Queen's University Institute of Intergovernmental Relations, 1979.
11. Fournier et al., *When Citizens Decide: Lessons from Citizen Assemblies on Electoral Reform*, Ch 4.

2. The Complex Normative Landscape of Electoral Systems

1. Some of this work is carried out in Jeremy Waldron, *Political Political Theory: Essays on Institutions* (Cambridge, MA.: Harvard University Press, 2016).
2. See for example Jeremy Waldron, "Bicameralism and the Separation of Powers," *Current Legal Problems* 65, no. 1 (2012): 31–57.
3. Andrew Rehfeld, *The Concept of Constituency* (Oxford: Oxford University Press, 2005).
4. See Peter Mair, *Ruling the Void: The Hollowing of Western Democracy* (London: Verso, 2013).
5. Daniel Weinstock, "Sites of Deliberation in Contemporary Electoral Systems," *Journal of Parliamentary and Political Law* 9 (2015): 291–306.
6. Michael Pal and Sujit Choudhry, "Is Every Ballot Equal? Visible Minority Vote Dilution in Canada," *IRPP Choices* 13, no. 1 (2007).
7. Melissa Williams, *Voice, Trust, and Memory: Marginalized Groups and the Failure of Liberal Representation.*
8. Many authors have in recent years argued that the main justification of democracy is epistemic. See for example David Estlund, *Democratic Authority:*

A Philosophical Framework (Princeton: Princeton University Press, 2009); Helen Landemore, *Democratic Reason* (Princeton: Princeton University Press, 2012). For a withering critique of the epistemic pretentions of democracy, see Jason Brennan, *Against Democracy* (Princeton: Princeton University Press, 2016).

9. Daniel Weinstock, "Sites of Deliberation."

10. Amartya Sen and Eric Maskin argued in the *New York Times* during the 2016 Republican Party primaries that Donald Trump would not have won as many contests as he did under a comparative voting system such as one of those imagined by Borda and Condorcet. See Amartya Sen and Eric Maskin, "How Majority Rule Might Have Stopped Donald Trump," http://www.nytimes.com/2016/05/01/opinion/sunday/how-majority-rule-might-have-stopped-donald-trump.html. For the best account we have of such systems, see Michael Dummett, *Principles of Electoral Reform* (Oxford: Oxford University Press, 1997).

11. Mark E. Warren and Hilary Pearse, eds., *Designing Deliberative Democracy* (Cambridge: Cambridge University Press, 2008).

3. Democratic Stability, Representation, and Accountability: A Case for Single-Member Plurality Elections in Canada

1 Nassim Nicholas Taleb, *Antifragile: Things That Gain from Disorder*, vol. 3 (Random House, 2012).

2 I acknowledge here that the standard of what is democratic has thankfully increased over time. Limited franchises and property requirements are, by objective standards, undemocratic. I wish to avoid, however, the argument about whether a country that did not have universal suffrage could be considered democratic, for two reasons. First, there is no clear difference between PR and non-PR countries on this measure. Most nearly every country has gradually expanded its understanding of what it means to be democratic. Second, if we wish to look back on countries and suggest that they are not democracies because they excluded one or another group in the past, we should be ready to acknowledge that no country today is democratic, given that in the future we may well think it abhorrent to prevent children from voting, or non-citizen residents of a country, or even perhaps non-citizen non-residents. In short, democracy is an expanding concept, but we can still classify countries by the standards of their time.

3 By this, I mean the fundamental challenges that face a country as a result of political decisions made about its institutions and laws at the time of its founding.

4 Seymour M. Lipset and Stein Rokkan, "Cleavage Structures, Party Systems, and Voter Alignments: An Introduction," in *Party Systems and Voter Alignments: Cross-National Perspectives* (The Free Press, 1967), 1–64.

5 Maurice Duverger, *Political Parties: Their Organization and Activity in the Modern State* (Methuen, 1959).

6 Gary W. Cox, *Making Votes Count: Strategic Coordination in the World's Electoral Systems*, vol. 7 (Cambridge: Cambridge University Press, 1997).

7 See, for example, Peter Russell's testimony to the Special Committee on Electoral Reform, available here: http://www.parl.gc.ca/Content/HOC/Committee/421/ERRE/Brief/BR8391090/br-external/RussellPH-e.pdf.

8 Andre Seigfried and Frank H. Underhill, *The Race Question in Canada*, no. 29 (McGill-Queen's Press, 1966).

9 Seigfried, 113–14, as quoted in Richard Johnston, "An Analytical History of the Canadian Party System," unpublished manuscript, ND.

10 Johnston, ND.

11 Johnston, ND, 134.

12 Johnston, ND, 134.

13 I am indebted here to personal correspondence with Richard Johnston, who provided this data point.

14 For an account of the few instances of successful electoral reform in Canada, see Harold John Jansen, "The Single Transferable Vote in Alberta and Manitoba," PhD diss., University of Alberta, 1998.

15 David Cameron and Richard Simeon, "Intergovernmental Relations in Canada: The Emergence of Collaborative Federalism," *Publius: The Journal of Federalism* 32, no. 2 (2002): 49–72.

16 Chris Cochrane was the first to introduce me to Orgell's Second Rule: "Evolution is cleverer than you are." It is discussed clearly in Daniel Dennett, *Darwin's Dangerous Idea: Evolution and the Meaning of Life* (New York: Touchstone, 1995), 74. The central intuition here is that things built up through trial and error contain much more wisdom than anything that is centrally imagined and planned.

17 G. Bingham Powell, *Elections as Instruments of Democracy: Majoritarian and Proportional Visions* (Yale University Press, 2000).

18 Cox, 1997.

19 Matt Golder and Benjamin Ferland, "Electoral Rules and Citizen-Elite Ideological Congruence," working paper, available at http://mattgolder.com/files/research/congruence.pdf.

20 André Blais, Peter Loewen, and Maxime Ricard, "The Government Life Cycle," *Democratic Reform in New Brunswick* (2007).

21 Golder and Ferland.

22 Blais et al. (2007).

23 Jeffrey Simpson, *The Friendly Dictatorship* (McClelland & Stewart, 2011).

24 Golder and Ferland provide a particularly strong and comprehensive review.

25 G. Bingham Powell Jr. and Georg S. Vanberg, "Election Laws, Disproportionality and Median Correspondence: Implications for Two Visions of Democracy," *British Journal of Political Science* 30, no. 3 (2000): 383–411; Arend Lijphart, *Patterns of Democracy: Government Forms and Performance in Thirty-Six Countries* (Yale University Press, 2012); Ian Budge and Michael D. McDonald, "Election and Party System Effects on Policy Representation: Bringing Time into a Comparative Perspective," *Electoral Studies* 26, no. 1 (2007): 168–79.

26 André Blais and Marc André Bodet, "Does Proportional Representation Foster Closer Congruence between Citizens and Policy Makers?," *Comparative Political Studies* 39, no. 10 (2006): 1243–62; Matt Golder and Jacek Stramski, "Ideological Congruence and Electoral Institutions," *American Journal of Political Science* 54, no. 1 (2010): 90–106.

27 Anthony Downs, "An Economic Theory of Political Action in a Democracy," *The Journal of Political Economy* (1957): 135–50.

28 Arthur Lupia, *Uninformed: Why People Seem to Know So Little about Politics and What We Can Do about It* (Oxford University Press, 2015).

29 John Zaller, *The Nature and Origins of Mass Opinion* (Cambridge University Press, 1992).

30 Gabriel S. Lenz, *Follow the Leader?: How Voters Respond to Politicians' Policies and Performance* (University of Chicago Press, 2013).

31 Christopher H. Achen and Larry M. Bartels, *Democracy for Realists: Why Elections Do Not Produce Responsive Government* (Princeton University Press, 2016).

32 R.M. Duch and R.T. Stevenson, *The Economic Vote: How Political and Economic Institutions Condition Election Results* (Cambridge University Press, 2008).

33 Raymond Duch, Wojtek Przepiorka, and Randolph Stevenson, "Responsibility Attribution for Collective Decision Makers," *American Journal of Political Science* 59, no. 2 (2015): 372–89.

34 R. Niebuhr, *The Children of Light and the Children of Darkness* (Charles Scribner's Sons, 1972).

35 University of Oklahoma, Institute of Group Relations, and Muzafer Sherif, *Intergroup Conflict and Cooperation: The Robbers Cave Experiment*, vol. 10 (Norman, OK: University Book Exchange, 1961); Henri Tajfel, *Social Identity and Intergroup Relations* (Cambridge University Press, 2010).

36 P.J. Loewen, "Affinity, Antipathy and Political Participation: How Our Concern for Others Makes Us Vote," *Canadian Journal of Political Science* 43, no. 3 (2010): 661–87; Achen and Bartels, 2016.

4. Electoral Reform Is Not a Rights Issue

1. Dennis Pilon, "A Referendum on Voting System Would Be Undemocratic and Immoral," *The Hill Times*, September 26, 2016, 18.

2. Mary Ann Glendon, *Rights Talk: The Impoverishment of Political Discourse* (New York: The Free Press, 1991), 3–4.

3. Eric Grenier, "The Pollcast: Green Party Leader Elizabeth May on Electoral Reform," *CBC News*, September 1, 2016, accessed October 15, 2016, http://www.cbc.ca/news/politics/grenier-pollcast-may-stemarie-1.3743037.

4. "Special Committee on Electoral Reform – July 28, 2016," House of Commons, accessed October 15, 2016, http://www.parl.gc.ca/HousePublications/Publication.aspx?Language=e&Mode=1&Parl=42&Ses=1&DocId=8395346&File=0.

5. "Submission to the Special Parliamentary Committee on Electoral Reform – August 19, 2016," Fair Vote Canada, accessed October 15, 2016, http://www.parl.gc.ca/Content/HOC/Committee/421/ERRE/Brief/BR8486811/br-external/FairVoteCanada-e.pdf.

6. "The Civil Rights Case for Voting Reform & Evaluating Key Options," Fair Voting BC, accessed October 15, 2016, http://www.parl.gc.ca/Content/HOC/Committee/421/ERRE/Brief/BR8430298/br-external/FairVotingBC-e.pdf, at 7.

7. "The Civil Rights Case for Voting Reform & Evaluating Key Options," 3.

8. Ibid.

9. Ibid, 4.

10. Ibid.

11. *Muldoon v. Canada*, [1988] F.C.J. No. 1003, [1988] 3 F.C. 628 (F.C.T.D.).

12. *Sauvé v. Canada (Chief Electoral Officer)*, [2002] S.C.J. No. 66, [2002] 3 S.C.R. 519 (S.C.C.).
13. *Haig v. Canada (Chief Electoral Officer)*, [1993] S.C.J. No. 84, [1993] 2 S.C.R. 995 (S.C.C.); *Reference re Yukon Election Residency Requirement*, [1986] Y.J. No. 14, 27 D.L.R. (4th) 146 (Y.T.C.A.); *Storey v. Zazelenchuk*, [1984] S.J. No. 800, 36 Sask. R. 103, 12 C.R.R. 261 (Sask. C.A.); *Arnold v. Attorney-General of Ontario*, [1987] O.J. No. 889, 61 O.R. (2d) 481 (Ont. H.C.J.).
14. *Harper v. Canada (Attorney General)*, [2004] S.C.J. No. 28, [2004] 1 S.C.R. 827 (S.C.C.).
15. *R. v. Bryan*, [2007] S.C.J. No. 12, [2007] 1 S.C.R. 527 (S.C.C.).
16. *Reference re Prov. Electoral Boundaries (Sask.)*, [1991] S.C.J. No. 46, [1991] 2 S.C.R. 158 (S.C.C.).
17. *Figueroa v. Canada (Attorney General)*, [2003] S.C.J. No. 37, [2003] 1 S.C.R. 912, 2003 SCC 37 (S.C.C.).
18. *Daoust v. Quebec (Chief Electoral Officer)*, [2011] Q.J. No. 12526, 2011 QCCA 1634 (Que. C.A.).
19. The Court was unanimous on the outcome but three justices wrote concurring reasons.
20. *Figueroa*, at para. 25. The concept was first recognized in *Haig*.
21. *Figueroa*, at para. 26.
22. *Figueroa*, at para. 29.
23. *Figueroa*, at para. 39.
24. *Figueroa*, at para. 101.
25. *Figueroa*, at para. 153.
26. *Figueroa*, at para. 154.
27. *Figueroa*, at paras. 154–57. Justice LeBel acknowledges the highly contested nature of these virtues.
28. *Figueroa*, at para. 158 [emphasis in italics is mine].
29. *Figueroa*, at para. 37.
30. *Daoust*, at para. 57.
31. *Daoust*, at para. 44.
32. Glendon, *Rights Talk*, 44–5.
33. Pilon, "A referendum on voting system would be undemocratic and immoral," 18.
34. See, for example, C. Neal Tate and Torbjorn Vallinder, eds., *The Global Expansion of Judicial Power* (New York: New York University Press, 1995).

35. See: Emmett Macfarlane, "Constitutional Constraints on Electoral Reform in Canada: Why Parliament Is (Mostly) Free to Implement a New Voting System," *Supreme Court Law Review* (forthcoming).

5. The Imaginary Worlds of Electoral System Reform

1. The argument is influenced by, but departs in important ways from, Gerald Gaus, *The Tyranny of the Ideal* (Princeton University Press, 2016). Gaus's work is a roadmap for thinking clearly about these sorts of debates. I am responsible for my interpretation, adaptation, and application of his argument.

6. Voter Choice and Accountability: A Case for Caution about Electoral Reform

1. Patrick Dunleavy and Helen Margetts, "Understanding the Dynamics of Electoral Reform," *International Political Science Review* 16, no. 1 (2005): 9–29.
2. Arend Lijphart, *Patterns of Democracy: Government Forms and Performance in Thirty-Six Countries* (New Haven: Yale University Press, 1999); G. Bingham Powell, *Elections as Instruments of Democracy: Majoritarian and Proportional Visions* (New Haven: Yale University Press, 2000).
3. G. Bingham Powell, *Elections as Instruments of Democracy: Majoritarian and Proportional Visions* (New Haven: Yale University Press, 2000).
4. Patrick Dunleavy and Helen Margetts, "Understanding the Dynamics of Electoral Reform," *International Political Science Review* 16, no. 1 (2005): 29.
5. Kathryn May, "Trudeau Effect? Same Complaints, but More Trust in Ottawa Than under Harper: Survey," *National Post*, September 5, 2016.
6. "Canadian Public Opinion on Governance 2016," Environics Institute on Governance, accessed on November 8, 2016, http://www.environicsinstitute.org/uploads/institute-projects/canadian%20public%20opinion%20on%20governance%202016%20-%20final%20report%20-%20june%2017-2016.pdf, 3.
7. Ibid.
8. "The International IDEA Handbook of Electoral System Design," International Institute of Democracy and Electoral Assistance, accessed on November 8, 2016, https://www.ifes.org/sites/default/files/esd_english_0.pdf, 9.
9. "Good Government," Green Party of Canada, accessed on November 8, 2016, https://www.greenparty.ca/en/platform#Good-Government.

10. "NDP Policy Book," New Democratic Party of Canada, accessed on November 8, 2016, http://xfer.ndp.ca/2016/documents/2016_PolicyBook_EN_WEB.pdf.

11. Ray M. Duch and R.T. Stevenson, *The Economic Vote: How Political and Economic Institutions Condition Election Results* (New York: Cambridge, 2008).

12. Bernard Manin, Adam Przeworski, and Susan C. Stokes, "Elections and Representation," in *Democracy, Accountability, and Representation*, eds. Adam Przeworski, Susan C. Stokes, and Bernard Manin (Cambridge: Cambridge University Press, 1999), 32.

13. Ibid.

14. Ibid, 40.

15. T. Hellwig, "Context, Information, and Performance Voting," in *Citizens, Context, and Choice: How Context Shapes Citizens' Electoral Choices*, eds. R.J. Dalton and C.J. Anderson (Oxford: Oxford University Press), 149–75

16. Maurice Duverger, *Political Parties: Their Organization and Activity in the Modern State*, trans. Barbara and Robert North (London: Methuen & Co., 1954).

17. Anthony Downs, *An Economic Theory of Democracy* (New York: Harper, 1957).

18. Stephen D. Fisher and Sara B. Hobolt, "Coalition Government and Electoral Accountability," *Electoral Studies* 29, no. 3 (2010): 358–369.

19. Ibid.

20. Bernard Manin, Adam Przeworski, and Susan C. Stokes, "Elections and Representation," in *Democracy, Accountability, and Representation*, eds. Adam Przeworski, Susan C. Stokes, and Bernard Manin (Cambridge: Cambridge University Press, 1999), 29–54.

21. R. Kenneth Carty, *Big Tent Politics: The Liberal Party's Long Mastery of Canada's Public Life* (Vancouver: UBC Press, 2015).

22. Sara B. Hobolt and Jeffrey A. Karp, "Voters and Coalition Governments," *Electoral Studies* 29, no. 3 (2010): 299.

23. Andrew Coyne, "On the Perils of Prorogation," *Maclean's*, October 12, 2010.

24. "Tories Begin Battle against Coalition," *CBC News*, December 2, 2008.

25. Bernard Manin, Adam Przeworski, and Susan C. Stokes, "Elections and Representation," in *Democracy, Accountability, and Representation*, ed. Adam Przeworski, Susan C. Stokes, and Bernard Manin (Cambridge: Cambridge University Press, 1999), 32.

7. Electoral System Reform: Implications for Internal Party Democracy

1. Much of the information presented in this chapter results from a series of in-country interviews conducted with party and elected officials in Australia, Ireland, and New Zealand between 2011 and 2015. For more on party organization and intra-party democracy in these countries, see William Cross, "Understanding Power-Sharing within Political Parties: Stratarchy as Mutual Interdependence between the Party in the Centre and the Party on the Ground," *Government and Opposition,* first view (2016).

2. Giovani Sartori, *Parties and Party Systems: A Framework for Analysis* (Cambridge: Cambridge University Press, 1976), 64.

3. New Zealand Electoral Act 1993, section 71.

4. The constitutions and rules of the New Zealand parties can be found on the website of the New Zealand Electoral Commission: "Register of Political Parties," New Zealand Electoral Commission, accessed on November 6, 2016, http://www.elections.org.nz/parties-candidates/registered-political-parties/register-political-parties.

5. Scott Pruysers and William Cross, "Candidate Selection in Canada: Local Autonomy, Centralization, and Competing Democratic Norms," *American Behavioral Scientist* 60 (2016): 781–98.

6. For an excellent overview of candidate selection in the Irish parties, see Theresa Reidy, "Candidate Selection," in *How Ireland Voted 2011: The Full Story of Ireland's Earthquake Election,* eds. Michael Gallagher and Michael Marsh (Houndmills: Palgrave Macmillan, 2011), 47–67.

7. Tim Colebatch, "Labor's Narrow Escape in Melbourne Ports, and a Preference Problem for the Coalition," *Inside Story,* September 16, 2016.

8. See William Cross, "The Increasing Importance of Region to Canadian Election Campaigns," in *Regionalism and Party Politics in Canada,* eds. Lisa Young and Keith Archer (Don Mills, Ontario: Oxford University Press, 2002), 116–28.

9. Recent New Zealand National governments have involved "confidence and supply" agreements with minor parties and their inclusion as government ministers outside of cabinet. The 2016 Irish election resulted in a minority Fine Gael government after lengthy attempts at coalition formation failed.

10. See, for example, Stephen Collins, "Any FF Coalition Now Needs Special Ardfheis Approval," *Irish Times,* February 11, 2016.

11. For more detail on the examples discussed here, see William Cross and André Blais, *Politics at the Centre: The Selection and Removal of Party Leaders in the Anglo-Parliamentary Democracies* (Oxford: Oxford University Press, 2012).

12. See William Cross and André Blais, "Who Selects the Party Leader?" *Party Politics* 18 (2012): 127–50.

8. Democratic Deliberation and Electoral Reform

1. For an excellent review of the now vast literature in deliberative democracy and the contrast between deliberative and aggregative conceptions of democracy, see Simone Chambers, "Deliberative Democratic Theory," *Annual Review of Political Science* 6 (2003): 307–26.

2. See Jonathan Quong, "On the Idea of Public Reason," in *The Blackwell Companion to Rawls*, eds. J. Mandle and D. Reidy (Oxford: Wiley-Blackwell, 2013).

3. The judicial system, especially when it addresses controversies about fundamental constitutional rights, may be a fourth site of democratic deliberation.

4. See Henry Richardson, *Democratic Autonomy* (Oxford: Oxford University Press, 2003).

5. See Daniel Weinstock, "Sites of Deliberation in Contemporary Electoral Systems: On the Deliberative Defense of Some Unfashionable Institutions," *Journal of Parliamentary and Political Law* 9 (2015): 295–6.

6. Weinstock, "Sites of Deliberation," 296–7.

10. What Is the Problem that Electoral Reform Will Solve?

1. The platform stated specifically, "We are committed to ensuring that 2015 will be the last federal election conducted under the first-past-the-post voting system. We will convene an all-party Parliamentary committee to review a wide variety of reforms, such as ranked ballots, proportional representation, mandatory voting, and online voting. This committee will deliver its recommendations to Parliament. Within 18 months of forming government, we will introduce legislation to enact electoral reform." "Electoral Reform," Liberal Party of Canada, accessed October 29, 2016, https://www.liberal.ca/real-change/electoral-reform/.

2. William Dunn, *Public Policy Analysis: An Introduction,* third ed. (New Jersey: Prentice Hall, 2004), 72.

3. "Tale of the Tape: Read a Full Transcript of Maclean's Debate," *Maclean's*, accessed October 29, 2016, http://www.macleans.ca/politics/ottawa/tale-of-the-tape-read-a-full-transcript-of-macleans-debate/.

4. "Frequently Asked Questions (FAQ) about Canadian Federal Electoral Reform," Government of Canada, last modified July 25, 2016, https://www.canada.ca/en/campaign/electoral-reform/learn-about-canadian-federal-electoral-reform/frequently-asked-questions-about-canadian-federal-electoral-reform.html.

5. Patrice Dutil, "The Imperative of a Referendum," in *Counting Votes: Essays on Electoral Reform,* ed. Lydia Miljan (Vancouver: Fraser Institute, 2016), 82, accessed October 29, 2016, https://www.fraserinstitute.org/sites/default/files/counting-votes-essays-on-electoral-reform-post.pdf.

6. Harold J. Jansen, "The Political Consequences of the Alternative Vote: Lessons from Western Canada," *Canadian Journal of Political Science* 37, no. 3 (2004): 647–69.

7. "Voter Turnout at Federal Elections and Referendums," Elections Canada, last modified October 15, 2015, http://www.elections.ca/content.aspx?dir=turn&document=index&lang=e&section=ele#ftn5; "Forty-second General Election: 2015 Official Voting Results," Elections Canada, last modified April 14, 2016, http://www.elections.ca/res/rep/off/ovr2015app/41/table4E.html.

8. Pierre Lortie, "The Principles of Electoral Reform," *Canadian Parliamentary Review* 16 (1993): 2–6.

9. Bernard Grofman and Peter Selb, "Turnout and the (Effective) Number of Parties at the National and District Levels: A Puzzle-Solving Approach," *Party Politics* 17 (2011): 93–117.

10. "Guiding Principles for Canadian Federal Electoral Reform," Government of Canada, last modified July 3, 2016, https://www.canada.ca/en/campaign/electoral-reform/learn-about-canadian-federal-electoral-reform/guiding-principles-for-canadian-federal-electoral-reform.html.

11. Dutil, "Imperative of a Referendum," 1.

12. Marie Vastel, "Trudeau ne garantit plus une réforme électorale majeure," *Le Devoir*, October 19, 2016, accessed October 20, 2016, http://www.ledevoir.com/politique/canada/482514/la-reforme-electorale-n-est-plus-garantie.

13. "Building the Country of Our Dreams: Tom Mulcair's Plan to Bring Change to Ottawa, 2015," New Democratic Party of Canada, accessed October 29, 2016, http://xfer.ndp.ca/2015/2015-Full-Platform-EN.pdf (NDP full 2015 election platform).

14. "6.1 Democratic Renewal and Proportional Representation," Green Party of Canada, accessed October 29, 2016, https://www.greenparty.ca/en/policy/vision-green/government/democratic-renewal (Green Party full 2015 election platform).

15. André Blais, "What Affects Voter Turnout?," *Annual Review of Political Science* 9 (2006): 11–25; André Blais and K. Aarts, "Electoral Systems and Turnout," *Acta Politica* 41 (2006): 180–96.

16. Blais and Aarts, "Electoral Systems"; Sergi Pardos-Prado, Carolina Galais, and Jordi Munoz, "The Dark Side of Proportionality: Conditional Effects of Proportional Features on Turnout," *Electoral Studies* 35 (2014): 253–264.

17. John Pepall, "First-Past-the-Post: Empowered Voters, Accountable Government," in *Counting Votes: Essays on Electoral Reform,* ed. Lydia Miljan (Vancouver: Fraser Institute, 2016), 1–20, as of October 29, 2016, https://www.fraserinstitute.org/sites/default/files/counting-votes-essays-on-electoral-reform-post.pdf.

18. "Canada: Parliamentary Elections 19 October 2015. OSCE/ODIHR Election Assessment Mission Final Report (Warsaw 2016)," Organization for Security and Co-operation in Europe [OSCE], accessed October 29, 2016, http://www.osce.org/odihr/elections/220661?download=true.

19. "Women Candidates in General Elections – 1921 to Date," Parliament of Canada, accessed October 29, 2016, http://www.lop.parl.gc.ca/About/Parliament/FederalRidingsHistory/hfer.asp?Language=E&Search=WomenElection.

20. Karen Bird, *The Political Representation of Women and Ethnic Minorities in Established Democracies: A Framework for Comparative Research,* Working Paper presented for the Academy of Migration Studies in Denmark (AMID) (Aalborg University, 2003).

21. Lydia Miljan and Taylor Jackson, "Consequences of the Alternative Vote," in *Counting Votes: Essays on Electoral Reform,* ed. Lydia Miljan (Vancouver: Fraser Institute, 2016), 45–79, as of October 29, 2016, https://www.fraserinstitute.org/sites/default/files/counting-votes-essays-on-electoral-reform-post.pdf.

22. Torsten Persson, Roland Gerard, and Guido Tabellini, "Electoral Rules and Government Spending in Parliamentary Democracies," *Quarterly Journal of Political Science* 2, no. 2 (2007): 155–88.

23. Jason Clemens, Taylor Jackson, Steve LaFleur, and Joel Emes, "Electoral Rules and Fiscal Policy Outcomes," in *Counting Votes: Essays on Electoral Reform,* ed. Lydia Miljan (Vancouver: Fraser Institute, 2016), 21–44, as of October 29, 2016,

https://www.fraserinstitute.org/sites/default/files/counting-votes-essays-on-electoral-reform-post.pdf.

24. See Clemens et al., "Electoral Rules," 32.

11. *The Electoral System and Parliament's Diversity Problem: In Defense of the Wrongfully Accused*

1. Anne Phillips, *The Politics of Presence* (Oxford: Oxford University Press, 1998).

2. Arend Lijphart, *Government Forms and Performance in Thirty-Six Countries* (New Haven: Yale University Press, 1999); G. Bingham Powell Jr., *Elections as Instruments of Democracy: Majoritarian and Proportional Views* (New Haven: Yale University Press, 2000).

3. Paul Warwic and Maria Zakharova, "Measuring the Media: The Risk of Inferring Beliefs from Votes," *British Journal of Political Science* 43 (2013): 157–75; Christopher Wlezien and Stuart N. Soroka, *Electoral Systems and Opinion Representation*, Nuffield College Working Paper Series in Politics (Oxford: Nuffield College, 2015).

4. Raymond M. Duch and Randolph T. Stevenson, *The Economic Vote: How Political and Economic Institutions Condition Election Results* (New York: Cambridge University Press, 2008).

5. André Blais and Marc André Bodet, "Does Proportional Representation Foster Closer Congruence Between Citizens and Policymakers?" *Comparative Political Studies* 39 (2006): 1243–62.

6. Stuart N. Soroka and Christopher Wlezien, "Opinion Representation and Policy Feedback: Canada in Comparative Perspective," *Canadian Journal of Political Science* 37, no. 3 (2004): 531–59; Stuart N. Soroka and Christopher Wlezien, *Degrees of Democracy* (New York: Cambridge University Press, 2010).

7. Pamela Paxton and Melanie M. Hughes, *Women, Politics and Power: A Global Perspective*, third ed. (Thousand Oaks, CA: Sage, 2017).

8. Melanee Thomas made this point in her submission to the Special Committee on Electoral Reform.

9. Karen Bird, "Patterns of Substantive Representation among Visible Minority MPs: Evidence from Canada's House of Commons," paper presented at the Midwest Political Science Association, Chicago, April 3, 2008; Karen Bird, "Toward an Integrated Perspective on Minority Representation: Views from Canada," *Politics & Gender* 8, no. 4 (2012): 529–35.

10. Manon Tremblay and Réjean Pelletier, *Que font-elles en politique?* (Sainte-Foy: Les Presses de l'Université Laval, 1995).

11. Data drawn from "Women in National Parliaments (as of 1 September 2016)," Inter-Parliamentary Union, accessed 24 October 2016, http://www.ipu.org/wmn-e/classif.htm.

12. Andrew Roberts, Jason Seawright, and Jennifer Cyr, "Do Electoral Laws Affect Women's Representation?" *Comparative Political Studies* 46, no. 12 (2012): 1555–81.

13. Jill Bystykzienski, "Women in Politics in Norway," *Women and Politics* 8 (1988): 73–95; Pippa Norris, *Politics and Sexual Equality* (Boulder, CO: Rienner, 1987).

14. These counter-examples are drawn from Roberts et al., "Do Electoral Laws Affect Women's Representation?"

15. Roberts et al., "Do Electoral Laws Affect Women's Representation?," 1557.

16. Pamela Paxton, Melanie M. Hughes, and Matthew Painter, "The Difference Time Makes: Latent Growth Curve Models of Women's Political Representation," *European Journal of Political Research* 49, no. 1 (2010): 25–52.

17. Richard E. Matland, "Women's Representation in National Legislatures: Developed and Developing Countries," *Legislative Studies Quarterly* 23 (1998): 109–25; Rob Salmond, "Proportional Representation and Female Parliamentarians," *Legislative Studies Quarterly* 31, no. 2 (2006): 175–204.

18. Salmond, "Proportional Representation and Female Parliamentarians."

19. Irene Bloemraad, "Accessing the Corridors of Power: Puzzles and Pathways to Understanding Minority Representation," *West European Politics* 36, no. 30 (2013): 652–70

20. Bloemraad, "Accessing the Corridors of Power."

21. Paxton and Hughes, *Women, Politics and Power*; Salmond, "Proportional Representation and Female Parliamentarians."

22. Elizabeth Goodyear-Grant and Julie Croskill, "Gender Affinity Effects in Vote Choice in Westminster Systems: Assessing 'Flexible' Voters in Canada," *Politics & Gender* 7, no. 2 (2011): 223–250; Kira Sanbonmatsu, "Do Parties Know that 'Women Win?' Party Leader Beliefs About Women's Electoral Chances," *Politics & Gender* 2 (2006): 431–50.

23. Melanee Thomas and Marc André Bodet, "Sacrificial Lambs, Women Candidates, and District Competitiveness in Canada," *Electoral Studies* 32, no. 1 (2013): 153–166.

24. Christine Cheng and Margit Tavits, "Informal Influences in Selecting Female Political Candidates," *Political Research Quarterly* 64, no. 2 (2011): 460–71; Manon Tremblay and Réjean Pelletier, "More Women Constituency Party

Presidents: A Strategy for Increasing the Number of Women Candidates in Canada?" *Party Politics* 7, no. 2 (2001): 157–90.

25. David Niven, "Party Elites and Women Candidates: The Shape of Bias," *Women and Politics* 19, no. 2 (1998): 57–80; Richard L. Fox and Jennifer L. Lawless, "Entering the Arena? Gender and the Decision to Run for Office," *American Journal of Political Science* 48, no. 2 (2004): 264–80.

26. Thomas and Bodet, "Sacrificial Lambs."

27. Mona Lena Krook, "Beyond Supply and Demand: A Feminist-Institutionalist Theory of Candidate Selection," *Political Research Quarterly* 63, no. 4 (2010): 707–20.

12. Indigenous Representation, Self-Determination, and Electoral Reform

1. Truth and Reconciliation Commission Canada, *Summary of the Final Report of the Truth and Reconciliation Commission Canada* (2015). Accessed October 24, 2016. http://www.myrobust.com/websites/trcinstitution/File/Reports/Executive_Summary_English_Web.pdf.

2. Susana Mas, "Trudeau Lays Out Plan for New Relationship with Indigenous People." CBC News, December 8, 2015, accessed October 24, 2016, http://www.cbc.ca/news/politics/justin-trudeau-afn-indigenous-aboriginal-people-1.3354747.

3. Michael Morden, "Indigenizing Parliament: Time to Re-Start a Conversation," *Canadian Parliamentary Review* (Summer 2016).

4. Tanya Talaga, "Behind the Scenes on the Push to Rock the Indigenous Vote," *Toronto Star*, October 23, 2015, accessed October 24, 2016, https://www.thestar.com/news/canada/2015/10/23/behind-the-scenes-on-the-push-to-rock-the-indigenous-vote.html.

5. Elections Canada, "On-Reserve Voter Turnout – 42nd General Election," accessed October 24, 2016, http://www.elections.ca/content.aspx?section=res&dir=rec/eval/pes2015/ovt&document=index&lang=e.

6. "Canada Elects Record Number of Indigenous Candidates to Parliament," *The Guardian*, October 21, 2015, accessed October 24, 2016, https://www.theguardian.com/world/2015/oct/22 canada-elects-record-number-of-indigenous-candidates-to-parliament.

7. The 4.3 per cent figure is based on the 2011 census. Statistics Canada, "Aboriginal Peoples in Canada: First Nations People, Métis and Inuit," accessed October 24, 2016, https://www12.statcan.gc.ca/nhs-enm/2011/as-sa/99-011-x/99-011-x2011001-eng.cfm.

8. Tim Fontaine, "Canada Discriminates against Children on Reserves, Tribunal Rules," CBC News, January 26, 2016, accessed October 24, 2016, http://www.cbc.ca/news/indigenous/canada-discriminates-against-children-on-reserves-tribunal-rules-1.3419480.

9. Jody Porter, "First Nations Children Get 30 Per Cent Less Funding than Other Children, Economist Says," CBC News, March 14, 2016, accessed October 24, 2016, http://www.cbc.ca/news/canada/thunder-bay/first-nations-education-funding-gap-1.3487822.

10. Andrew Parkin, *International Report Card on Public Education: Key Facts on Canadian Achievement and Equity* (Toronto: Environics, 2015), 18–19, accessed on October 24, 2016, http://www.environicsinstitute.org/uploads/institute-projects/environics%20institute%20-%20parkin%20-%20international%20report%20on%20education%20-%20final%20report.pdf.

11. Matthew McClearn, "Water Systems at Risk," *The Globe and Mail*, August 30, 2016, accessed October 24, 2016, http://www.theglobeandmail.com/news/national/indigenous-water/article31589755/. See also Human Rights Watch, "Make It Safe: Canada's Obligation to End the First Nations Water Crisis," June 7, 2016, accessed October 24, 2016, https://www.hrw.org/report/2016/06/07/make-it-safe/canadas-obligation-end-first-nations-water-crisis; "Water Woes on First Nations Unacceptable, Say 74% of Canadians Polled," CBC News, accessed October 24, 2016, http://www.cbc.ca/news/canada/manitoba/first-nations-water-supply-poor-poll-1.3811339.

12. Environics Institute, *Canadian Public Opinion on Governance 2016* (Toronto: Environics, 2016), 17, accessed October 24, 2016, http://environicsinstitute.org/uploads/institute-projects/canadian%20public%20opinion%20on%20governance%202016%20-%20final%20report%20-%20june%2017-2016.pdf.

13. Environics Institute, *Canadian Public Opinion on Aboriginal Peoples* (Toronto: Environics, 2016), 43, accessed October 24, 2016, http://www.environicsinstitute.org/uploads/institute-projects/canadian%20public%20opinion%20on%20aboriginal%20peoples%202016%20-%20final%20report.pdf.

14. Hon. Maryam Monsef, Special Committee on Electoral Reform (hereafter "ERRE"), House of Commons Canada, Session 3, July 6, 2016, accessed October 24, 2016, http://www.parl.gc.ca/content/hoc/Committee/421/ERRE/Evidence/EV8385950/ERREEV03-E.PDF, 3.

15. See *inter alia*, Testimony of Pippa Norris, ERRE, Session 16, August 23, 2016, accessed October 24, 2016, http://www.parl.gc.ca/content/hoc/Committee/421/ERRE/Evidence/EV8400432/ERREEV16-E.PDF, 9.; Testimony of Kirk Cameron, ERRE, Session 30, September 26, 2016, accessed October 24,

2016. http://www.parl.gc.ca/content/hoc/Committee/421/ERRE/Evidence/
EV8442039/ERREEV30-E.PDF, 1–2.

16. Canada, Royal Commission On Electoral Reform and Party Financing, *Final Report Volume I: Reforming Electoral Democracy* (Ottawa: Minister of Supply and Services, 1991); Canada, *Report of the Royal Commission on Aboriginal Peoples: Restructuring the Relationship*, vol. 2 (Ottawa: Supply and Services Canada, 1996); Law Commission of Canada, *Voting Counts: Electoral Reform for Canada* (Ottawa: Supply and Services Canada, 2004).

17. Testimony of Georges Erasmus, ERRE, Session 34, September 30, 2016, accessed October 24, 2016. http://www.parl.gc.ca/content/hoc/Committee/421/ERRE/Evidence/EV8464898/ERREEV34-E.PDF, 38.

18. Elyse Skura, "Indigenous People Need 'Direct Representation' in Parliament, Argues Nunavut Tunngavik," CBC News, October 18, 2016, accessed on October 24, 2016, http://www.cbc.ca/news/canada/north/inuit-indigenous-electoral-reform-1.3809306.

19. See, e.g., Kiera L. Ladner and Michael McCrossen, "The Electoral Participation of Aboriginal People," Elections Canada Working Paper Series on Electoral Participation and Outreach Practices (Ottawa: Elections Canada, 2007), 23–24.

20. Pam Palmater, "The Power of Indigenous People Has Never Come through Voting in Federal Elections," rabble.com, August 9, 2015, accessed October 24, 2016, http://rabble.ca/blogs/bloggers/pamela-palmater/2015/08/power-indigenous-peoples-has-never-come-voting-federal-electi.

21. See, e.g., Jennifer Dalton, "Nation-to-Nation Recognition, Not Electoral Reform, Key to Increasing Indigenous Voter Turnout," rabble.com, May 12, 2016, accessed October 24, 2016, http://rabble.ca/news/2016/05/nation-to-nation-recognition-not-electoral-reform-key-to-increasing-indigenous-voter-tu.

22. "Ngā Māngai—Māori Representation," *The Encyclopedia of New Zealand*, accessed October 24, 2016, http://www.teara.govt.nz/en/nga-mangai-maori-representation/page-2.

23. Statistics New Zealand, "How Is Our Māori Population Changing?" Accessed October 24, 2016, http://www.stats.govt.nz/browse_for_stats/people_and_communities/maori/maori-population-article-2015.aspx.

24. See, e.g., Susan A. Banducci, Todd Donovan and Jeffrey A. Karp, "Minority Representation, Empowerment, and Participation," *The Journal of Politics* 66, no. 2: 534–56 (2004).

25. Karen Bird, "Ethnic Quotas and Ethnic Representation World-Wide," *International Political Science Review* 35, no. 1: 12–26.

26. Brian F. Crisp, Betul Demirkaya, Leslie A. Schwindt-Bayer, and Courtney Millian, "The Role of Rules in Representation: Group Membership and Electoral Incentives," *British Journal of Political Science* (April 2016, first view online publication).

27. New Zealand Electoral Commission, "About the 2011 Referendum on the Voting System," accessed October 24, 2016, http://www.elections.org.nz/events/past-events-0/2011-referendum-voting-system/about-2011-referendum-voting-system.

28. *Reforming Electoral Democracy*, 169–92.

29. Charlottetown Accord (1992), Article 22, accessed October 24, 2016, https://www.saic.gouv.qc.ca/documents/positions-historiques/positions-du-qc/part3/Document27_en.pdf.

30. Ibid., Article 9.

31. Ibid., Article 41.

32. *Restructuring the Relationship*, 358–63.

33. Ibid., 363.

34. *Voting Counts*, 117–23

35. For theoretical arguments linking "descriptive representation" (the presence of representatives from disadvantaged groups in legislative bodies) to "substantive representation" (legislators' active advocacy for a disadvantaged group's distinctive interests), see, e.g., Melissa S. Williams, *Voice, Trust and Memory: Marginalized Groups and the Failings of Liberal Representation* (Princeton: Princeton University Press, 1998) and Jane J. Mansbridge, "Should Blacks Represent Blacks and Women Represent Women? A Contingent 'Yes,'" *The Journal of Politics* 61, no. 3: 628–57.

36. For a more detailed discussion, see Melissa S. Williams, "Sharing the River: Aboriginal Representation in Canadian Political Institutions," in David Laycock, ed., *Representation and Democratic Theory* (Vancouver: University of British Columbia Press, 2004), chapter 5.

37. Quoted in Michael A. Murphy, "Representing Indigenous Self-Determination," *University of Toronto Law Journal* 58 (2008): 197.

38. See Michael Morden, "Indigenizing Parliament: Time to Re-Start a Conversation," *Canadian Parliamentary Review* (Summer 2016): 30.

39. For a scholarly treatment of citizens' assemblies on electoral reform, see Mark E. Warren and Hillary Pearse, eds., *Designing Deliberative Democracy: The*

British Columbia Citizens' Assembly (Cambridge: Cambridge University Press, 2008).

40. B.J. Siekierski, "A Citizens' Assembly on Electoral Reform? Monsef Doesn't Rule it Out," *iPolitics*, April 26, 2016, accessed October 24, 2016, http://ipolitics.ca/2016/04/26/a -citizens-assembly-on-electoral-reform-monsef-doesnt-rule-it-out/.

13. Addressing Representational Deficits in Canadian Legislatures

1. Sue Thomas, "Introduction," in *Women and Executive Office: Past, Present, and Future, Third Edition*, eds. Sue Thomas and Clyde Wilcox (New York: Oxford University Press, 2014), 2–3.
2. Marian Sawer, Manon Tremblay and Linda Trimble, "Introduction: Patterns and Practice in the Parliamentary Representation of Women," in *Representing Women in Parliament: A Comparative Study,* eds. Marian Sawer et al. (New York: Routledge, 2006), 18; Linda Trimble, "When Do Women Count? Substantive Representation of Women in Canadian Legislatures," in *Representing Women in Parliament: A Comparative Study,* eds. Marian Sawer et al. (New York: Routledge, 2006).
3. Thomas, "Introduction," 2; Rainbow Murray, "Quotas for Men: Reframing Gender Quotas as a Means of Improving representation for All," *American Political Science Review* 108 (2014): 520–32; Iris Marion Young, *Inclusion and Democracy* (Oxford: Oxford University Press, 2000).
4. Livianna Tossutti and Jane Hilderman, "Representing Canadians: Is the 41st Parliament Still a Vertical Mosaic?" in *Canadian Democracy from the Ground Up: Perceptions and Performance,* eds. Elisabeth Gidengil and Heather Bastedo (Vancouver: UBC Press, 2014).
5. The figures in this paragraph are taken from Erin Tolley, "Visible Minority and Indigenous Members of Parliament," in *Canadian Election Analysis: Communication, Strategy, and Democracy,* eds. Alex Marland and Thierry Giasson (Vancouver: UBC Press, 2015), 50–51.
6. The figures in this paragraph come from Tolley, "Visible Minority and Indigenous Members of Parliament."
7. All of the numbers cited in this paragraph are taken from Joanna Everitt, "LGBT Activism in the 2015 Federal Election," in *Canadian Election Analysis: Communication, Strategy, and Democracy,* eds. Alex Marland and Thierry Giasson (Vancouver: UBC Press, 2015), 48–49. It is, of course,

possible that there are LGBT MPs who have chosen not to make their sexual orientation or gender identity public. While their presence may increase substantive representation, it does not contribute to the descriptive representation of LGBT Canadians.

8. Richard E. Matland, "Institutional Variables affecting Female Representation in National Legislatures," *Journal of Politics* 55 (1993): 737–55.

9. Brenda O'Neill, "Unpacking Gender's Role in Political Representation in Canada," *Canadian Parliamentary Review* (Summer 2015): 22–31.

10. Richard E. Matland and Donley T. Studlar, "The Contagion of Women Candidates in Single-member District and Proportional Representation Electoral Systems: Canada and Norway," *Journal of Politics* 58 (1996): 707–33.

11. Pippa Norris, "Choosing Electoral Systems: Proportional, Majoritarian and Mixed Systems," *International Political Science Review* 18 (1997): 297–312.

12. Norris, "Choosing Electoral Systems"; Wilma Rule, "Electoral Systems, Contextual Factors and Women's Opportunity for Election to Parliament in Twenty-Three Democracies," *The Western Political Quarterly* 40 (1987): 477–98.

13. Rule, "Electoral Systems, Contextual Factors and Women's Opportunity for Election to Parliament."

14. Matland, "Institutional Variables."

15. Karen Bird, "The Political Representation of Visible Minorities in Electoral Democracies: A Comparison of France, Denmark, and Canada," *Nationalism and Ethnic Politics* 11 (2005): 425–65.

16. Andrew Griffith, "Visible Minority Candidates in the 2015 Election: Making Progress," *Policy Options* (2015). http://policyoptions.irpp.org/2015/10/17/visible-minority-candidates-in-the-2015-election-making-progress/. Accessed October 22, 2016.

17. Tolley, "Visible Minority and Indigenous Members of Parliament."

18. Tolley, "Visible Minority and Indigenous Members of Parliament."

19. The electoral quotient is the province's population divided by its number of seats.

20. Richard E. Matland and Donley T. Studlar, "Gender and the Electoral Opportunity Structure in the Canadian Provinces," *Political Research Quarterly* 51 (1998): 117-40; Gary F. Moncrief and Joel A. Thompson, "Urban and Rural Ridings and Women in Provincial Politics in Canada," *Canadian Journal of Political Science* 24 (1991): 831–37.

21. Matland and Studlar, "Gender and the Electoral Opportunity Structure."

22. Tolley, "Visible Minority and Indigenous Members of Parliament."

23. Jerome H. Black, "The 2006 Federal Election and Visible Minority Candidates: More of the Same?" *Canadian Parliamentary Review* (Autumn 2008): 30–36.

24. Joanna Everitt and Michael Camp, "In Versus Out: LGBT Politicians in Canada," *Journal of Canadian Studies* 48 (2014): 226–51.

25. Michael Pal and Sujit Choudhry, "Still Not Equal: Visible Minority Vote Dilution in Canada," *Canadian Political Science Review* 8 (2014): 85–101.

26. Pal and Choudhry, "Still Not Equal: Visible Minority Vote Dilution in Canada."

27. O'Neill, "Unpacking Gender's Role."

28. See Alfred A. Hunter and Margaret Denton, "Do Female Candidates 'Lose Votes'? The Experience of Female Candidates in the 1979 and 1980 Canadian General Elections," *Canadian Review of Sociology and Anthropology* 21 (1984): 395–406; Elizabeth Goodyear-Grant, "Who Votes for Women Candidates and Why? Evidence from Recent Elections," in *Voting Behaviour in Canada*, eds. Cameron Anderson and Laura Stephenson (Vancouver: UBC Press, 2010).

29. Jerome H. Black and Lynda Erickson, "Ethno-racial Origins of Candidates and Electoral Performance: Evidence from Canada," *Party Politics* 12 (2006): 541–61.

30. Everitt and Camp, "In Versus Out."

31. Jerome H. Black and Lynda Erickson, "Women Candidates and Voter Bias: Do Women Politicians Need to Be Better?" *Electoral Studies* 22 (2002): 81–100.

32. Jerome H. Black, "Immigrant and Minority Political Incorporation in Canada: A Review with Some Reflections on Canadian-American Comparison Possibilities," *American Behavioral Scientist* 55 (2011): 1160–88; O'Neill, "Unpacking Gender's Role."

33. Christine Cheng and Margit Tavits, "Informal Influence in Selecting Female Political Candidates," *Political Research Quarterly* 64 (2011): 460–71.

34. Bird, "The Political Representation of Visible Minorities."

35. Black, "Immigrant and Minority Political incorporation"; Livianna S. Tossutti and Tom Pierre Najem, "Minorities and Elections in Canada's Fourth Party System: Macro and Micro Constraints and Opportunities," *Canadian Ethnic Studies* 34 (2002): 85–112.

36. Melanee Thomas and Marc André Bodet, "Sacrificial Lambs, Women Candidates, and District Competitiveness in Canada," *Electoral Studies* 32 (2013): 153–66.

37. Linda Trimble and Jane Arscott, *Still Counting: Women in Politics across Canada* (Peterborough: Broadview Press, 2003), 58.
38. This is the title of a book on the under-representation of women. Jennifer L. Lawless and Richard L. Fox, *It Takes a Candidate: Why Women Don't Run for Office* (New York: Cambridge University Press, 2005).
39. Susan Abrams Beck, "Acting as Women: The Effects and Limitations of Gender in Local Governance," in *The Impact of Women in Public Office*, ed. Susan J. Carroll. (Bloomington: Indiana University Press, 2001); Janine Brodie, *Women and Politics in Canada* (Toronto: McGraw-Hill Ryerson Limited, 1985); Rick Wilford, Robert Miller, Yolanda Bell, and Freda Donoghue, "In Their Own Voices: Women Councillors in Northern Ireland," *Public Administration* 71 (1993): 341–55.
40. Tina Minor, "Political Participation of Inuit Women in the Government of Nunavut," *Wicazo Sa Review* 17 (2002): 65–90.
41. Jacqui Briggs, "'What's in It for Women?' The Motivations, Expectations and Experiences of Female Local Councillors in Montreal, Canada and Hull, England," *Local Government Studies* 26 (2000): 71-84; Linda Trimble, "Politics Where We Live: Women and Cities," in *Canadian Metropolitics: Governing Our Cities*, ed. James Lightbody (Toronto: Copp Clark Ltd., (1995); Laura Van Assendelft, "Women in Local Government," in *Gender and Women's Leadership: A Reference Handbook* (Volume 1), ed. Karen O'Connor (Los Angeles: Sage, 2010).
42. Jane Taber, "A Workplace Designed by Men for Men? Ask Female MPs About It," *Globe and Mail* (Toronto), 29 January 2016. http://www.theglobeandmail.com/news/politics/mps-balancing-motherhood-inspire-workplace-changes-in-legislatures/article28448787/.
43. Andrea Huncar, "Maternity Leave for MLAs to be Introduced by Alberta Government," CBC News, 7 March 2016. http://www.cbc.ca/news/canada/edmonton/maternity-leave-for-mlas-to-be-introduced-by-alberta-government-1.3479937.
44. Briggs, "'What's in It for Women?'"; Susan J. Carroll and Kira Sanbonmatsu, "Entering the Mayor's Office: Women's Decisions to Run for Municipal Positions," in *Women and Executive Office: Pathways and Performance*, ed. Melody Rose (Boulder: Lynne Rienner Publishers, 2013).
45. Louise Carbert, *Rural Women's Leadership in Atlantic Canada: First-Hand Perspectives on Local Public Life and Participation in Electoral Politics* (Toronto: University of Toronto Press, 2006), 105–12.

46. Edward S. Greenberg, ed., *Political Socialization* (New Brunswick: AldineTransaction, 2009 [1970]); Elisabeth Gidengil, Brenda O'Neill and Lisa Young, "Her Mother's Daughter? The Influence of Childhood Socialization on Women's Political Engagement," *Journal of Women, Politics and Policy* 31 (2010): 334–55.

47. Gidengil et al., "Her Mother's Daughter?" 348–50.

48. Jennifer L. Lawless and Richard L. Fox, *It Still Takes a Candidate: Why Women Don't Run for Office* (Cambridge: Cambridge University Press, 2010); Melanee Thomas, "The Complexity Conundrum: Why Hasn't the Gender Gap in Subjective Political Competence Closed?" *Canadian Journal of Political Science* 45 (2012): 337–58.

49. Jennifer L. Lawless, "Women's Political Ambition," in *Gender and Women's Leadership: A Reference Handbook* (Volume 1), ed. Karen O'Connor (Los Angeles: Sage, 2010).

50. Thomas, "The Complexity Conundrum."

51. Angela Howard Frederick, "Bringing Narrative In: Race-Gender Storytelling, Political Ambition, and Women's Paths to Public Office," *Journal of Women, Politics and Policy* 34 (2013), 132.

52. Jennifer L. Lawless, Richard L. Fox, and Gail Baitinger, "Women's Underrepresentation in U.S. Politics: The Enduring Gender Gap in Political Ambition," in *Women and Executive Office: Past, Present, and Future, Third Edition*, eds. Sue Thomas and Clyde Wilcox (New York: Oxford University Press, 2014); Paru Shah, "Stepping Up: Black Political Ambition and Success," *Politics, Groups, and Identities* 3 (2015): 278–94.

53. Laura Van Assendelft, "Entry-Level Politics? Women as Candidates and Elected Officials at the Local Level," in *Women and Executive Office: Past, Present, and Future, Third Edition*, eds. Sue Thomas and Clyde Wilcox (New York: Oxford University Press, 2014).

54. Shah, "Stepping Up"; Gbemende Johnson, Bruce I. Oppenheimer and Jennifer L. Selin, "The House as a Stepping Stone to the Senate: Why Do So Few African American House Members Run?" *American Journal of Political Science* 56 (2012): 387–99.

55. Jennifer L. Lawless and Richard L. Fox, *Running From Office: Why Young Americans Are Turned Off to Politics* (Oxford: Oxford University Press, 2015).

56. Lawless and Fox, *Running From Office*, 131.

57. See for example Barbara Burrell, "Campaign Financing: Women's Experience in the Modern Era," in *Women and Elective Office: Past, Present, and Future, Second Edition*, eds. Sue Thomas and Clyde Wilcox (Oxford: Oxford

University Press, 2005); Rebekah Herrick, "Is There a Gender Gap in the Value of Campaign Resources?" *American Politics Research* 24 (1996): 68–80.

58. Sylvia Bashevkin, *Toeing the Lines: Women and Party Politics in English Canada, Second Edition* (Toronto: Oxford University Press, 1993).

59. Candice J. Nelson, "Women's PACs in the Year of the Woman," in *The Year of the Woman: Myths and Realities,* eds. Elizabeth A. Cook et al. (Boulder: Westview Press, 1994), 181–96.

60. Elections Canada provides an explanation of campaign finance rules for federal elections at http://www.elections.ca/content.aspx?section=res&dir=ces&document=part6&lang=e. See also Section 18 of the Canada Elections Act (S.C. 2000, c. 9).

61. The federal Conflict of Interest Act (S.C. 2006, c. 9, s. 2) contains rules regarding post-employment activities for former public office holders.

62. Joanna Everitt and Michael Camp, "One Is Not Like the Others: Allison Brewer's Leadership of the New Brunswick NDP," in *Opening Doors Wider: Women's Political Engagement in Canada*, ed. Sylvia Bashevkin (Vancouver: UBC Press, 2009); Joanna Everitt and Michael Camp, "Changing the Game Changes the Frame: The Media's Use of Lesbian Stereotypes in Leadership Versus Election Campaigns," *Canadian Political Science Review* 3 (2009): 24–39; Linda Trimble, Daisy Raphael, Shannon Sampert, Angelia Wagner and Bailey Gerrits, "Politicizing Bodies: Hegemonic Masculinity, Heteronormativity, and Racism in News Representations of Canadian Political Party Leadership Candidates," *Women's Studies in Communication* 38 (2015): 314–30.

63. Donald P. Haider-Markel, *Out and Running: Gay and Lesbian Candidates, Elections, and Policy Representation* (Washington: Georgetown University Press, 2010), 58–59.

64. Donald P. Haider-Markel and Chelsie Lynn Moore Bright, "Lesbian Candidates and Officeholders," in *Women and Executive Office: Past, Present, and Future, Third Edition*, eds. Sue Thomas and Clyde Wilcox (New York: Oxford University Press, 2014), 265.

14. Public Consultation on Electoral Reform Through Referenda or Plebiscite: Recent Experience in British Columbia

1. Election Act, RSBC 1996, c 106, s. 12(1)(d).
2. Referendum Act, RSBC 1996, c 400, s. 4.

3. Referendum Act, RSBC 1996, c 400, s. 1(1), which reads: "If the Lieutenant Governor in Council considers that an expression of opinion is desirable on any matter of public interest or concern, the Lieutenant Governor in Council may, by regulation, order that a referendum be conducted in the manner provided for in this Act."

4. British Columbia, Statement of Votes, 36th Provincial General Election, May 28, 1996, 10.

5. British Columbia Citizens Assembly on Electoral Reform. *Making Every Vote Count: Technical Report*, December 2004, 116–18

6. British Columbia, Report of the Chief Electoral Officer on the 39th Provincial General Election and Referendum on Electoral Reform, May 12, 2009, 30.

7. British Columbia Electoral Boundaries Commission, Amendment to the Preliminary Report, February 14, 2008, 130–36.

8. British Columbia, Report of the Chief Electoral Officer on the 2011 HST (Harmonized Sales Tax) Referendum, June 13–August 26, 2011, 3–4.

9. British Columbia, Report of the Chief Electoral Officer on the 2015 Metro Vancouver Transportation and Transit Plebiscite, March 16–July 2, 2015, 3.

10. Referendum Act, RSBC 1996, c. 400, s. 4.

11. Ibid., s. 6.

12. British Columbia, Report of the Chief Electoral Officer on the 38th Provincial General Election 2005 Referendum on Electoral Reform, May 17, 2005, 34.

13. Ibid.

14. British Columbia, Report of the Chief Electoral Officer on the 39th Provincial General Election and Referendum on Electoral Reform, May 12, 2009, 35–37.

15. British Columbia, Report of the Chief Electoral Officer on the 38th Provincial General Election 2005 Referendum on Electoral Reform, May 17, 2005, 190.

16. British Columbia, Report of the Chief Electoral Officer on the 39th Provincial General Election and Referendum on Electoral Reform, May 12, 2009, 191.

17. British Columbia, Report of the Chief Electoral Officer on the 2011 HST (Harmonized Sales Tax) Referendum, June 13–August 26, 2011.

18. British Columbia, Report of the Chief Electoral Officer on the 38th Provincial General Election 2005 Referendum on Electoral Reform, May 17, 2005, 48-57.

19. British Columbia, Report of the Chief Electoral Officer on the 39th Provincial General Election and Referendum on Electoral Reform, May 12, 2009, 45-49.

20. British Columbia, Report of the Chief Electoral Officer on the 2011 HST (Harmonized Sales Tax) Referendum, June 13–August 26, 2011.

21. British Columbia, Report of the Chief Electoral Officer on the 2015 Metro Vancouver Transportation and Transit Plebiscite, March 16 – July 2, 2015.

22. British Columbia, Report of the Chief Electoral Officer on the 2011 HST (Harmonized Sales Tax) Referendum, June 13–August 26, 2011.
23. British Columbia, Report of the Chief Electoral Officer on the 2015 Metro Vancouver Transportation and Transit Plebiscite, March 16 – July 2, 2015.
24. British Columbia, Independent Panel on Internet Voting, Recommendation Report to the Legislative Assembly of British Columbia, February 2014, 47–49.

15. Should We Have a Referendum?

1. Olivier Beaud, *La puissance de l'État* (Paris: Presses Universitaires de France, 1994), 365.
2. They are also very different from issues like abortion or divorce in a country like Ireland or conscription in Canada during World War II. In such cases, holding a referendum or plebiscite appears as a way for the party in power to resolve an issue that divides the party internally (On the referendum as a "*recours des partis*" see Francis Hamon, *Le Référendum:* Étude *comparative* (Paris: LGDJ, 2012) and Lawrence LeDuc, *The Politics of Direct Democracy: Referendums in Global Perspective* (Toronto: Broadview Press, 2003), 47–48 and 163.
3. According to a recent poll, 65 per cent of Canadians agree that a national referendum is needed before Parliament can change the present electoral system, while 18 per cent consider such a step to be unnecessary and 17 per cent express no opinion on the matter. See Ryan Maloney, "Most Canadians want electoral reform referendum, Forum poll suggests," *Huffington Post*, July 11, 2016.
4. Vernon Bogdanor, *The People and the Party System. The Referendum and Electoral Reform in British Politics* (Cambridge: Cambridge University Press, 1981), 14.
5. A. V. Dicey, "Ought the referendum to be introduced into England?," *Contemporary* Review (1890), 507. Cited by Bogdanor, *The People and the Party System: The Referendum and Electoral Reform in British Politics* (Cambridge: Cambridge University Press, 1981), 15.
6. Bogdanor, *The People and the Party System*, 69
7. "Referendum the only legitimate way to reform the electoral system: Ambrose," Conservative Party of Canada, accessed on December 28, 2015, http://www.conservative.ca/referendum-the-only-legitimate-way-to-reform-the-electoral-system-ambrose/.
8. See the motion from the Minister for Democratic Institutions, M. Monsef: Canada, House of Commons, *Notice Paper*, 42nd Leg, 1st Sess, No 53 (May 11, 2016).

9. Louis Massicotte, "Electoral Reform in Canada," in *To Keep or Change First Past the Post? The Politics of Electoral Reform*, ed. André Blais (Oxford: Oxford University Press, 2008), 121.

10. In its attempt at reforming the electoral system, the Quebec government opted for a somewhat different approach, setting up a Special Committee of the National Assembly composed of MNAs from all parties and eight citizens acting as advisors. See Massicotte, "Electoral Reform in Canada," 122.

11. On the British Columbia and Ontario cases, see Mark E. Warren and Hilary Pearse, eds., *Designing Deliberative Democracy: The British Columbia Citizens' Assembly* (Cambridge: Cambridge University Press, 2008); Patrick Fournier et al., *When Citizens Decide: Lessons from Citizens' Assemblies on Electoral Reform* (Oxford: Oxford University Press, 2011). On PEI, see Jeannie Lee, "The Prince Edward Island on Electoral Reform," *Canadian Parliamentary Review* (Spring 2006): 4–8.

12. The alternative would have been for the governments to commit themselves to endorse the reform proposal made by the independent commission/citizens' assembly and have it go through the legislative process. Governments have shown themselves very reluctant to do this. Moreover, opting for a referendum may seem to follow the logic behind these two models, which is to insulate the process of reform from the parties.

13. In all the cases mentioned above where there was a referendum, the vote in favour of reform failed to reach the required level of popular consent. For some observers, one reason for this lack of success may be found in the reluctance of elected representatives to participate actively in the referendum campaigns. This absence of leadership in favour of reform may itself be related to the fact that politicians had been sidelined in the process of elaboration. If true, this would count as a significant drawback of the second reform model (see R. Kenneth Carty in this volume).

14. "Special Committee on Electoral Reform," Parliament of Canada, accessed on November 8, 2016, http://www.parl.gc.ca/Committees/en/ERRE/About. Note that the Conservatives voted against the motion, stating that they had not been consulted. Conservative MP and spokesperson on electoral reform Scott Reid argued that no level of cross-party support (even if it were to include all the parties represented in the House of Commons) could be an acceptable substitute for a referendum. See "Conservatives to vote 'no' on changes to electoral reform committee," *Global News*, June 2, 2016.

15. In the last federal elections, the Liberals received 39.47 per cent of the vote; the Conservatives: 31.89 per cent; the NDP: 19.71 per cent ; the BQ: 8.2 per cent and the Green Party: 3.45 per cent.

16. New Zealand Parliament, Royal Commission on Electoral Reform, *Towards a Better Democracy* (Wellington, 1986), Chapter 9, 187.

17. The requirement concerning reserved provisions was introduced in Section 189 of the Electoral Act (1956). The Royal Commission recommended retaining the requirement. In its report, the Commission stated that the reserved provisions should cover the elements of the Act pertaining to (a) the right to vote and be a candidate; (b) the method of voting; (c) the method for the determination of the number of seats and their boundaries; (d) the term of Parliament; and (e) the tenure of the electoral commissioner. See Royal Commission on Electoral Reform, *Towards a Better Democracy*, 9, 292.

18. If we translate the 75 per cent requirement in terms of the present composition of the Canadian House of Commons, it would require that the reform proposal be supported by 253 MPs out of a total of 338 MPs. There are currently 183 Liberal MPs; 98 Conservative MPs; 44 NDP MPs; 10 Bloc Québécois MPs; 1 Green MP; and 1 Independent.

19. See Royal Commission on Electoral Reform, *Towards a Better Democracy*, 9, 288: "All the changes that have been recognised as amending the reserved provisions since 1956 have in fact been made by agreement between the major parties in the House (which is what in practical terms the 75 per cent requirement amounts to and what its principle probably requires)".

20. Royal Commission on Electoral Reform, *Towards a Better Democracy*, Appendix A, 81, 83.

21. Note that if we see the problem as essentially one of partisan partiality seriously, then we should accept that no threshold would be high enough to secure an impartial process as long as the parties remain the main actors of the reform process. If partisan partiality is the problem, the solution must be to select a non-partisan process.

16. A Modest Case for Constitutional Limits on Electoral Reform in Canada

1. There are several versions of this claim, the most authoritative of which can be found in *Figuerora v Canada (Attorney General)*, [2003] 1 SCR 912, para. 81, where the majority reasoned that "the *Charter* aside, the choice among electoral processes is, as LeBel J. states, a political one—and not one in which the Court

should involve itself." This version of the claim is qualified insofar as it mentions the *Charter* (*Canadian Charter of Rights and Freedoms*, Part 1 of the *Constitution Act, 1982*, being Schedule B to the *Canada Act 1982* (UK), c 11), but for the purposes of the analysis that follows, it is pertinent because the qualification does not consider any constitutional provisions outside of that text.

2. I have decided to limit my analysis to the constitutional provisions addressed in the main text because they are the ones that most obviously apply to the question at hand. I do not intend to imply that Parliament's ability to engage in electoral reform may not also be limited by, for instance, section 3 of the *Charter* or by the preamble to the *Constitution Act, 1867*. I have simply not engaged those issues in this chapter.

3. *Constitution Act, 1867* (UK), 30 & 31 Vict, c 3, reprinted in RSC 1985, App II, No 5.

4. Michael Pal, "Constitutional Amendment After the *Senate Reference* and the Prospects for Electoral Reform" (2016) 76 SCLR 353 and Yasmin Dawood, "The Process of Electoral Reform in Canada: Democratic and Constitutional Constraints" (2016) 76 SCLR 330.

5. Although, to my knowledge, no one has done an exegesis of these provisions like the one in the main text, others, including Pal, "Constitutional Amendment," 362 and Dawood "The Process of Electoral Reform," 348, have discussed them.

6. *Constitution Act, 1982*, being Schedule B to the *Canada Act 1982* (UK), c 11.

7. For a suggestion of this possibility, see Dawood, "The Process of Electoral Reform," 348.

8. 2014 SCC 32.

9. *Reference re Senate Reform*, para. 26.

10. The Court reasoned that the section 38(2) opt out provision did not apply in this instance, since the proposed reform would "not affect the legislative powers, property rights, or any other rights or privileges of the legislature or government of a province" *Reference re Senate Reform*, para. 83.

11. *Reference re Senate Reform*, para. 77.

12. *Reference re Senate Reform*, para. 71.

13. *Reference re Senate Reform*, paras. 72–73.

14. *Reference re Senate Reform*, para. 76.

15. *Reference re Senate Reform*, para. 77.

16. *Reference re Senate Reform*, para. 82.

17. *Reference re Senate Reform*, para. 55.

18. P.B. Waite, ed., *The Confederation Debates in the Province of Canada: 1865: A Selection*, 2nd ed. (Montreal: McGill-Queen's Press, 2006), 10–11.

19. It is significant that in the *Reference re Senate Reform*, the Court referred to the Senate as a "core institution of the Canadian federal structure of government" and reasoned that "changes that affect its fundamental nature and role" (para. 77) could not be undertaken unilaterally by Parliament. By implication, the analysis would extend to changes bearing on the fundamental nature and role of any other core institution. The House of Commons is one such body. For a similar argument, which claims that this aspect of the reasoning in the *Reference re Senate Reform* applies to the House of Commons, see Pal, "Constitutional Amendment," 359–60.

20. See the references in Pal, "Constitutional Amendment," footnote 28.

21. *Re: Resolution to amend the Constitution*, [1981] 1 SCR 753 [hereinafter "*Patriation Reference*"].

22. *Patriation Reference*, 909.

23. *Patriation Reference*, 888 (internal citations omitted).

24. Patrice Dutil, "The Imperative of a Referendum," Fraser Institute, accessed November 14, 2016, https://www.fraserinstitute.org/sites/default/files/the-imperative-of-a-referendum.pdf.

25. Dutil, "The Imperative," 18.

26. *Patriation Reference*, 905.

27. *Patriation Reference*, 905.

28. Dutil, "The Imperative," 19.

17. Which Procedure for Deciding Election Procedures?

1. I have sought a formulation that is neutral between purely consequentialist and deontological justifications of democratic institutions. That procedures embody or express certain values or norms can be characterized as (non-causal) outcomes of the procedure. See Ronald Dworkin, *Law's Empire* (Cambridge, MA: Harvard University Press, 1986), chapter 4; Richard J. Arneson, "Democracy Is Not Intrinsically Just," in *Justice and Democracy*, ed. Keith Dowding et al. (Cambridge: Cambridge University Press, 2004).

2. James Wycliffe Headlam, *Election by Lot at Athens* (Cambridge: Cambridge University Press, 1891); Bernard Manin, *The Principles of Representative Government* (Cambridge: Cambridge University Press, 1997); Oliver Dowlen, *The Political Potential of Sortition: A Study of the Random Selection of Citizens for Public Office* (Exeter: Imprint Academic, 2008).

3. See Dennis F. Thompson, "Who Should Govern Who Governs? The Role of Citizens in Reforming the Electoral System," in *Designing Deliberative*

Democracy: The British Columbia Citizens' Assembly, ed. Mark E. Warren and Hilary Pearse (Cambridge: Cambridge University Press, 2008), 20–49.

4. Hélène Landemore, *Democratic Reason: Politics, Collective Intelligence, and the Rule of the Many* (Princeton, NJ: Princeton University Press, 2012).

5. Josiah Ober, *Democracy and Knowledge: Innovation and Learning in Classical Athens* (Princeton, NJ: Princeton University Press, 2008).

6. Mark E. Warren and Hilary Pearse, *Designing Deliberative Democracy: The British Columbia Citizens' Assembly* (Cambridge: Cambridge University Press, 2008); Patrick Fournier, Henk van der Kolk, R. Kenneth Carty, André Blais, and Jonathan Rose, *When Citizens Decide: Lessons from Citizens' Assemblies on Electoral Reform* (Oxford: Oxford University Press, 2011).

7. Manin, *The Principles of Representative Government*.

8. John A. Simmons, *Moral Principles and Political Obligation* (Princeton, NJ: Princeton University Press, 1979); Allen Buchanan, "Political Legitimacy and Democracy," *Ethics* 112 (2002): 689–719.

9. See Peter Singer, *Democracy and Disobedience* (Oxford: Oxford University Press, 1974), 24–26, 45–49.

10. It is true that allowing for a three-stage selection process mediating by self-selection introduces a non-random element that will cause departures from full descriptive representativeness. Those disposed to agree to serve may not be descriptively representative of the population in some respects: they tend to be more educated and politically engaged (Fournier et al., *When Citizens Decide: Lessons from Citizens' Assemblies on Electoral Reform*).

11. See Peter Stone, *The Luck of the Draw: The Role of Lotteries in Decision Making* (Oxford: Oxford University Press, 2011); Gil Delannoi, Oliver Dowlen, and Peter Stone, "The Lottery as a Democratic Institution," in *Studies in Public Policy* (Dublin, Policy Institute, 2013).

12. See also the literature on deliberative polls (James S. Fishkin, *When the People Speak: Deliberative Democracy and Public Consultation* (Oxford: Oxford University Press, 2009).

13. Fred Cutler, Richard Johnston, R. Kenneth Carty, André Blais, and Patrick Fournier, "Deliberation, Information, and Trust: The British Columbia Citizens' Assembly as Agenda Setter," in *Designing Deliberative Democracy: The British Columbia Citizens' Assembly*, ed. Mark E. Warren and Hilary Pearse (Cambridge: Cambridge University, 2008), 166–91; Fournier et al., *When Citizens Decide: Lessons from Citizens' Assemblies on Electoral Reform*, 130–32.

Contributors

Arash Abizadeh is Associate Professor of Political Science, McGill University

Keith Archer is the Chief Electoral Officer of British Columbia

Ken Carty is Professor Emeritus of Political Science, University of British Columbia

Christopher Cochrane is Associate Professor of Political Science, University of Toronto

William Cross is the Hon. Dick and Ruth Bell Chair for the Study of Canadian Parliamentary Democracy in the Department of Political Science, Carleton University

Elisabeth Gidengil is the Hiram Mills Professor in Political Science, McGill University

Elizabeth Goodyear-Grant is Associate Professor, Political Studies, and Director, Institute of Intergovernmental Relations, Queen's University

Hoi L. Kong is Associate Professor of Law, McGill University

Dominique Leydet is Full Professor in the Department of Philosophy, Université du Québec à Montréal

Peter Loewen is Director of the School of Public Policy and Governance, University of Toronto

Emmett Macfarlane is Assistant Professor of Political Science, University of Waterloo

Contributors

Colin M. Macleod is Associate Professor in Law and the Department of Philosophy, University of Victoria

Lydia Miljan is Associate Professor of Political Science, University of Windsor

Andrew Potter is Director of the McGill Institute for the Study of Canada

Erin Tolley is Assistant Professor in the Department of Political Science, University of Toronto

Angelia Wagner is SSHRC Postdoctoral Fellow at the Centre for the Study of Democratic Citizenship, McGill University

Mark E. Warren is the Harold and Dorrie Merilees Chair in the Study of Democracy in the Department of Political Science, University of British Columbia

Daniel Weinstock is James McGill Professor in the Faculty of Law, McGill University

Melissa S. Williams is Professor of Political Science and Founding Director of the Centre for Ethics, University of Toronto